Defense Spending and Economic Growth

Defense Spending and Economic Growth

EDITED BY
James E. Payne
and Anandi P. Sahu

LONDON AND NEW YORK

First published 1993 by Westview Press

Published 2018 by Routledge
52 Vanderbilt Avenue, New York, NY 10017
2 Park Square, Milton Park, Abingdon, Oxon OX14 4RN

Routledge is an imprint of the Taylor & Francis Group, an informa business

A CIP catalog record for this book is available from the Library of Congress.

ISBN 13: 978-0-367-01100-0 (hbk)

ISBN 13: 978-0-367-16087-6 (pbk)

Contents

Tables and Figures

Tables

Figures

Preface

This book examines the impact defense spending has on economic growth. While defense spending was not deliberately invented as a fiscal policy instrument, its importance in the composition of overall government spending and thus in determining employment is now easily recognized. In light of the collapse of the Soviet Union and the consequent reduction in the threat to the security of the United States, maintaining defense spending at the old level seems indefensible. The media has concentrated on the so-called peace dividend. However, as soon as the federal government is faced with defense cuts, it realizes the macroeconomic ramifications of such a step. Based on studies included in this volume, we examine the effects of defense spending on economic growth and investigate how the changed world political climate is likely to alter the importance and pattern of defense spending both for developed and developing countries.

The volume consists of fourteen chapters and is divided into five parts. The introductory part, besides presenting a background regarding the importance of defense spending in developed and developing countries, analyzes the different issues addressed in the book, relates them to the central theme and provides conclusions regarding the overall significance of defense spending for the economic growth of a nation. While studies included in this volume are fairly detailed, we recognize that not *all* points of view are equally represented. We have attempted to convey mainstream views without sacrificing the diversity of opinions.

We acknowledge the unqualified support of the contributing authors without which this volume would not have been possible. We also appreciate the cooperation and support provided by Eastern Kentucky University and Oakland University that enabled the timely completion of the project.

James E. Payne
Anandi P. Sahu

PART ONE

Introduction

1

Defense Spending and Economic Growth: An Evaluation of the Overall Impact

James E. Payne and Anandi P. Sahu

Defense spending has been an important component of government expenditures both for highly industrialized developed countries and for less developed poorer countries. While it is for the less developed countries, often called LDCs, that spending on defense has been a subject of controversy, its role in the development process of industrialized countries is no less important.

For developed countries, an increase in defense spending implies a rise in the aggregate demand. This, in turn, leads to increased production of goods and services to fulfill the increased demand, resulting in higher income and employment in the economy. In addition, the military R&D can lead to spillover of new defense technology to the civilian sector of the economy, increasing private sector productivity. Benefits of defense spending may, however, be unevenly distributed across different geographical regions of the economy.

In the context of developing and underdeveloped countries, issues raised by defense spending are somewhat different. Increased defense spending is not necessarily considered to be conducive to economic growth of less developed countries. It has been argued that much of developing countries' defense demand is met by imports. Defense spending may thus take resources away from productive investment and deter their economic growth and prosperity. Even when defense goods are produced domestically, one needs to investigate the extent to which spillover from the defense sector favorably affects the civilian sector of the economy.

The recent developments in Eastern Europe and the former Soviet Union have generated a need for a re-examination of the traditional wisdom regarding the importance of defense spending. In particular, there is a need to investigate the possible effects of defense spending on economic growth in light of the immense weakening of the superstructure supporting the arms race. There is thus a need to examine the entire spectrum of issues associated with defense spending in light of recent political and economic developments.

In what follows we analyze theoretical and empirical issues associated with the effects of defense spending on economic growth both for industrialized and developing countries. Based on the evidence presented in this volume, we provide broad answers to the often asked question: does defense spending promotes economic growth in industrialized countries and retard economic progress in less developed countries? We also analyze the implications of the recent economic and political developments in Eastern Europe and the Soviet Union for the arms race, and their consequent effects on economic development of industrialized economies.

Importance of Defense Spending

During the cold war era, military expenditures increased globally, NATO and Warsaw Pact countries leading the way. However, worldwide military spending has been falling since the late 1980s. Table 1.1, abridged from Table 11.1, displays this global defense spending pattern.

As the above table shows the downward trend in military spending is unmistakable. In fact, the annual growth rate of total world military spending declined from a nearly 4 percent per annum increase during 1960-70 to about 3.0 percent annual decline during 1987-90.

Theoretical Underpinnings

It is worthwhile to examine why we should expect a link between defense spending and economic growth. Ram (Chapter 2) provides a survey of the theoretical linkages between defense expenditures and economic growth. In particular, he concentrates on two channels: (1) aggregate supply effects and (2) aggregate demand effects. With

TABLE 1.1
Trends in Global Military Spending

Year/Period	Developing Countries	Industrialized Countries
Military Expenditures (US$ Billions)		
1960	35	385
1970	75	545
1980	137	618
1984	155	750
1987	132	838
1990	123	762
Annual Growth Rates (%)		
1960-70	7.9	3.5
1970-80	6.2	1.3
1980-90	-1.1	2.1
1980-84	3.1	5.0
1984-87	-5.2	3.8
1987-90	-2.3	-3.1

Source: Abridged from Biswas (Table 11.1)

respect to long-run economic growth, the aggregate supply effects dominate.

The Supply-side Effects

The supply-side considerations are rooted in the opportunity costs of scarce resources. In this case, defense expenditures divert resources from more productive uses. Ram highlights several ways in which resources are directly diverted. Private consumption could be reduced if defense expenditures are devoted to the production of non-consumption items such as weapons. Also, private consumption could be harmed if the social value attached to defense expenditures is smaller than the social value (utility) of consumption that is displaced. Depending upon the resource constraints that a country faces, defense expenditures could either "crowd-out" or "crowd-in" private investment and savings. Moreover, public expenditures on education and health as well as research and development could be adversely affected by increases in defense expenditures. Increases in defense expenditures, in particular, arms imports, affect many LDCs' balance of payments by using scarce foreign exchange reserves that could be used in the importation of capital and necessary intermediate goods. In addition to these direct effects of defense expenditures upon economic growth, there are several indirect effects that should be mentioned. Defense expenditures could generate negative externalities with respect to the environment, lead to the militarization of society, as well as create an arms race mentality for threatened countries. On the other hand, positive externalities from the defense to the civilian sector may exist in the form of advancing technology, human capital formation, and infrastructure.

Technological Changes and Economic Growth. Mueller and Atesoglu (Chapter 4) present a theoretical model of the determination of the effects of defense spending and technological change upon economic growth. Their model divides the economy into two sectors: civilian and defense. The defense sector is postulated to generate either positive or negative externalities upon the civilian sector. Positive externalities would entail such items as technological breakthroughs and a better trained labor force. Negative externalities would cover such items as labor shortages for specialized skilled labor and potential "crowding out" effects associated with investment resources.

Mueller and Atesoglu derive a single equation expression for economic growth by incorporating the effects of the factors of production (labor and capital), technological change, and defense spending. Given that the rate of technological change and marginal factor productivity in the two sectors may differ, Mueller and Atesoglu find that, theoretically, the effect of the defense spending growth upon output is indeterminate. They next examine the comparative statics of their model. Both the size of the defense sector and the rate of growth in defense spending affect economic growth. The effect of defense spending size depends upon the relative productivity of the factors of production in the two sectors as well as the relative rate of technological advancement in the two sectors. The effect of growth in defense spending depends upon the marginal external product of defense spending on the civilian sector. In particular, if the relative rate of technological advancement in the defense sector falls then a reduction in the size of the defense sector would improve overall economic growth. As Mueller and Atesoglu suggest, only empirical estimation of their growth model could validate the impact of defense spending upon overall output growth.

The Demand-side Effects

In addition to affecting economic growth from the supply-side, defense expenditures could have affects from the demand-side. In the absence of capacity constraints, increases in defense expenditures could increase aggregate demand thereby real output and economic growth. If capacity constraints are binding then increases in defense expenditures could generate inflationary pressures. As Ram emphasizes, the positive or negative effects of defense expenditures upon economic growth is largely an empirical question tailored to the specifics of the country under inquiry.

The Arms Race and Economic Growth

The arms race and the rivalry have been said to have an impact on economic growth of rival nations. Anderton (Chapter 3) incorporates economic growth endogenously into an arms race model. Indeed, current resource allocations influence an economy's future production possibilities. Such considerations are important in analyzing a country's propensity to wage war or continue ongoing military efforts. Moreover, decisions to undergo an arms race, arms control or war will affect a country's economic growth. Anderton's simulation analysis yield several interesting conclusions. First, the country with the greater defense spillover to the civilian sector relative to its rival is in a stronger economic and military position, *ceteris paribus*. Second, the country with better quality of weaponry can outperform it rival in the long run given equal resources and growth patterns. Third, weapon technology oriented towards the "offensive" effectively increases the respective countries military burdens and hinders economic growth, all else equal. In conclusion, Anderton suggests that even minor increases in defense burdens in the short run have dramatic effects when compounded over the long run. A case in point is the recent economic collapse of the Soviet Union.

Effects on Industrialized Economies

As observed several times in the preceding section, only empirical evidence can shed light on whether defense spending has a significant effect on the economic growth of an economy.

Supply-side Effects on Economic Growth in the U.S. Meyer and Raines (Chapter 5) examine the effects of projected declines in U.S. defense spending on productive capacity as well as the contribution of both defense and non-defense research and development to productivity growth. Though defense spending has both demand-side and supply-side effects, Meyer and Raines focus upon the supply-side effects. In their investigation Meyer and Raines use the Washington University Macroeconometric Model, consisting of 350 equations, to simulate reductions in defense spending over the decade 1992 to 2001 as advanced by the Congressional Budget Office.

In order to concentrate on the long-run effects of reductions in defense spending, Meyer and Raines allow for an accommodative monetary policy in order to maintain the level of aggregate demand and hence employment. They find that GDP increases due in large part to increases in investment and private capital stock. The resulting transfer of government workers to the private sector produces an increase in private sector output at a rate greater than the increase in GDP. The increment to the compound annual growth rate of GDP by 2001, resulting from anticipated cuts in defense spending, is only 0.06 percentage points. Meyer and Raines point to several factors that limit the long-run increase in output. The direct saving from the defense cuts is partially offset by declines in both private and foreign saving. The decline in defense spending lowers interest rates which in turn depreciates the U.S. dollar. The stimulation of net exports absorbs resources released from the cut in defense purchases. The lower interest rates stimulate residential construction as well as consumption spending. The net result of these opposing effects is that only a small fraction of resources released by the government sector ends up in private capital formation and thus in enhancing productive capacity.

Another avenue of investigation undertaken by Meyer and Raines is the impact of defense related research and development on economic growth. Civilian applied research and development has an important impact upon private capital while both defense and nondefense research and development have no discernible impact. However, if resources earmarked for applied defense research and development are reallocated to civilian research and development as well as public infrastructure, private productivity could be enhanced.

The Effect on Employment in OECD Countries. Dunne (Chapter 6) investigates the relationship between defense expenditures and employment for 14 OECD countries. Using annual data over the time frame 1962-1985, Dunne employs a general dynamic modelling strategy to examine the effect on employment. He finds little or no evidence that defense expenditures influence employment at the macroeconomic level. However, such a finding is subject to question with respect to the quality of the data, model specification, and the ever present concern of structural change. At the micro level, Dunne points out the problem of differing structural adjustment and policy responses across countries, indeed making a comparative analysis difficult. How do defense expenditures affect industrial structure as well as company specific production? What is the regional distribution of defense expenditures? What is the impact of the defense industry upon local communities? These are a few of the questions raised by Dunne that are often concealed by macroeconomic aggregates. In conclusion, Dunne finds that cuts in defense expenditures provide an opportunity, not a cost, for society.

Demand-side Effects on the U.S. Economy. Unlike the work of Meyer and Raines which deals with the supply-side effects and the long-run implications of defense spending, Payne, Ross, and Olszewski (Chapter 7) analyze the demand-side effects and the resulting short-run dynamics. Payne, Ross, and Olszewski examine the macroeconomic effects of both defense and nondefense spending in the United States. The authors outline the possible macroeconomic effects of changes in these two components of federal government spending. Using a five variable vector autoregressive (VAR) model, they evaluate the effects of both real defense and nondefense expenditures upon real GNP, the real money supply, inflation, and the three-month Treasury bill rate. Multivariate Granger-causality tests found no significant relationship between the variables representing the macroeconomy and both defense and nondefense expenditures. Further examination of the forecast error variance decompositions of the VAR model presented evidence that inflation has a slight yet significant impact on both defense and nondefense expenditures. While the current political climate is very conducive to defense budget reductions, evidence provided by Payne, Ross and Olszewski suggest that the macroeconomic effects will be minimal.

The Effect on Trade and Employment in the U.S. Haveman, Deardorff, and Stern (Chapter 8) analyze the possible sectoral impacts of a "peace dividend" on trade and employment for the United States. Using the computational general equilibrium Michigan Model of World Production and Trade, Haveman, Deardorff, and Stern conduct two experiments: (1) 25% unilateral reduction of military spending in the United States and (2) 25% multilateral reduction of military spending in 18 Western industrialized and 16 developing countries. Both of these policy experiments stress the reallocation of the resources stemming from the reduced military spending in order to maintain existing level of final demand for goods and services. In general, there are three policies to accompany a reduction in military spending that would result in a neutralizing effect upon aggregate demand. The first policy simply redistributes the reduction in military spending to other forms of government spending. The second policy is to accompany the reduction in military spending with a reduction in taxes. The reduction in taxes would in turn stimulate civilian consumption expenditures. The third policy applies the resources saved from the reduction in military spending to the federal budget deficit. The resulting reduction in the federal budget deficit would put downward pressure on interest rates which could possibly stimulate private investment expenditures. Since their model can formally allow for changes in interest rates and taxes, Haveman, Deardorff and Stern implement the above policies by exogenously changing the composition of final demand.

Haveman, Deardorff and Stern's first scenario assumes the reduction in military spending is absorbed proportionally by consumption, investment, and nonmilitary government expenditures while the second scenario examines the reallocation of military spending to other forms of government spending while maintaining constant levels of consumption and investment spending. The third scenario redistributes the reduction in military spending to consumption while keeping other components of final demand constant. The fourth scenario focuses upon the redistribution of the reduction in military spending to investment expenditures. The first three scenarios of a unilateral reduction in military spending find that both exports and imports decline as well as some dislocation of the labor force. However, the fourth scenario yields different results. The increase in private investment leads to an increase in both exports and imports as well as an increase in employment. The next policy experiment undertaken by Haveman, Deardorff and Stern is a 25% multilateral reduction in military spending by Western industrialized and developing countries. The employment effects are similar to the first scenario of a unilateral reduction while the trade sector responds differently. U.S. exports fall while imports rise due to a relatively large appreciation of the U.S. dollar. The overall results suggest that a 25% multilateral reduction in military spending has a larger impact on the U.S. economy than a unilateral reduction of the same size. At the sectoral level some industries carry a higher burden of the adjustment costs associated with reduced military spending.

Faulty Estimates of Soviet Economic Growth and the U.S. Military Spending. It has been conjectured that huge amount of resources were diverted to the military sector in the U.S. based on faulty estimates of Soviet military and economic capabilities. Boettke (Chapter 9) suggests that the Soviet system was unlikely to continue even in the absence of military pressure from the West. Specifically, he points out that the increasing emphasis on measuring macroeconomic aggregates did not aid in understanding the Soviet economic performance in that most economists did not focus upon the structural composition from which such aggregates emerged. In fact, CIA estimates of Soviet economic growth were drastically overestimated. If the CIA estimates were correct then Gorbachev's reforms would not have been needed. Boettke argues that the military-industrial complex in the West benefitted from the overestimation of the Soviet military and economic capabilities. As a result, the Cold War effort distorted the U.S. economic structure and its long-run capabilities. Now that the Soviet Union is dismantled economically and politically, Boettke asks: can the U.S. reallocate resources effectively from military to civilian uses? Can reigning military-political self-interests change to accommodate a "peace-dividend"?

Regional Sensitivities to Defense Purchases. As pointed out earlier, defense spending has regional implications. Taylor (Chapter 10) investigates the sensitivity of state employment to defense-related industries. With legislators representing regions whose economies are dependent upon the defense industry one can easily see the vested interests that would prevail in any policy discussion of defense expenditure cutbacks. Indeed, defense cuts could potentially have severe redistributive effects on defense dependent regional economies. Thus, understanding the potential redistributive effects of defense cuts can aid policymakers in formulating assistance aid to minimize the short-run impact of defense industry cutbacks.

Addressing the potential shortfalls of analyzing defense sensitivity with contract data, Taylor implements the input-output approach. At the aggregate level, Taylor finds the U.S. economy to be relatively insensitive to defense purchasing. Taylor suggests that the U.S. would lose roughly .03 percent of its employment if defense purchases fell by 1 percent. At the state level, Taylor finds Connecticut, Washington and Kansas the most sensitive states to defense cuts, while Alaska, Delaware, and Hawaii are the least sensitive. Indeed, much of the variation of state sensitivity to defense purchases is directly related to the industrial composition of states. Finally, Taylor points out that even though a state is relatively insensitive to defense cuts, specific communities within the states may be highly sensitive to such cuts.

Effects on Less Developed Countries

As discussed by Ram (Chapter 2), Mueller and Atesoglu (Chapter 3) and Anderton (Chapter 4), there is a theoretical basis for expecting defense spending to have somewhat different impact on the economic growth of less developed countries. Biswas (Chapter 11) empirically investigates this impact within the context of a simple neoclassical production function with labor, capital, and military expenditures as inputs. For a sample of 74 less developed countries over the time period 1981-1989, Biswas finds that defense spending has a significant and positive impact upon economic growth. This result runs counter to earlier work done by Biswas and Ram for the time periods 1960-1970 and 1970-1977, based on a sample of 58 less developed countries.

Arms Imports and Economic Growth. As was noted earlier, defense spending by less developed countries often took the form of arms imports from industrialized countries. Looney and Frederiksen (Chapter 12) investigate whether or not future "peace dividends" resulting from reductions in defense spending in 62 developing countries will aid in the economic growth. In particular, Looney and Frederiksen examine three hypotheses: (1) whether military spending and arms imports hurt or helped economic growth, (2) whether military spending/arms imports affected changes in a country's external debt situation, and (3) whether or not military spending has an uniform impact across countries faced with varying resource constraints. Using data for 62 countries over the time period 1981-89, Looney and Frederiksen employ discriminant analysis to study the effect of defense spending. They divide their sample into two groups: high growth and low growth countries based on relative resource constraints. High growth countries have less of their government budget allocated to defense spending. Moreover, a lower share of their imports are armaments.

For the entire sample of countries, Looney and Frederiksen find that both debt and military expenditures contribute to overall economic growth while arms imports do not have a significant impact. Next, the sample of countries were divided into sub-groups. As the low growth/resource-constrained countries were eliminated from the sample, the regression results for the high growth/resource-unconstrained countries suggested investment, debt and military expenditures to have a positive impact on economic growth. However, even for the high growth countries, arms imports had a marginally significant and negative impact on growth. In contrast, as the high growth/resource unconstrained countries were eliminated from the sample the regression results for the low growth/resource constrained countries implied that investment and debt were important determinants of growth. For the low growth countries neither military expenditures or arms imports were significant factors in determining to economic growth. These findings suggest that defense spending has a dual role in the development process depending in large part on a country's level of economic development as well as endowment of resources.

World Peace, Terrorism and Peace Dividends

The breaking out of global peace raises some other interesting questions. Is terrorism a curse of the past? Are we overemphasizing the peace dividend? Chapters 13 and 14 examine these questions.

Deterring Terrorism. Scott (Chapter 13) investigates terrorism and its deterrence through reputation building on the behalf of governments. Given the latest surge in this means of negotiation, it is timely to consider whether or not a government should negotiate with terrorists. Scott demonstrates that governments cannot build reputations of not bargaining in a model with complete information. However, one may be able to build a reputation under incomplete (asymmetric) information. Based on an adaptation of the chain store model advanced by Selten (1978), and Kreps and Wilson (1982), Scott concludes that under incomplete information early government counterattacks discourages later terrorist attacks. This particular result does not hold with complete information. Finally, Scott suggests that the adaptation of existing game theory models to terrorist behavior can be of tremendous use in the derivation of optimal policies when dealing with terrorism.

World Peace and "Peace Dividends." Sahu and Kleiman (Chapter 14) discusses what to expect from a stable world peace. He points out that the end of Cold War has not necessarily ushered in an era of eternal global bliss. It may have merely changed the character of the military conflict -- a change from dealing with the prospect of devastating thermonuclear war to many small conflicts. While peace dividends can translate into domestic prosperity, a *complete* transfer of resources from war efforts to peaceful uses may be premature. It appears almost definite, at least in the near term, that the defense budget would be reduced. However, the reduced resources would be more directed towards increasing mobility and speed with which the U.S. armed forces can reach areas of armed conflicts globally. The role that the United Nations plays in such conflicts is also likely to be drastically altered eventually, with some possibility of the U.N. having its own armed forces to enforce Security Council resolutions. However, in the near term, industrial nations of the world led by the U.S. would continue to *enforce* peace globally, mostly with the consent of the U.N.

The Overall Impact of Defense Spending

Studies included in this volume show that there are theoretical bases for expecting defense spending to have an effect on economic growth both for industrialized and less developed countries. While the economic growth could be affected both from the supply-side and the demand-side, the net effect of the diverse forces on economic growth of a nation is theoretically ambiguous. Measuring the impact of defense spending on economic growth then ultimately becomes an empirical question.

Most studies cited in this volume suggest that defense spending has rather modest effect on the economic growth of an industrialized nation. According to one estimate, a 1-percent increase in the defense spending in the U.S. leads to a less than 0.03 percent increase in employment nationally.[1] In fact, defense spending does not appreciably affect other macroeconomic variables such as real GNP, inflation and interest rates.[2] Only for less developed countries, do the evidence presented in this volume suggest that defense spending has a significant impact on economic growth.[3] For the LDCs, while military expenditures seem to contribute to overall economic growth, arms imports do not have a significant impact.[4] Only for the resource-unconstrained developing countries, arms imports has a marginally negative effect on economic growth.

In light of the weak link between defense spending and economic growth for developed countries, one should realistically expect that a reduction in defense spending would not make a significant difference either. Studies included in this volume, in fact, suggest that the effect of the anticipated cuts in the U.S. defense spending on economic growth is rather modest. By the end of 1990s, the increment to long-term annual growth rate of GDP is only about 0.06 percentage points.[5] The annual GDP growth rate averaged about 3% during the 1970s and is currently about 2.25%. If we are looking to raise the long-term growth even to the 3% level, the defense cuts are likely to make only a small contribution toward this objective.

While the defense cutbacks do not seem to herald a new period of economic prosperity and the economic impact of a *peace dividend* may have been overemphasized, transfer of resources from production of military goods to civilian goods is still desirable. Smaller defense spending leads to greater private sector investment and consumption, leading to a better standard of living. Indeed, one study finds that the defense cutbacks would lead to a 23% increase in investment in equipment by 2001.[6]

The defense cuts, however, mask some harsh realities at the

regional level. Defense-based communities may be very hard hit. While the average impact of the cutbacks is only modest at the national level, some industries/communities are 20 times more sensitive to changes in defense purchases than the national average.[7] There is thus a need to ameliorate the negative effects of the reduction in defense budget on these industries/communities.

The change in global political and military climate has made the world and the Western nations less paranoid about a nuclear war. However, small conflicts are unlikely to go away. The change in the nature of the potential conflicts will shape the military objectives to be achieved by the reduced level of defense spending.[8] Greater cooperations among nations to solve world conflicts, and even human calamities, is a likely outcome of the of the changes in the Eastern Europe and the Soviet Union. Moreover, the military rivalries may be replaced by economic rivalries in the near term. Overall, are we better off relative to the Cold War era? We surely think so. While the much talked of "peace dividend" may not bring a large economic dividend, the changed environment forms a good basis for economic prosperity based on consumption, rather than on production of war goods.

Notes

1. See Taylor (Chapter 10).
2. See Payne, Ross and Olszewski (Chapter 7).
3. See Biswas (Chapter 11).
4. See Looney and Frederiksen (Chapter 12).
5. See Meyer and Raines (Chapter 5).
6. See Meyer and Raines (Chapter 5).
7. See Taylor (Chapter 10).
8. See Sahu and Kleiman (Chapter 14).

PART TWO

Theoretical Underpinnings

2

Conceptual Linkages Between Defense Spending and Economic Growth and Development: A Selective Review

Rati Ram

This paper describes some of the major theoretical linkages between defense expenditure and economic growth and development.[1] The primary objective is to state the nature of these conceptual linkages, and, therefore, discussion of the empirical aspects is minimal. Since the paper is largely a compilation of the linkages that have been suggested by various scholars, there is not much that can be regarded as "new". Moreover, the coverage is somewhat selective, and not all points of view are necessarily included. Two broad categories of connections between defense spending and economic growth are discussed. These are (a) aggregate-supply-side linkages, and (b) connections related to aggregate demand. Some thoughts are also expressed on defense expenditures and economic growth in the post-Cold-War era.

Aggregate-Supply-Side Linkages

Much of the discussion in the literature on the subject deals with what may be called aggregate-supply considerations, which typically deal with defense spending in terms of its "opportunity cost" or the alternatives that are sacrificed. Although these arguments often suggest an adverse effect of defense (military) outlays on economic growth, some positive linkages can also be postulated. The following paragraphs state the major arguments.

Diversion of Resources from Other Uses

Perhaps the most common argument in this category suggests that defense (military) expenditure displaces an equal amount of civilian resource-use. The traditional "guns-butter tradeoff" paradigm indicates that if more "guns" are produced, a smaller amount of "butter" is a necessary consequence. For example, United Nations (1978, p. 1) stated, "The cost of the arms race is enormous....Public services, health, education, housing, protection of the environment, and social and economic progress generally, all need the resources which the arms race consumes."[2] Deger (1986, p. 243) points out "It is then quite easy to claim that that specific amount (of military outlays) could have been used for more 'productive expenditure', for example on investment or on human capital or in the enhancement of entitlements. In a sense this is the most potent form in which the argument against militarization is conducted; its appeal is obvious." In her typical position about military expenditure, Sivard (1989, p. 7) writes "A multitude of economic, social, and political repercussions results from the enormous diversion of resources to economically non-productive use. One of the more direct effects is the squeeze on budgets for other responsibilities of governments." One of the most eloquent expositions of this view is attributed to Dwight Eisenhower, who is cited by Russett (1983, pp. 48-49) as having said, "Every gun that is made, every warship launched, every rocket fired signifies, in the final sense, a theft from those who hunger and are not fed, those who are cold and are not clothed. This world in arms...is spending the sweat of its laborers, the genius of its scientists, the hopes of its children."

Although a plausible view, the proposition that military expenditures divert resources from more productive uses seems a bit too general and undifferentiated.

While it is definitionally true that defense outlays displace other uses of those resources, it is not obvious how overall economic well-being (or growth) is affected by that fact. The usual propositions about such a displacement imply either that the (marginal) contribution of defense expenditure to social welfare is zero or that it is lower than the marginal contribution of other types of expenditures. It seems appropriate to compare such contributions before one can conclude how the diversion of resources to defense affects social and economic well-being.

In its commonest form, the argument focuses on "unproductive" output of defense outlays, and some of the most familiar examples are bombs, guns, warships, missiles, and tanks. However, not all defense expenditure is directed toward such products; a substantial part obviously goes toward meeting consumption needs of defense personnel and their families and construction of various categories of infrastructure. If defense outlays displace civilian consumption and investment, they also generate some investment and perhaps a substantial amount of consumption in the defense sector.[3]

To the extent the argument refers to displacement of other forms of public expenditure, several points need consideration. For example, it is not obvious that government revenue is unrelated to the magnitude of defense expenditure. Although the direction of causation between government revenue and government expenditure is somewhat uncertain, it is reasonable to believe that projected military expenditure is taken into consideration when the revenue target or the tax levels are set.[4] Therefore, if military expenditure were lower, it is not inevitable that total government revenue and expenditure would remain unchanged and expenditure on other public services would be correspondingly larger. Some or all of reduced military outlays could be reflected in lower taxes and reduced government revenue; some may also be reflected in smaller growth of money supply.[5] Even if the revenue level is treated as independent of defense expenditure, it is difficult to say which categories of public expenditure would be increased if defense outlays are reduced, and the position may differ greatly across countries.[6]

In general, it might be said that unless the socially optimal level of defense spending is zero, not all defense outlays can be regarded as worthless and not all alternative uses of resources will be necessarily better. Therefore, it seems appropriate to consider more specific arguments regarding the adverse effect of defense expenditure on growth and well-being in terms of the alternatives it displaces.

Reduction in Private Consumption

The core of the reasoning in this regard is quite simple. It states that defense expenditure diverts scarce resources away from other uses, which causes a reduction in private (civilian) consumption and lowers the well-being of the society. This statement is true but needs two caveats. First, private (and public) consumption will not be reduced by the full amount of defense outlays but will be reduced only to the extent defense expenditure is devoted to production of non-consumption items, namely, defense capital and non-consumable defense output like bombs, guns, and tanks.[7] Second, as is true of most other arguments, since production of national defense is likely to have some social value, reduction in well-being will occur to the extent the social value of defense outlays is smaller than the social value (utility) of the consumption it displaces. Note also that the displacement is likely to have an impact on current well-being and not on economic growth.

Reduction in Private and Public Saving and Investment

This proposition is based on the consideration that use of resources for defense leaves a smaller amount for other purposes, and is therefore likely to lower private (and public) saving and investment. Since saving and investment are often regarded as important sources of economic growth, the adverse effect on growth is a logical implication.

The argument has some obvious validity. However, one needs to state three qualifications that are similar to those mentioned in regard to the displacement of consumption. First, it is not likely that defense outlays lower saving and investment by an equal amount, and the quantitative impact of these outlays needs a careful assessment.[8] Second, some defense expenditure goes toward capital-formation in infrastructure and other areas, and that should be taken into consideration. Third, as for all such arguments, growth consequences of the reduction in savings and investment may be compared with social returns on defense outlays. Deger (1986, pp. 87-111) considers at some length how military expenditure could affect saving and investment. His discussion shows that the relationships are not as simple as might appear, and the magnitude of the impact of military expenditure depends on (a) whether the operative constraint on growth is aggregate demand or aggregate supply, (b) capacity-utilization rate, (c) short-run versus long-run considerations, (d) impact of defense spending on time preference, and (e) the extent to which defense expenditure is covered by inflationary finance. In particular, he pointed out (Deger 1986, p. 111) the difference between the position in developed countries (DCs) and less-developed countries (LDCs) and stated, "LDC military expenditure may not crowd out investment from the demand side in the same way as in OECD countries....an expansion in milex (military expenditure) may not mean an equivalent fall in investment....If military spending reduces the absorptive capacity of the civilian sector, then investment will suffer even though investable funds are available." United Nations (1978, p. 43) discussed the issue and concluded at a somewhat general level "In most countries, therefore, there is scope for significant rises in investment if military budgets are reduced."

Diversion of Public Expenditure from Education and Health

This is one important argument made in most discussions relating to the adverse effect of defense spending on economic growth. Since human-capital formation through education and health is perhaps a major source of economic growth, especially in LDCs, defense spending is believed to lower growth by reducing public expenditure on human-capital formation. Besides other scholars, Deger (1986, pp. 112-116, 120-121) discusses the nature of the relationship between defense expenditure and public outlays on health and education. After considering the alternatives of financing government expenditure through taxation, domestic borrowing, creation of high-power money by borrowing from the central bank, and foreign transfers, he states (p. 121) "The overall conclusion seems to be that there is not much flexibility for a low income, rural-oriented LDC with backward financial institutions to increase its total budget rapidly...unlike DCs, LDCs' governments will find it difficult to resist a cut in human capital expenditures." Askari and Glover (1977, p. 60) conclude "...these (military) expenditures also absorb resources that are needed for social development, such as public expenditures on education and health."

Despite the diversity of considerations bearing on this issue, it is reasonable to say that increased defense spending probably does reduce public outlays on education and health and, therefore, tends to lower economic growth and development. However, in addition to the point about the economic value of national defense, the magnitude of the impact is an empirical question and the impact may differ significantly across countries.

It may also be noted that defense spending does contribute to some human-capital formation in education and health because defense personnel receive good physical training and undergo a significant process of skill-formation of various kinds. However, since most of their human-capital assets are applied to the defense sector, it is still true that public outlays on education and health in the civilian sector are reduced and economic growth may be adversely affected except to the extent that military human-capital may generate positive externalities (spillovers) for the civilian sector.[9]

Reduction in Private Spending on Education and Health

This argument is similar to the one which says that defense expenditure lowers private consumption. The underlying idea is that increased military expenditure reduces the resources available for private spending. Therefore, private expenditure on all items, including education and health, is likely to be reduced. Since outlays on these two items are important for economic growth, there will be an adverse effect on growth.

It is possible to argue that increased military expenditure may *raise* private outlays on education and health. That may happen if (a) as is likely, increased military outlays reduce public spending on education and health, and (b) public and private expenditures on these two items are "substitutes" in the sense that a reduction in one increases the other. However, such a reasoning is unlikely to be realistic, especially relative to the LDCs, since (a) "complementarity" between public and private spending on education and health seems more likely, and (b) even if there is some substitutability in this sense, the effect of reduced private disposable income may outweigh the "substitution" effect of lower public spending on these items.

Reduction in Public Research and Development (R&D) Outlays

It is well known that, due to large positive spillovers (externalities) of R&D products, the public sector has an important role in R&D, especially in LDCs. Therefore, the argument goes, increased defense spending is likely to lead to lower R&D outlays in the public sector, and an adverse effect on growth is likely in view of the critical contribution of technical change toward economic growth. The argument does not obviously consider public R&D outlays in the defense sector, but refers to R&D outlays directed primarily toward civilian products. Besides many other scholars, Ruth Sivard has explained this point well. In Sivard (1989), for example, she points out (p. 5) "Six times as much public research money goes for research on weapons as for research on health protection" and (p. 9) "Public investment in military research, now estimated at $100 billion a year, has produced a series of technological marvels...Public financing of health research, by comparison, has been a neglected step-child." United Nations (1978) similarly noted (p. 46) "...it is in the field of research and development that the diversion of productive resources to military ends is most massive," and (pp. 28-29) "The potential benefits...from the redeployment of R and D resources which effective disarmament would permit are so many, differentiated, and unforeseeable that one cannot give an adequate picture of them...there are enormous needs, unexplored in almost every respect, waiting to be dealt with in the systematic, large-scale and purpose-oriented fashion which has so far been the almost exclusive privilege of military research."

In view of the difficulty of expanding government revenue or funding defense expenditure through deficit finance or external transfers, it seems likely that increased defense expenditure lowers public R&D outlays in the civilian sector and may have an adverse effect on growth. However, the quantitative significance of this aspect, as of most others, is a matter of judgement and empirical research, and is likely to vary across countries.

Apart from the direct effect of defense expenditure on public (non-defense) R&D outlays, an indirect effect on technical progress could occur through its adverse impact on investment. If defense spending lowers aggregate investment and if, as Deger (1986, p. 94) suggests, new technology is "embodied" in capital, technical progress and economic growth could be adversely affected by defense expenditure.

There is a belief that even though non-defense public R&D outlays may be reduced due to an increase in defense expenditure, defense R&D projects make an important contribution toward technical progress in the civilian sector. However, that is one possible dimension of positive externalities of defense expenditure, and is discussed in a later sub-section.

Adverse Effect on Balance-of-Payment Position of LDCs

Since practically no LDC is self-sufficient in regard to its defense needs, the argument suggests that military outlays use scarce foreign exchange, accentuate balance-of-payment difficulties, reduce import of necessary capital and intermediate goods, and hurt economic growth.

Several points related to this argument may be noted. First, it is suggested that foreign-exchange cost of defense imports is likely to be substantial for many LDCs. Second, the opportunity cost of these may not be import of "luxury" consumption items, and imports of capital or intermediate goods are likely to be affected. Third, if any part of defense imports is covered by external assistance, either the country's debt burden may increase or the political implications of such assistance may be adverse and might not be any better than a direct expenditure of foreign exchange. Fourth, while the quantitative importance of this aspect would certainly vary across countries, an unfavorable effect seems likely in most cases. Fifth, adverse balance-of-payment implications of defense outlays may occur due to import of defense equipment and technology and also because of diversion to military use of domestic products that could have been exported to earn foreign exchange. However, like all other real costs of defense expenditure, one has to evaluate the consequences after considering the social and economic value of provision of national defense.

Diversion of Skilled Manpower from Civilian Use

Somewhat related to the argument about the reduction of civilian R&D effort is the suggestion that the defense sector diverts highly skilled persons from other uses, and such diversion is harmful for LDCs who face scarcity of high-skill personnel. Askari and Glover (1977, p. 54), for example, express the view "The operation of modern military equipment requires a heavy input of skilled manpower, a resource typically in short supply in underdeveloped countries...The cost of the military effort of the developing countries is increased in proportion to the skilled manpower required by the military establishments..." Similarly, United Nations (1978, p. 30) stated "...it is evident that the over-all drain on highly qualified manpower resources is often larger than either military budget figures or over-all figures for military-related employment suggest." Increasing technological sophistication of modern warfare and rising skill intensity of defense establishments tend to make this argument stronger.

Although defense sector does seem to employ large numbers of high-skill personnel in most countries and may do so on an increasing scale in the future, it is not evident that all or most of them are "diverted" from non-defense employment. Many of them receive training during the course of military employment. It is true, however, that even if these persons receive their training in the defense sector, they had high-skill potential and could have been similarly trained for non-defense employment and might then have made a larger contribution to economic growth.

Negative Spillover (Externality) Effects of Military Expenditure

Besides the direct effects of defense outlays on economic growth and well-being, many scholars have discussed the positive and negative spillover ("externality" or "spinoff") effects of military expenditures. They include Askari and Glover (1977), Benoit (1973, 1978), Bremer and Hughes (1990, pp. 25-32), Chan (1987), de Haan (1987), Deger (1986, pp. 186-196), Deger and Sen (1983), Kennedy (1983, pp. 194-211), Lindgren (1988, pp. 175-178), and United Nations (1978, pp. 45-57). The negative aspects are discussed here, and the potentially positive effects are mentioned in the following sub-section.

First, it is believed by some scholars that defense activities have an adverse effect on environment due to nuclear tests and other experimental explosions, toxic discharges, and use of a wide range of non-renewable resources that include both energy and raw materials.[10]

Second, it is pointed out that high defense outlays may tend to generate or strengthen a powerful military-industrial complex which influences public policy in a manner that is not conducive to the well-being of the society at large. For example, it may encourage excessive militarization, incite military intervention or aggression in foreign countries, and try to derive benefit for itself at the cost of the society.[11] Although non-defense activities may also generate similar interest-groups, high military expenditures are believed to lead to more powerful and perhaps more dangerous vested interests.

Third, it is possible that high levels of military expenditures tend to be associated with repressive regimes that may be dominated or supported by the military establishment. United Nations (1978, p. 56), for example, noted "Militarization often goes hand in hand with social tension. As a means of domestic repression it is not least characteristic of countries where considerable social differences and extreme exploitation of large sectors of the population prevail."[12]

In a Marxist or neo-Marxist perspective, military establishment is a means of exploitation and repression both domestically and internationally. It is a tool that capitalism uses to establish and perpetuate its many exploitative mechanisms.[13]

Fourth, due to governments' budgetary constraints, military expenditures may encourage inflationary finance and lead to serious economic distortions. United Nations (1978, pp. 40-41), for example, noted "Large military expenditures...tend to aggravate inflationary tendencies...Galloping inflation and the disruption of monetary systems have often in the past been associated with wars and rapid increases in military expenditure...Theory and data are not at the point where the role of the military expenditure in stimulating inflation can be quantified, but consideration of the various ways in which it can have an effect suggests that its contribution is not inconsequential."

Fifth, it is suggested that defense procurement and management systems are often such as to involve waste, inefficiency and extravagance in the use of resources. Therefore, apart from the diversion of resources, an unfavorable effect on growth is generated due to inefficiency in the management of defense outlays. An impressionistic illustration of such a situation could perhaps be provided from the United States where government investigations indicated that, for some items, defense contractors were paid amounts that were vastly in excess of reasonable market prices.

Sixth, due to the presence of a military-industrial group or simply due to the nature of defense operations, upper-income classes may gain more from defense outlays than lower-income people. Such a pattern may make intracountry income distribution worse. Since income distribution is an important dimension of economic development, defense outlays may generate a negative spillover relative to development.

Last, it could be argued that high defense spending by DCs tends to curtail development assistance to LDCs, and thus constitutes a negative externality for the LDCs.

In a more general perspective, defense spending by one country may constitute a negative externality if such spending makes others feel more threatened or less secure and impels them to increase their own defense expenditures. Such is indeed the general character of what is called the "arms race". Of course, conversely, defense spending by one country could constitute a positive externality for others if it provides additional security to them or otherwise lowers their defense burden.

As an aside, the possible adverse effect of defense imports on balance-of-payment position of LDCs could also be treated as a negative "spillover" of the defense establishment. However, as done in an earlier sub-section, it seems more appropriate to treat that as a direct effect.

Positive Externalities (Spillovers) of Defense Expenditure

Although almost all supply-side considerations discussed in this section suggest an adverse effect of defense outlays on economic growth and well-being, quite a few positive spillover effects have been indicated in the literature. These are mentioned in the following paragraphs.

Technology Spillover. A positive spillover that is frequently mentioned is the beneficial effect of defense R&D outlays on the rest of the economy. It is argued that new technology produced in the defense sector benefits civilian productivity also, and it is pointed out that military innovations in air transportation, nuclear power generation, radar usage, space technology and other areas have been adapted to civilian use and constitute an important spillover of defense expenditure.

While the possibility of such spillovers is evident, their quantitative importance is uncertain. A strong repudiation of the significance of such positive externalities is offered by the United Nations (1978, pp. 46-47):

> In the case of technological innovation...the true impact of high military expenditures has mostly been clouded in myth....A sober assessment indicates that the claims are grossly exaggerated....In fact it is remarkable how many inventions of the greatest civil importance... owed absolutely nothing of their origin and very little, if anything, of their subsequent development to military R and D....The truly remarkable fact is how little that is new, not how much, has come to the civilian sector from military R and D efforts....There can be no doubt that in the final analysis technological innovation in the civilian sector and, with it, growth are not furthered by military research and development but are greatly impaired by it.

Human-Capital Spillover. This is another area in which a substantial positive spillover of defense outlays on the rest of the economy is suggested, and it is argued that defense sector undertakes several forms of human-capital formation that are useful to the civilian economy.

First, skill and training imparted in the military can be put to civilian use later. For example, training in the air force enables pilots to fly civil planes after retirement; technicians trained in the army, navy and air force become useful skilled personnel for the economy when they leave military service; and health professionals may render service to the society after retirement.

Second, the training in discipline and physical improvement that military service gives to most employees becomes a valuable human-capital asset for the society at large not merely after their retirement but, through a kind of demonstration effect, even during their employment with the military.

Third, good care is taken of the nutrition and health needs of defense personnel and sometimes even the members of their families. Their stock of health is, therefore, better than that of comparable persons in the rest of the economy, especially in LDCs where general nutrition and health levels are low. This stock is a useful human-capital asset for the society at least after they leave military service.

Fourth, many defense personnel receive general schooling during their service. The effect of this human-capital formation is also a spillover for the rest of the economy.

Infrastructure Spillover. Many roads, bridges, communications networks, airports, water works, and townships are built for military use. Many of these are used by the civilian population too. These may constitute an important external benefit of defense outlays for the rest of the economy.

Employment Spillover. It is suggested that since open or "disguised" unemployment or underemployment is common in most LDCs, defense activities attenuate this problem by putting the "surplus" manpower to use. This is a positive spillover of defense outlays in the sense that the problem of unemployment is made less severe.

Although a plausible proposition, several scholars have expressed reservations about the "employment benefit" of defense expenditure. United Nations (1978, pp. 44-45) pointed out that (a) in a basic sense, labor constitutes a real resource that can be put to work if released from military-related activities, (b) people in LDCs are unemployed or underemployed because of structural problems that are aggravated by high military expenditures, and (c) increasing technological sophistication and high capital-intensity and equipment-intensity of defense activities implies that a given expenditure generates smaller employment in defense-related activities than in the rest of the economy.

Security Spillover. As is obvious, defense outlays are expected to produce national defense and to generate a more secure social and economic environment. Thus, like maintenance of internal law and order and promotion of well-functioning markets, defense outlays can have a substantial positive impact on growth. Rapid economic growth, this argument suggests, is not likely under threats of external aggression or insecurity, and defense outlays generate a more secure and more productive environment.

The argument has an obvious appeal. Defense outlays probably do have social and economic value. However, the optimal level of defense outlays is not obvious, and the "arms race" may raise defense expenditure above the level that would be optimal in a more stable international environment. Thus, the marginal value of defense spending may remain uncertain.

Direct Use of Military for Civilian Purposes. There are several circumstances in which the military sector renders a direct service to the civilian population. Some examples include (a) use of military hospitals and schools by civilians, (b) army deployment in situations of grave internal disorder, and (c) use of army personnel and equipment in special situations caused by natural disasters like tornados, floods, fires, earthquakes, and maritime emergencies.

Help in Resource Mobilization. Military activities may sometimes create a stronger national sentiment, unity of purpose, keener sense of sacrifice, and a higher state of alertness. These may facilitate resource mobilization both for defense and non-defense purposes.[14]

Increase in Aggregate Demand. In demand-deficit contexts, defense outlays may increase aggregate demand and may stimulate real activity and economic growth. Although this can be perceived as a positive spillover of defense, it is discussed in a separate section.

Role as a High-Productivity Sector. If the defense sector is technologically more advanced than the rest of the economy, it could act as a "modern" sector that may facilitate overall growth. In particular, if input productivity is higher in defense than in the rest of the economy, expansion of defense outlays may improve the growth rate in a Feder-type (1983) framework since defense output is a part of total product (GNP or GDP). An empirical assessment of the presence and the magnitude of such an effect, however, indicates a somewhat uncertain picture.[15]

Models of Supply-Side Effects

Some of the considerations discussed in this section have been incorporated in formal models of the defense-growth linkage. Besides several other scholars, de Haan (1987, pp. 91-94, 96-97), Deger (1986, pp. 193-200), Deger and Sen (1983), and Faini et al. (1984) have provided such models. Leontief and Duchin (1983) employ an input-output framework, and Bremer and Hughes (1990) have developed a fairly general simulation model.[16]

Cross-Country Differences in the Effects of Defense Expenditure on Growth

Despite the conceptual generality of what Deger (1986) termed as allocation-effect, spillover-effect and resource-mobilization effect of defense outlays, the magnitude and even the sign of the overall effect may be uncertain and may vary greatly across countries. Therefore, Frederiksen and Looney (1982) have suggested a distinction between resource-abundant and resource-constrained LDCs. For the former, they indicated the impact of defense expenditure may be positive or non-negative while for the latter it is likely to be negative. Biswas and Ram (1986) distinguished between low-income and middle-income LDCs. In a somewhat similar spirit, Deger (1986, pp. 203-209) suggested the possibility that the relation between defense expenditure and growth is nonlinear, and hypothesized that high- and low-income countries can derive and absorb the benefits of military expenditure, while middle-income countries tend to suffer more than they gain.[17] Empirical evidence on the importance of these distinctions and classifications, however, seems ambiguous.

Defense-Growth Linkages Related to Aggregate Demand

The basic argument is couched in a Keynesian framework. The general scenario is of some slack in the employment of resources (labor and/or capital) and of an "aggregate demand constraint" on expansion of real output. In such a situation, defense outlays may increase aggregate demand and, due to the multiplier effect, may raise real output by a multiple of the magnitude of demand increase.

In this mode of thought, many of the supply-side considerations discussed in the previous section are regarded as unimportant due to the belief that there are idle resources in the economy; defense expenditures simply cause utilization of these resources and expansion of real output. Therefore, defense outlays lead to higher output and enhance economic growth.

The magnitude of the impact of defense expenditure on output and growth depends on the structural parameters. In a post-Keynesian model, de Haan (1987, pp. 88-91) shows that the influence of defense spending on growth will depend on the *effect* of such spending on four expenditure-equations parameters, namely, savings ratio, government budget ratio, current account ratio, and the capital coefficient. His general conclusion is that the effect of defense expenditure (and of disarmament) on economic growth is analytically uncertain. Deger (1986, pp. 200-203) also discusses the potential role of defense spending in economic growth through aggregate demand.

Conceptual validity and empirical importance of the aggregate demand aspect of defense expenditure seem highly context-dependent. For most developed countries, the argument is likely to have some validity, especially in recessionary periods, in a short-run framework. However, its significance is doubtful in a longer horizon even for the DCs. For most LDCs, the real constraint is likely to lie on the supply side, and considerations of resource-diversion seem to have stronger relevance than the demand-raising role of military expenditure.

One may note the possibility that, as an aggregate-demand measure, defense spending could be used, especially by DC governments, as a stabilization tool. However, since defense outlays lack the kind of flexibility that is needed for stabilization measures, their role as a discretionary countercyclical policy device is likely to be limited. Lindgren (1988, pp. 179-184) provides an interesting discussion of linkages between military expenditures and business-cycles and "electoral cycles".

Defense Expenditures and Economic Growth After the Cold War

With the disintegration of the Soviet Union and the end of the Cold War, a new era in world history has begun, and international situation regarding military expenditures is likely to undergo a major restructuring. Several questions may be considered in this context.

First, one might ask whether the defense-growth nexus would change in any significant manner. Although the question cannot be adequately discussed within the limits of this paper, it seems unlikely that the nature of the relationship between military spending and economic performance will be altered in any major way. The broad character of the allocation and the spillover (spinoff) effects of defense outlays may be predicted to remain largely the same.

Second, it could be considered whether cessation of the superpower rivalry is likely to lead to a more secure world order and to lower military expenditures. Although this aspect also needs a lengthy discussion, a few brief remarks are offered. It seems reasonable to say that military expenditures of the United States and other industrial economies would decline. However, it is uncertain whether defense expenditures of LDCs will be reduced in any significant manner.[18] McNamara (1991, p. 26) noted "The past 45 years have seen some 125 wars and conflicts in the Third World...That (superpower) rivalry has undeniably been a contributing factor...Many of these conflicts, however,...have had their roots in historical enmities within and among developing countries...In view of the diverse reasons countries have for going to war, we must conclude that...conflicts within and among nations will not disappear even though East and West cease to fight their proxy wars in the South." While the wars and conflicts incited and encouraged by the superpowers are likely to decline, it is not obvious that developing countries will necessarily feel less threatened. On the contrary, some of them may feel a greater external threat because of the loss of "balance" that existed between the two superpowers.[19] Therefore, it is not clear that LDC defense outlays will fall significantly.

Third, it might seem that reduced military outlays in the United States and other DCs could induce them to increase development assistance to LDCs. Such a scenario also appears generally unlikely except in terms of some unusual international agreement. In fact, since political considerations motivated by the superpower rivalry seem to have been a major factor even in development assistance, such assistance to LDCs may decline despite the "peace dividend" reaped by DCs.

Last, it is relevant to ask whether the character of international arms trade or military aid may change in such a manner as to benefit the LDCs and, if nothing else, to reduce the burden on their foreign exchange resources. This, too, is a difficult aspect, but there seems little basis for optimism.[20] During the Cold War, most of the major concessional military transfers were apparently motivated by "power bloc" considerations. Those factors will become less important, and it is difficult to say how costs of LDC arms imports will change. Monopoly of modern arms technology by one country or a group of countries may make its acquisition more difficult, especially for those LDCs who may not wish to support the position of the monopolist(s) on various international issues. For neutral and "nonaligned" nations, the real costs of security could increase after the Cold War.

Concluding Remarks

This paper endeavors to provide a broad synoptic perspective on conceptual linkages between defense expenditure and economic growth and well-being. Several other papers in this volume deal with some of these issues in greater detail.[21] Although I have discussed the linkages in general terms, the focus is on less-developed countries. From the supply-side perspective, the resource-diversion arguments have been stated, and possible existence of many kinds of positive and negative externalities (spillovers or spinoffs) has been mentioned. A brief discussion is also provided about the potential role of defense outlays in stimulating demand, especially in the presence of idle resources.

It is obviously difficult to give an assessment of the overall effect which is likely to vary across countries. It is not easy even to venture a general conjecture about the direction of the overall effect. By way of a quick summary of the various effects, three points could be made. First, the aggregate-demand consideration is probably a short-run aspect and does not seem important in a discussion of economic growth in the "medium" or the "long" run. Moreover, LDCs are unlikely to be characterized by idle resources except perhaps in a short-run cyclical context or in regard to unskilled labor. Second, while there are likely to be several positive externalities of defense outlays, some negative spillovers are also possible; the balance could well be positive in many countries, but its magnitude is a matter of empirical assessment. Last, therefore, the net impact of defense expenditure on economic well-being and growth will depend on the balance between social usefulness (utility) of national defense and the real opportunity cost of material and human resources devoted to defense. Despite the simplicity of the concept of "opportunity cost", its quantification relative to defense outlays is difficult because the foregone alternatives are not easily measured. Quantification of the social usefulness of national defense is even more elusive. A scientific assessment of the net economic effect of defense outlays thus remains a hazardous undertaking both theoretically and empirically. Although most defense expenditures may be "unproductive" in a perfect world, given the state of external insecurity perceived by countries, a nonzero defense expenditure is likely to be optimal in almost all cases. However, it is difficult to assess, in any reasonably scientific mode, the extent to which the actual exceeds the optimal. Ambiguities in the reported empirical results may at least partly be a reflection of the underlying conceptual issues that are difficult to capture in standard econometric models.

A few observations are also made on the consequences of the end of the Cold War for the level of defense expenditures and the structure of the defense-growth nexus. The author's conjecture is that, although there is always scope for hope, neither the defense-growth nexus is likely to undergo a significant structural change nor the LDCs in general have reason to be optimistic about a substantial reduction in their defense outlays despite the cessation of superpower rivalry and a sizable fall in DC military expenditures.

Notes

1. An important distinction is sometimes made between "growth" and "development"; while the former is typically measured in terms of "average" (per capita) income, the latter also takes into account the distributional aspects and status of low-income (poor) groups. In this paper, the terms are used synonymously except in a few contexts.

2. There are actually several related studies by the United Nations, both before and after the cited (1978) volume. However, their general tenor is similar, and quotes from the 1978 volume provide a fair representation of those studies.

3. Russett (1970, pp. 140-141) presents one estimate of the "opportunity cost" of defense expenditure in the United States for the period 1939-68. He indicated that a dollar spent on defense reduces personal consumption by 42 cents, fixed capital formation by 29 cents,

exports by 10 cents, federal civil programs by 5 cents, and state and local government programs by 13 cents. His estimates have been criticized by Caputo (1975) and others.

4. The multicountry study by Ram (1988) provides some evidence on patterns of Granger-causality between government revenue and government expenditure.

5. Empirical estimates reported by Deger (1986, p. 71) from data for twenty-seven countries are interesting in this context. He interpreted the estimates as suggestive of "a definite positive effect of the defence burden on the tax effort"; one-dollar increase in military expenditure appears to increase the tax revenue by 85.8 cents.

6. Of course, public expenditure on highly productive items like education and health *could* increase, but it is not evident that it necessarily would. Deger (1986, p. 123) reports some estimates of the effect of military outlays on public educational spending, and states qualitatively that the defense burden "is probably strongly detrimental to human capital formation."

7. Note 3 indicates one estimate of the opportunity cost of defense expenditure in terms of private consumption. With the increasing technical sophistication of military gear, very high costs of modern weapons, and rising equipment-intensity of defense outlays, this reasoning may tend to acquire greater significance.

8. In particular, note the possibility suggested by Deger (1986, p. 105) "the problem for LDCs is that even if sufficient funds are available, the amount of investment is often limited by the economy's ability to absorb capital."

9. This aspect is discussed later in the text.

10. A brief discussion of the environmental aspects is provided by United Nations (1978, pp. 30-32).

11. See United Nations (1978, pp. 54-56) for an analysis of the role of military institutions in internal affairs of a country.

12. A different perspective is suggested by Deger and Smith (1983) who stated "The coercive power provided by a strong military may enable the state to increase the rate of exploitation of available resources." Deger (1986, pp. 222-223) similarly suggests the possibility that the military might be the only force which could impart "cohesion, unity, and leadership" in some LDCs, and the military could use its power against the dominant vested interests.

13. See Smith (1977) for an analysis of the connections between military expenditures and capitalism.

14. This is suggested by Deger (1986) and other scholars.

15. Biswas and Ram (1986) attempted such an empirical assessment. Their results show a mixed and uncertain position. The

paper by Biswas in this volume contains an update of the Biswas-Ram exercise.

16. Some of these models include aggregate-demand aspects also.

17. Note that while Frederiksen and Looney (1982) and Biswas and Ram (1986) focussed attention on LDCs, Deger (1986) considers both DCs and LDCs.

18. Kaldor (1991) discusses prospects for reduction of military expenditures in the DCs and the LDCs after the Cold War.

19. McNamara (1991) makes several specific suggestions for increasing international security and lowering LDC military expenditures.

20. Deger and Sen (1991) provide a discussion of the linkages between military aid and developmental assistance. They also consider several questions regarding military aid and LDC arms imports.

21. The papers by Anderton, Mueller and Atesoglu, and Meyer and Raines seem especially relevant.

References

Askari, Hossein, and Michael Glover (1977), *Military Expenditures and the Level of Economic Development*, Austin: University of Texas at Austin.

Benoit, Emile (1973), *Defense and Economic Growth in Developing Countries*, Lexington, MA: Lexington Books.

_____ (1978), "Growth and Defense in Developing Countries," *Economic Development and Cultural Change* Vol. 26, pp. 271-280.

Biswas, Basudeb, and Rati Ram (1986), "Military Expenditures and Economic Growth in Less Developed Countries: An Augmented Model and Further Evidence," *Economic Development and Cultural Change*, Vol. 34, pp. 361-72.

Bremer, Stuart A., and Barry B. Hughes (1990), *Disarmament and Development*, Englewood Cliffs, NJ: Prentice Hall.

Caputo, David A. (1975), "New Perspectives on the Public Policy Implications of Defense and Welfare Expenditures in Four Modern Democracies: 1950-1970," *Policy Sciences*, Vol. 6, pp. 423-46.

Chan, Steve (1987), "Military Expenditures and Economic Performance," in *World Military Expenditures and Arms Transfers 1986*, pp. 29-37, Washington, DC: U.S. Arms Control and Disarmament Agency.

De Haan, Hendrik (1987), "Military Expenditures and Economic Growth: Some Theoretical Remarks," in Christian Schmidt, ed.,

The Economics of Military Expenditures, pp. 87-97, New York, NY: St. Martin's Press.

Deger, Saadet (1986), *Military Expenditure in Third World Countries: The Economic Effects*, Boston, MA: Routledge & Kegan Paul.

_____, and Somnath Sen (1983), "Military Expenditure, Spin-off and Economic Development," *Journal of Development Economics*, Vol. 13, pp. 67-83.

_____, and Somnath Sen (1991), "Military Expenditure, Aid, and Economic Development," in *Proceedings of the World Bank Annual Conference on Development Economics 1991*, pp. 159-186, Washington, DC: World Bank.

_____, and Ron Smith (1983), "Military Expenditure and Growth in Less Developed Countries," *Journal of Conflict Resolution*, Vol. 27, pp. 335-53.

Faini, Riccardo, Patricia Annez and Lance Taylor (1984), "Defense Spending, Economic Structure, and Growth: Evidence Among Countries and Over Time," *Economic Development and Cultural Change*, Vol. 32, pp. 487-98.

Feder, Gershon (1983), "On Exports and Economic Growth," *Journal of Development Economics*, Vol. 12, pp. 59-73.

Frederiksen, Peter C., and Robert E. Looney (1982), "Defense Expenditures and Economic Growth in Developing Countries: Some Further Empirical Evidence," *Journal of Economic Development*, Vol. 7, pp. 113-25.

Kaldor, Mary (1991), "After the Cold War: Obstacles and Opportunities in Cutting Arms Budgets," in *Proceedings of the World Bank Annual Conference on Development Economics 1991*, pp. 141-56, Washington, DC: World Bank.

Kennedy, Gavin (1983), *Defense Economics*, New York, NY: St.Martin's Press.

Leontief, Wassily, and Faye Duchin (1983), *Military Spending*, New York, NY: Oxford University Press.

Lindgren, Goran (1988), "Armaments and Economic Performance," in Peter Wallensteen, ed., *Peace Research: Achievements and Challenges*, pp. 169-97, Boulder, CO: Westview Press.

McNamara, Robert S. (1991), "Reducing Military Expenditures in the Third World," *Finance and Development*, Vol. 28, pp. 26-28.

Ram, Rati (1988), "A Multicountry Perspective on Causality Between Government Revenue and Government Expenditure," *Public Finance/Finances Publiques*, Vol. 43, pp. 261-70.

Russett, Bruce M. (1970), *What Price Vigilance?: The Burdens of National Defense*, New Haven, CT: Yale University Press.

_____ (1983), *The Prisoners of Insecurity*, San Francisco, CA: W.H. Freeman & Company.

Sivard, Ruth Leger (1989), *World Military and Social Expenditures 1989*, Washington, DC: World Priorities.

Smith, Ron P. (1977), "Military Expenditure and Capitalism," *Cambridge Journal of Economics*, Vol. 1, pp. 61-76.

United Nations (1978), *Economic and Social Consequences of the Arms Race and of Military Expenditures*, New York, NY: United Nations.

3

A Theory of Defense Spending and Economic Growth

Michael J. Mueller and H. Sonmez Atesoglu

This paper presents a neoclassical model of defense spending and economic growth. The theoretical approach adopted is based on the production function framework recently developed by Feder (1982) to explain the role of exports in economic growth. This framework was used by Ram (1986) to examine the relationship between government spending and economic growth. More recently Feder's theoretical framework and its extensions were used by Atesoglu and Mueller (1990) to describe the connection between defense spending and economic growth in the United States.

The theoretical approach discussed here allows for the effects of defense spending and technological change in determining economic growth in addition to the traditional factors of production. Defense production is thought of as generating externalities for the civilian sector. The civilian sector may benefit from favorable spillovers from the defense sector such as technological discoveries and trained labor. The civilian sector may be hampered because of unfavorable spillovers such as shortages of specialized workers and scientists due to defense sector demands or lack of investment funds because of high interest rates brought about by the financing needs of the defense sector. These effects are outside the control of the civilian sector and are considered as generating externalities that impact the civilian sector.

The effects of technological change have been neglected in the earlier studies of defense spending and economic growth mentioned above. The incorporation of technological change allows the proposed theory of defense spending and economic growth to be comparable to the neoclassical theory of economic growth which, as discussed by Solow (1957), pays special attention to the role of technological change. In the following section of the paper a two sector production model of the economy is discussed which includes defense spending as an externality in the civilian sector and which explicitly allows for technological change in both the civilian and defense sectors of the economy. This model yields a single equation account of economic growth by recognizing the effects of the factors of production, technological change, and defense spending. In the third section, comparative static effects of defense spending and technological change are illustrated by graphical rendition of the model. Concluding remarks are in the final section.

Theoretical Model

The economy is assumed to have two sectors: defense and civilian. The defense sector is postulated to generate externalities that effect the civilian sector. These effects can be positive or negative and are outside the control of the civilian sector. The two sector production model of the economy is given by the following aggregate production functions,

$$D = A(t)F(L_d, K_d), \tag{1}$$

$$C = B(t)G(L_c, K_c, D), \tag{2}$$

where D is defense sector output, C is civilian output, and A(t) and B(t) give Hicks neutral technical change in the respective sectors. Hicks neutral technical change, also called output-augmenting technical change, is such that the shares of income going to the factors of production and the factor ratios do not change as a result of technical change. Subscripts represent the sectors and L_i is labor input in the ith sector and K_i is capital stock in the ith sector. The production functions are assumed to have continuous first and second derivatives, and to be strictly increasing with respect to L, K, and t but the derivatives of G with respect to the external effect, D, are of unknown sign.

Total output, Q, is:

$$Q = D + C, \tag{3}$$

where civilian output, C, includes all economic production that is not classified as defense output, i. e. it includes nondefense government output as well as all private sector output. Total inputs are given by:

$$L = L_d + L_c, \tag{4}$$

$$K = K_d + K_c, \tag{5}$$

where L and K are total amounts of labor and capital used in the economy.

Technical change in the defense sector may not be the same as in the civilian sector. However, it is assumed that they are proportional to each other according to:

$$A(t)/B(t) = 1 + \phi, \tag{6}$$

where ϕ, the technological change proportionality factor, is an unknown constant.

The marginal productivities of labor and capital may not be the same in both sectors. The marginal productivity of a factor of production is the additional output resulting from the use of an additional unit of the factor while not changing the amount of the other factors used, the level of technology, or, in the case of the civilian sector, the size of the defense sector. Allowance is made for differences in marginal productivities between sectors by assuming that the marginal productivity of factors used in the defense sector is equal to $(1 + \delta)$ times the corresponding marginal factor productivity in the civilian sector, i.e.,

$$F_l/G_l = F_k/G_k = 1 + \delta, \tag{7}$$

where the F_i's and the G_i's are the marginal products of labor and capital in the two sectors, respectively. The factor productivity differential, δ, is an unknown constant. The assumption in equation (7) that the productivity differential is the same for labor and capital is a simplification necessary to derive a single equation description of total output growth from the two sector model.

Assuming technical progress proceeds at a constant exponential rate by letting $B=e^{\lambda t}$, it is possible to derive (see appendix) the following relationship between the total output growth rate, the growth rate of L, K, D, and technological change:

$$dQ/Q = \lambda + e^{\lambda t}G_l(dL/L)(L/Q) + e^{\lambda t}G_k(dK/K)(K/Q) + (\theta + e^{\lambda t}G_d)(dD/D)(D/Q) + \theta\lambda(D/Q), \quad (8)$$

where θ is a constant involving the two parameters δ and ϕ.

$$\theta = (\phi+\delta+\delta\phi)/(1+\phi+\delta+\delta\phi). \quad (9)$$

Finally, equation (8) is written in elasticity terms. Letting ε_i indicate elasticity of output with respect to the ith input gives:

$$dQ/Q = \lambda + \varepsilon_l(dL/L) + \varepsilon_k(dK/K) + \varepsilon_d(dD/D) + \theta\lambda(D/Q). \quad (10)$$

The elasticities are thus defined as:

$$\varepsilon_l = e^{\lambda t}G_l(L/Q);\ \varepsilon_k = e^{\lambda t}G_k(K/Q);\ \varepsilon_d = (\theta+e^{\lambda t}G_d)(D/Q). \quad (11)$$

It is appropriate to express the result in elasticities because of the assumption of Hicks neutral technical change which means constant factor shares. Assuming a perfectly competitive economy, elasticities are also factor shares and viewing equation (10) empirically, the elasticities are parameters.

Notice that λ appears in equation (10) as an exponent within the elasticities, as well as a separate term and a multiplier in the last term. λ comes from the assumption, stated before equation (8) above, that technical progress in the civilian sector, B(t), proceeds at a constant exponential rate, i.e. $B(t)=e^{\lambda t}$. So $e^{\lambda t}$ is the technological change factor and $(e^{\lambda t}-1)C(t)$ is the amount, in terms of civilian output, C, that the production function, equation (2), shifts up over period t. Since technical progress in the defense sector is defined as $A(t)=(1+\phi)B(t)$ by equation (6), the amount the defense sector production function shifts up is given by $(1+\phi)(e^{\lambda t}-1)D$. The technological change factor in the defense sector, $(1+\phi)e^{\lambda t}$, is different than the civilian sector factor unless ϕ equals zero. λ itself is a percentage rate of technical change per unit time since $dB/B=\lambda$ and is thus denominated in the same units, percentages, as the rates of growth dL/L, dK/K, and dD/D. Also, notice using the definition of A, that $dA/A=\lambda$. Thus λ is the common, economy-wide, rate of technical change. That both sectors have the same rate of technical change is a result of the specific functional forms used in the derivation and not of the underlying properties of the production functions. In the discussion which follows, the terminology rate of technical change means λ and technological change factor means $e^{\lambda t}$ or $(1+\phi)e^{\lambda t}$.

Equation (10) predicts a positive relationship between economic growth, (dQ/Q), capital growth, (dK/K), and employment growth (dL/L), providing that the marginal products of capital and labor are positive in the civilian sector. The technological change factor, $e^{\lambda t}$, is of course positive even if λ is negative. (If λ is negative, $e^{\lambda t}$ is less than one so the production function is shifted down over time since $G(L_c,K_c,D)$ is being multiplied by a number between zero and one.) However, since λ is thought of as the average percentage rate of technical progress over the long run, it is expected to be positive. The predicted sign of the defense growth effect, (dD/D), depends on the signs of θ and the marginal external product of defense spending in the civilian sector, G_d. The predicted sign of the defense size effect, D/Q, depends on the sign of θ. There is no a priori assumption about the sign of G_d because defense spending is being treated as an externality and may have a positive, negative, or zero effect. Equation (9) shows that the sign of θ depends on the signs of δ and ϕ. Since δ is positive, negative, or zero depending on the relative productivity of capital and labor in the two sectors, and likewise for ϕ depending on the relative rates of technological change, there is no theoretical basis for an a priori assumption about the sign of θ. The sign of the defense spending growth effect and of the defense size effect are indeterminate.

Comparative Statics

Given the description of predictions the model yields in the above paragraph, the comparative statics of equation (10) with respect to changes in the growth rate of capital and labor are straightforward. An increase in dK/K and/or dL/L will cause an increase in dQ/Q since both have positive elasticities of output.

Defense Size Effect

The effect of a change in defense spending growth, dD/D, on overall economic growth is complex. It helps to start by looking at the effect of different relative sizes of the defense sector, D/Q. This is the last term in equation (10). Assuming λ is positive, the effect of a larger defense sector on economy-wide growth can be positive or negative depending on the sign of θ. Only in the case where both δ and ϕ are positive is it possible to know the sign of θ without knowing the magnitudes of δ and ϕ. In which case it would be positive and a larger defense sector would mean faster economic growth. A likely case is lower productivity in the defense sector than in the civilian sector, δ negative, and a larger technological change factor in the defense sector than in the civilian sector, ϕ positive. In this case the sign of θ is indeterminate. So a larger defense sector could have a positive or negative effect on economy-wide growth.

It is of course possible that ϕ could change over time. It might be expected to decrease as the US reduces expenditures on defense research as part of the overall reduction in military expenditures in the 1990's. The derivative, $d\theta/d\phi$ gives the effect of changes in ϕ. That derivative is $(1+\delta)/(1+\phi+\delta+\delta\phi)^2$ and it is positive unless δ is less than -1. A value of -1 for δ is unlikely because that means the marginal products of factors used in the defense sector are negative. Thus a smaller D/Q combined with a reduction in ϕ, the current likely scenario in the US, could change θ from positive to negative -- if it is currently positive. The result would be greater economy-wide growth rates as D/Q falls.

Defense Growth Effect

In the short run, the effect of a change in dD/D on economic growth depends on the sign of θ, the sign of G_d, and the sign of λ. In the long run it also depends on how the change in dD/D effects the relative size of the defense sector, D/Q. As usual, in the following discussion λ is taken to be positive.

The short run defense growth effect depends on ε_d as defined in equations (11). Theoretically, its sign is given by $(\theta+e^{\lambda t}G_d)$ since D/Q is always positive. The effect may be positive or negative depending on the signs of θ and G_d. This is illustrated in Figures 3.1, 3.2 and 3.3 which show economic growth, dQ/Q, as a function of the growth rate of defense spending, dD/D, holding constant the other variables in equation (10). In Figure 3.1, the upper line shows the relationship for a defense sector of size $(D/Q)_0$, a positive θ, and a positive slope, ε_d. When the rate of growth of defense spending declines and/or changes from positive to negative, as is likely in the US in the 1990's, initially economic growth will fall from a to b as indicated by arrow 1 due to the short run effect of the defense growth effect. In Figure 3.2, where ε_d is positive but θ is negative, the lower line shows that the short run effect of a decline in dD/D is a decrease in economic growth from a to b as arrow 1 shows. However, in Figure 3.3 where both θ and G_d are negative so ε_d is negative, the lower line shows the short run effect of a decrease in dD/D is an increase in economic growth from a to b. So in the short run, changes in the rate of growth of defense spending stimulate or depress the growth rate of the economy depending on the direction of the externality effect, G_d, and the sign of θ.

In the long run, changes in the growth rate of defense spending

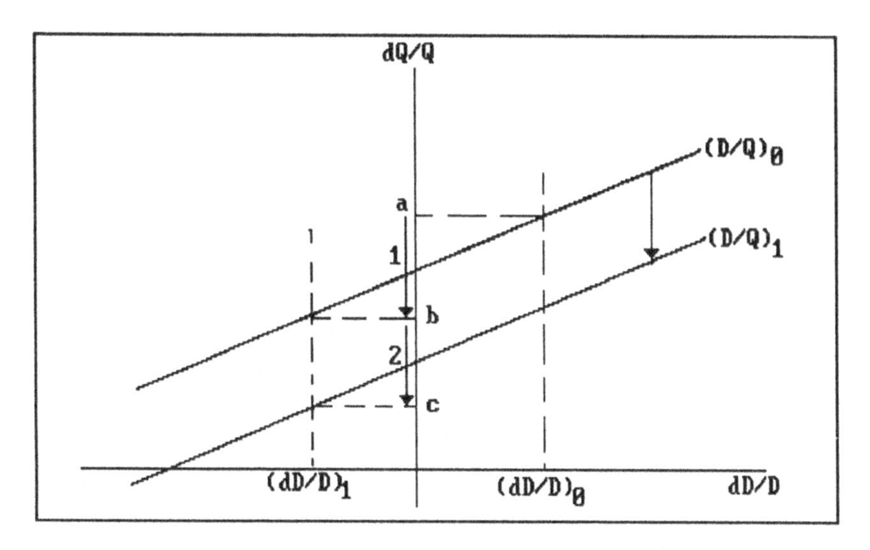

FIGURE 3.1 Economic Growth Changes With $\varepsilon_d>0$, $G_d>0$, and $\theta>0$.
[Given a Reduction in Defense Spending Growth. Note: $(D/Q)_0>(D/Q)_1$]

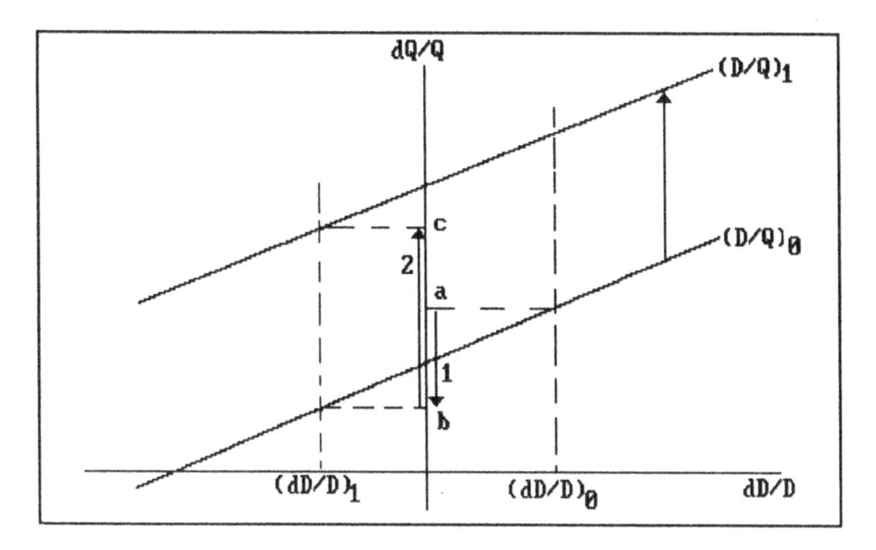

FIGURE 3.2 Economic Growth Changes With $\varepsilon_d>0$, $G_d>0$, and $\theta<0$.
[Given a Reduction in Defense Spending Growth. Note: $(D/Q)_0>(D/Q)_1$]

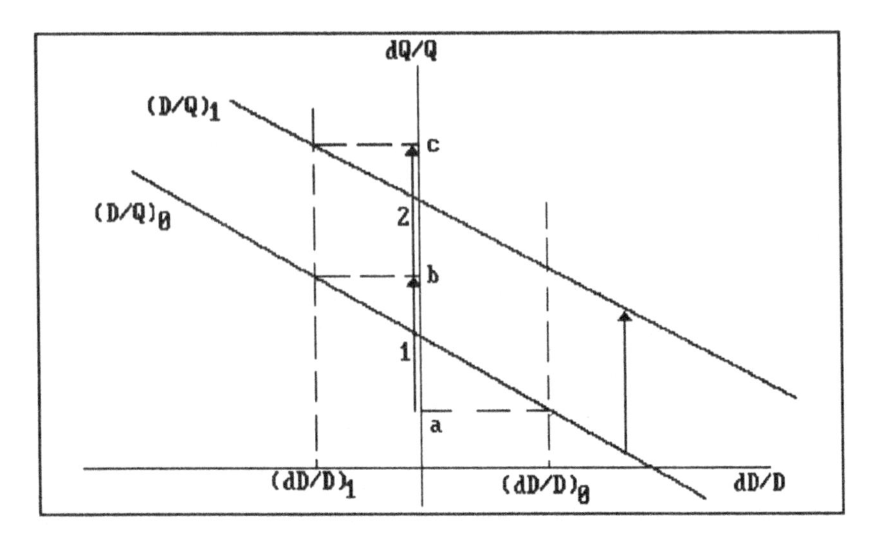

FIGURE 3.3 Economic Growth Changes With $\varepsilon_d<0$, $G_d<0$, and $\theta<0$.
[Given a Reduction in Defense Spending Growth. Note: $(D/Q)_0>(D/Q)_1$]

cause changes in the size of the defense sector, D/Q. The direction of that change is not obvious as the derivative of D/Q with respect to D shows.

$$d(D/Q)/dD = (\beta/\lambda\theta Q)[d(dD/dt)/dD - \beta(dD/dt)/Q - \lambda - \lambda\theta D/Q], \qquad (12)$$

where $\beta=(\theta+e^{\lambda t}G_d)$ and it is assumed dK/K and dL/L are constant. Depending on the signs and magnitudes of the terms in equation (12), d(D/Q)/dD could be positive or negative.

Figures 3.1, 3.2 and 3.3 show three of the possible cases. In all the figures it is assumed that d(D/Q)/dD is positive. In the case presented in Figure 3.1, θ is positive so the decline in the growth rate of defense spending causes a decline in the size of the defense sector, and this results in an downward shift to the line labeled $(D/Q)_1$. The short run reduction in economy-wide growth is reinforced by the negative defense size effect as shown by arrow 2.

In Figure 3.2, with θ negative, a reduction in the rate of growth of defense spending shifts the line upward to $(D/Q)_1$. The short run reduction in economy-wide growth is countered by the defense size effect as arrows 1 and 2 indicate. The defense size effect and the defense growth effect act in opposite directions on the growth rate of the economy. Since only the direction of the short run and long run effects are known, the net result on dQ/Q could be positive or negative.

A net positive effect, from a to c, is shown in the figure.

In Figure 3.3, both θ and G_d are negative so ε_d is also negative and the slope of the line is negative. A reduction in defense spending growth shifts the line upward to $(D/Q)_1$. The long run effect on the economic growth rate, from b to c, reinforces the short run effect from a to b so the overall effect is an increase in the economy-wide growth rate as arrows 1 and 2 indicate.

All the other cases relating the two defense effects and their impact on economic growth can be visualized, but the general conclusion is that overall economic growth may be stimulated or retarded by changes in the rate of growth of defense spending. However, following the discussion above under the defense size effect, the most likely situation for the U. S. can be described. It consists of reduced dD/D, a falling D/Q, positive λ, and negative θ. This still leaves the sign of G_d for which there is no likely value as noted above. The cases shown in Figures 3.2 and 3.3 are exactly the two situations which result from the most likely situation. If one believes the defense sector has a negative external effect on the civilian sector then Figure 3.3 is appropriate and optimism about future domestic economic growth is warranted. However, if it is thought that the externality is positive, than either figure is appropriate because the magnitude of G_d comes into play, and only cautious optimism is called for.

Technological Change

Both the technological change rate, λ, and the technological change proportionality factor, ϕ, have effects on the economy's rate of growth. As explained above, the technological change rate is assumed to be positive but the sign of ϕ may be positive or negative and its effects are indirect through the sign of θ. Reference to equations (10) and (11), shows that the greater the technological change rate the faster is the growth rate of the economy, dQ/Q, provided θ and G_d are both positive. This case is illustrated in Figure 3.1. If θ and/or G_d are negative, the net result of a greater λ depends on the magnitude of the terms, but the increase in dQ/Q will be smaller. (It is unlikely that the net result would be negative because this means technological improvements have a negative effect on the growth rate of the economy, an implausible possibility.) Thus, a negative external effect of defense spending, $G_d<0$, can act as a drag on the growth rate of the economy through its impact on the effects of technological rate of change. However, the magnitude of the drag depends on the growth rate of defense spending, dD/D. If the growth rate of defense spending is negative, in these circumstances the drag effect is reversed.

Changes in the rate of technological change, λ, are long run structural shifts in the economy and even sizable changes in defense spending are not likely to have significant short or medium run effects on λ. However, changes in the rate of defense spending may well have major, immediate effects on the technological change proportionality factor, ϕ. This follows because a significant portion of defense spending is directed toward military research and development in order to keep advancing defense technology. With reductions in defense spending, $dD/D<0$, it is likely that ϕ will change from positive to negative. That is, the shift upward in the defense sector production function will become proportionately smaller than that in the civilian sector. Since $d\theta/d\phi$ is positive, a decrease in ϕ will decrease θ and, as suggested above, may change it from positive to negative. The effect of such a change in the sign of θ is seen by comparing Figure 3.1, where θ is positive, with Figures 3.2 and 3.3. In Figure 3.2 the sign of θ is negative but G_d is positive and assumed large enough that the slope remains positive. Figure 3.3 shows the change from positive θ when G_d is also negative. In both cases, the decrease in ϕ causes the long run defense size effect of a reduction in defense spending to switch direction from Figure 3.1. In the case in Figure 3.3, the slope also changes sign. Thus, the likely decrease in ϕ may result in faster economic growth as the movement from point a to point c shows in Figures 3.2 and 3.3.

Conclusions

A two sector model of the economy composed of a civilian and a defense sector with technological change in both sectors and with defense spending acting as an externality in the civilian sector shows that the effect of a change in defense spending on the growth rate of the economy is not straightforward. However, important insights are gained. Given the very likely scenario that U. S. defense spending is reduced, the size of the defense sector as a proportion of the whole economy falls over time, the economy-wide rate of technological change is positive, and that the parameter θ is negative, the model shows that, regardless of the sign of the external effect of defense production, the growth rate of the economy may well be enhanced. However, this conclusion must be highly qualified, as the following discussion makes clear, and empirical studies are needed to resolve the remaining uncertainties.

Both the size of the defense sector and the rate of defense spending growth affect the overall growth rate of the economy. The direction of the size effect depends on the relative productivity of factors in the two sectors and the relative rate of technological advance in the two sectors. The direction of the rate of growth effect also depends on relative productivity and technological advance and on the sign of the marginal external product of defense spending in the civilian sector. Defense spending has both a short run and long run effect on the economic growth rate of the overall economy. Immediate changes in defense spending result in eventual changes in the size of the defense sector. The direction of the effect of these long and short run effects on the growth rate of the economy is uncertain because of dependence on parameters whose signs are an empirical question.

In general, improvements in the rate of technological change in the economy will increase the economy's growth rate, however the defense sector may act as somewhat of a drag, slowing down the effects of technological change depending on the signs of the defense size and spending effects. Also, if the relative rate of technological advance in the defense sector falls, a reduction in the size of the defense sector will improve the rate of growth of the overall economy. Thus, with a reduction in defense spending, technological considerations suggest the economy-wide growth rate will be improved. The conclusions are unclear because the signs and magnitudes of key parameters are not predictable from the theory. Further research involving estimation of the derived relationships is called for to help eliminate some possibilities and more accurately delineate predictions.

Appendix

This appendix shows the derivation of equations (8) and (9).

The total differential of $Q = D + C$ gives:

$$dQ = FdA + AF_l dL_d + AF_k dK_d + GdB + BG_l dL_c + BG_k dK_c + BG_d dD. \quad \text{(A1)}$$

Eliminating F_l and F_k using equation (7) and collecting terms yields:

$$dQ = G_l(AdL_d + BdL_c) + G_k(AdK_d + BdK_c) + \delta A(G_l dL_d + G_k dK_d) + BG_d dD + FdA + GdB. \quad \text{(A2)}$$

From equations (4) and (5), $dL = dL_d + dL_c$ and $dK = dK_d + dK_c$. Using this, equation (6), and equation (7) gives:

$$dQ = BG_l dL + BG_k dK + B(\phi/(1+\delta))(F_l dL_d + F_k dK_d) + A(\delta/(1+\delta))(F_l dL_d + F_k dK_d) + BG_d dD + FdA + GdB. \quad \text{(A3)}$$

Now using equation (7), the total differential of equation (1), $dD = FdA + AF_l dL_d + AF_k dK_d$, and collecting terms yield:

$$dQ = BG_l dL + BG_k dK + [(\delta+\phi/(1+\phi))/(1+\delta) + BG_d]dD + [1-(\delta+\phi/(1+\phi))/(1+\delta)]FdA + BdG. \quad \text{(A4)}$$

Using $dA = dB + \phi dB$ and simplifying gives:

$$dQ = BG_l dL + BG_k dK + [(\delta+\phi/(1+\phi))/(1+\delta) + BG_d]dD + dB[(1/(1+\delta))F+G]. \quad \text{(A5)}$$

Dividing each side of equation (A5) by Q, it can be written in terms of growth rates:

$$dQ/Q = BG_l(dL/L)(L/Q) + BG_k(dK/K)(K/Q) + [(\delta+\phi/(1+\phi))/(1+\delta) + BG_d](dD/D)(D/Q) + dB[(1/(1+\delta))F+G]/B((1+\phi)F+G), \quad \text{(A6)}$$

where $Q = AF + BG = B((1+\phi)F+G)$ is used in the last term. Assuming technical progress proceeds at a constant exponential rate, let $B=e^{\lambda t}$. Substituting this in equation (A6) gives:

$$dQ/Q = e^{\lambda t}G_l(dL/L)(L/Q) + e^{\lambda}G_k(dK/K)(K/Q) + [(\delta+\phi/(1+\phi))/(1+\delta) + e^{\lambda t}G_d](dD/D)(D/Q) + \lambda[(1/(1+\delta))F+G]/((1+\phi)F+G). \quad \text{(A7)}$$

Since $G = C/B$, $F = D/B(1+\phi)$, and $C = Q - D$, it is possible to write equation (A7) as:

$$dQ/Q = e^{\lambda t}G_l(dL/L)(L/Q) + e^{\lambda}G_k(dK/K)(K/Q) + [(\delta+\phi/(1+\phi))/(1+\delta) + e^{\lambda t}G_d](dD/D)(D/Q) + \lambda/((1+\delta)(1+\phi))(D/Q) + \lambda(C/Q). \quad \text{(A8)}$$

Now, using $C = Q - D$, collecting terms, and some algebraic manipulation yields:

$$dQ/Q = \lambda + e^{\lambda t}G_l(dL/L)(L/Q) + e^{\lambda t}G_k(dK/K)(K/Q) + (\theta + e^{\lambda t}G_d)(dD/D)(D/Q) + \theta\lambda(D/Q), \quad \text{(A9)}$$

where θ is a constant involving the two parameters δ and ϕ.

$$\theta = (\phi+\delta+\delta\phi)/(1+\phi+\delta+\delta\phi). \qquad \text{(A10)}$$

Equation (A9) is equation (8) of the main text and equation (A10) is equation (9).

References

Atesoglu, H.S. and Mueller, M.J. (1990), "Defence Spending and Economic Growth," *Defence Economics*, Vol. 2, pp. 19-27.

Feder, G. (1982), "On Exports and Economic Growth," *Journal of Development Economics*, Vol. 12, pp. 59-73.

Ram, R. (1986), "Government Size and Economic Growth: A New Framework and Some Evidence from Cross Section and Time Series Data," *American Economic Review*, Vol. 76, pp. 191-203.

Solow, R.M. (1957), "Technical Change and the Aggregate Production Function," *The Review of Economics and Statistics*, Vol. 39, pp. 312-20.

4

Arms Race Modelling and Economic Growth

Charles H. Anderton

The interdependence between military spending and economic growth is one of the most interesting, yet frustrating topics in social science research. It is interesting because military spending may be an important ingredient in the economic and military rise and fall of nations throughout history (Kennedy, 1987). It is frustrating because there are many variables that significantly affect military spending and economic growth and it is difficult to adequately grasp the links between them.

A simple guns versus butter tradeoff suggests that more military spending can reduce capital accumulation and technology development, dampening economic growth. If resources are diverted from consumption rather than investment, however, military spending might have a negligible impact on economic growth. It is even possible for technological spillovers and labor training effects from military spending to be greater than an equal use of resources in civilian production, leading to enhanced economic growth. A priori we might expect to find a negative, negligible or positive relationship between military spending and economic growth, and a post hoc justification for whatever relationship we find.

The unpleasant ambiguity of our a priori expectations are magnified when we consider other variables that influence the military spending/economic growth relationship: (1) the state of the economy (full employment or idle resources; developed or less developed), (2) economic and political system, (3) culture and social organization, (4) magnitude and composition of military spending, and (5) presence or absence of arms rivalry and war.

Despite the theoretical and empirical obstacles, some useful research on military spending and economic growth has been undertaken. Necessarily the researchers cut the web of interdependence at some point and focussed on a subset of relevant variables. We do the same in this chapter. Our focus is arms rivalry and economic growth. We build a simple model of arms rivalry and link it to the economies of the rivals via an economic growth equation. We use the model to illustrate and explore, via simple simulations, a variety of arms race/economic growth issues including the relationship between an arms race and economic growth during war.[1]

Review of the Literature[2]

Before developing our model of arms rivalry and economic growth, it is important to see what ground has been cultivated already. Three broad classes of studies of military expenditures and economic growth can be distinguished: (1) developed country studies, (2) developing country studies, and (3) theoretical arms race models that incorporate economic growth as a key variable.

Developed Country Studies

Dumas (1986) argues that military production in the U.S. (and other nations) diverts resources from the civilian sector at the expense of civilian capital and technology formation, leading to long-term economic deterioration. Gold and Adams (1990) and Weidenbaum (1989) reject this view; they argue that defense spending in the U.S. can not compellingly explain the peaks and valleys of U.S. economic performance or the change in U.S. economic position relative to other countries.

Cross-national empirical studies seem to indicate that countries with low defense burdens tend to have higher investment or economic growth than countries with high defense burdens[3] (Smith 1977 and 1980; DeGrasse 1983; Szymanski 1973; Bezdek 1975; Leontief and Duchin 1983; Rothschild 1973; See Gold and Adams 1990:279-280 for criticisms of this literature). Counterexamples are cited, however, e.g., Weidenbaum (1989:15) argues that South Korea devotes a larger share of its GNP to defense than Japan, but it has a more rapid growth rate. A key empirical question in this debate is, what goes down (if anything) when a nation's defense burden rises?

Russett (1970) initiated much empirical work on the question when he took various U.S. public and private expenditures as percentages of GNP and regressed them against the U.S. defense burden for the 1939-1968 period. He concluded that a greater U.S. defense burden took place mostly at the expense of consumption, although there were significant displacements of investments in durable equipment and housing.

Boulding (1973) also studied the question. He chose two years, 1929 and 1969, which have a good deal of comparability for the U.S. (low unemployment, business cycle peak). A major difference between 1929 and 1969 is the percent of full employment GNP allocated to defense: 0.6 percent in 1929 and 8.2 percent in 1969. Boulding found that when the U.S. defense burden rose, there was no significant decline in the gross private domestic investment share of full employment GNP; rather, it was the private consumption share that fell. Weidenbaum (1990) extended Boulding's analysis up through 1988, concluding that Boulding's result continues to hold.

Other authors argue that the relationship between the defense burden and investment in the U.S. depends on the time period of the study. For example, Hollenhorst and Ault (1971) maintain that only the World War II period shows a strong negative relationship between military spending and investment; other periods show a positive or negligible relationship. Nardinelli and Ackerman (1976) argue that there is a negligible relationship between defense spending and civilian economic growth in the U.S. for the 1905-1973 period, however a strong negative relationship is found for the 1946-1973 subperiod.

Military spending can also affect economic growth via its impact on technology. This raises another key empirical question addressed in the literature: does military R&D and technological progress occur at the expense of civilian R&D and technological progress?

Some authors answer the question in the negative. Weidenbaum (1974:134-140) and Striner et al. (1958:16-17) cite positive contributions of military R&D to civilian products and technology. Lederman (1971:3), Rosenberg (1976) and Trebilcock (1969) argue that military R&D has had a positive contribution to U.S. economic growth, productivity and consumer living standards. Weidenbaum (1990) presents a scatter plot of the annual percentage changes in U.S. military and civilian R&D for the 1955-1988 period. He concludes that changes in military and civilian R&D are just as likely to be in the same direction as in opposite directions.

On the other hand, Solo (1970), Etzioni (1971), DeGrasse (1983), Dumas (1989), and others argue that military R&D is negatively related to the rate of commercial R&D, of course not denying that there are examples of successful transference of military technology to civilian uses. Dumas (1989:24) maintains that there is a negative 'diversion' effect and a positive 'spin-off' effect of military R&D on civilian technological progress, and it is the net effect that matters. He argues that the net effect is generally negative:

> If spin-off were the more powerful effect, nations heavily engaged in military R and D would have a considerable advantage in developing civilian technology over nations that do comparatively little military R and D. We would therefore see nations like Great Britain and the Soviet Union at the forefront of civilian technology, while nations like Japan and West Germany lagged far behind. But, of course, just the opposite situation obtains. (Dumas 1989:24).

Reppy (1989) maintains that there are technological and institutional features of the defense market that determine whether the net effect of military R&D on civilian technology is positive or negative. She turns to empirical evidence to evaluate the relative importance of the opposing tendencies. Aggregate productivity studies and patent studies suggest little or no benefit to the civilian economy from military R&D. Preliminary data from international trade competitiveness studies, however, show a stronger U.S. performance in military-related high technology product groups than in product groups based on civilian technology. Reppy suggests that general conclusions about military R&D and innovation are hard to make because each technology and industry is potentially a special case.

Developing Country Studies

Emile Benoit's (1973) pathbreaking study of the relationship between defense burden and economic growth in developing countries has spurred much research in the field. Benoit empirically tested the hypothesis that the defense burden is inversely correlated with the rate of growth of civilian national product. His controversial result is summarized as follows:

> ...the evidence does not indicate that defense has had any adverse effect on growth in developing countries....The crucial evidence in this matter was the finding that the average 1950-1965 defense burdens (defense as a percent of national product) of 44 developing countries were positively, not inversely, correlated with their growth rates over comparable time periods: i.e., the more they spent on defense, in relation to the size of their economies, the faster they grew -- and vice versa (Benoit 1973:xix).[4]

Benoit considered several beneficial and adverse effects of defense on civilian economic growth, suggesting that the net effect is what counts. On the positive side, defense programs make tangible contributions to LDC civilian economies by: (1) feeding, clothing, and housing people who would otherwise have to be fed, housed, and clothed by the civilian economy; (2) providing education, medical care, and vocational and technical training that may have high civilian utility; (3) engaging in a variety of public works -- roads, dams, river improvements, airports, communication networks, etc. -- that may in part serve civilian uses; and (4) engaging in scientific and technical specialities such as hydrographic studies, mapping, aerial surveys, dredging, meteorology and so on, which would otherwise have to be performed by civilian personnel (Benoit 1978:277). On the negative side, Benoit identified three types of adverse effects: (1) diversion of resources away from civilian investment, (2) diversion of resources to a relatively unproductive military/government bureaucracy, and (3) the "income shift" -- higher defense lowers civil GNP therefore starting civil economic growth at a lower base than would have otherwise been the case (Whynes 1979:70). In spite of difficulties in quantifying the effects and some ambiguous statistical evidence, Benoit concluded that defense spending is likely to have a positive net effect on economic growth in developing countries.

Other analysts support Benoit's position. Kennedy (1974) reviewed a large number of LDC's and concluded that the "growth rates for GDP of individual countries did not seem to have been affected by their defense allocations." (Kennedy 1974:188). Whynes (1979:72) finds a correlation coefficient of +0.224 between defense burden and per capita income in LDC's using 1977 data (the figure for the developed country sample is -0.355). Weidenbaum (1974:128) cites a Rand Corporation study of Latin America that suggests that nations with larger defense spending have greater economic growth.

On the other hand, Chatterji (1992) reports studies critical of Benoit's findings: Ball (1983), Lim (1983), Deger and Smith (1983), Nabe (1983), Biswas and Ram (1986), and Adams, Behrman and Boldin (1991). To these we can add others such as: Boulding (1974) who concludes that there is no relationship between defense burden and economic growth in the high growth countries, and a negative relationship in the low growth countries; Frederiksen and Looney (1983) who find a positive correlation between defense and growth for some LDCs and a negative correlation for others; and Chowdhury (1991:80) who maintains that "the relationship between defense spending and economic growth cannot be generalized across countries. The actual relationship may vary from one country to another due to the use of a different sample period, as well as differences in the socioeconomic structure and type of government in each country."

While it is difficult to reach any firm conclusions from this literature, a review by Grobar and Porter (1989) offers some perspective:

> ...efforts at reestimating Benoit's correlation coefficients for different samples of LDCs and different time periods all fail to reproduce Benoit's results. In place of Benoit's positive correlations, researchers regularly find negative or statistically insignificant correlation coefficients....[W]hile studies by Weede (1983) and Deger and Sen (1983) find some limited evidence of positive effects of military spending through human capital formation and technological "spin-off" effects, the models that allow military spending to affect growth through multiple channels (such as those of Deger 1986; Deger and Smith 1983; and Faini et al. 1984) find that, while military spending may stimulate growth through some channels, it retards it through others, and the net effect is negative. (Grobar and Porter 1989:342-343).

Arms Race Models and Economic Growth

While most arms race models include resource constraints, very few explicitly incorporate economic growth as a key variable. Of those that do, most treat the economic growth as exogenous; i.e., it is given, and unaffected by resource allocation decisions (see Anderton 1990a, Seiglie 1988, Saris and Middendorp 1980, Lambelet et al. 1979, Luterbacher 1976, Gregory 1974). A few arms race modelers explicitly incorporate economic growth endogenously (e.g., Fischer 1984, Wolfson 1985, Wolfson and Shabahang 1991, Anderton 1986: ch. 31). In the endogenous models, today's resource allocations affect tomorrow's production opportunities via capital accumulation and technology development. How tomorrow's production opportunities are affected influences the ability of a nation to continue waging an arms race and the nation's preference for arms control or war. Arms racing, arms control or war, in turn, affect a nation's economic growth.

Fischer (1984) presents a two-nation von Neuman growth model of an arms race. Table 1 presents an example of nation J's economy. When J's civilian industry uses one unit of civilian goods as input, it produces b units of civilian goods as output with no externalities. When J's military sector uses one unit of civilian goods as input, it produces c units of security as output. J also inputs d units of security goods from nation L representing a negative security externality imposed on J from L's security production.

Table 4.1 reflects the arms race/economic growth dilemma: devoting

TABLE 4.1
Fischer's von Neumann Economy for Nation J

Industries Operated by J	Inputs from J		Outputs to J		Inputs from L		Outputs to L	
	1	2	1	2	1	2	1	2
1. civilian	1	0	b	0	0	0	0	0
2. military	1	0	0	c	0	d	0	0

Source: Fischer (1984), p. 54

more resources to the military increases security but reduces economic growth; devoting more resources to civilian production increases future production potential but reduces current security.

Fischer derives reaction functions from the von Neuman model. He finds that when arms technology is relatively less threatening in an arms rivalry, resource allocations to the military will be relatively low and the economic growth rates of the rivals will be relatively high. Fischer also finds that if the production of arms reduces the security of the other country more than it increases a country's own security, then the economies of the rivals will be contracting.

Wolfson (1985) investigates how an arms race can be a form of economic warfare, where the rival with the stronger economy can subdue its foe. Wolfson's idea is shown in an over-simplified fashion in Figure 4.1. M_J and M_L are J and L's stocks of military goods. C_J is J's civilian production, which includes consumption and real investment. Quadrant I shows the amount of military goods that J needs to deter L. Any point on or to the left of the J deters line represents a weapons vector where J can deter L. Quadrant II shows J's production possibilities frontier. Ç represents the minimum civilian production that J needs to maintain its resource base. If C_J<Ç, then real investment will be lower than that needed to maintain J's capital stock, and its economy will begin to crumble. When nation L produces M^1_L military goods, J can minimally deter by producing M^1_J military goods. When L increases its military to M^2_L, J can still minimally deter by producing M^2_J; however, J's civilian production is at Ç which is just enough to maintain J's resource base. When L produces M^3_L, J needs to produce M^3_J to minimally deter. Military production at M^3_J, however, implies civilian production at C_3 which is not enough to maintain J's economy. As J's economy crumbles (PPF shifts in), its ability to sustain its position in the arms rivalry is destroyed.

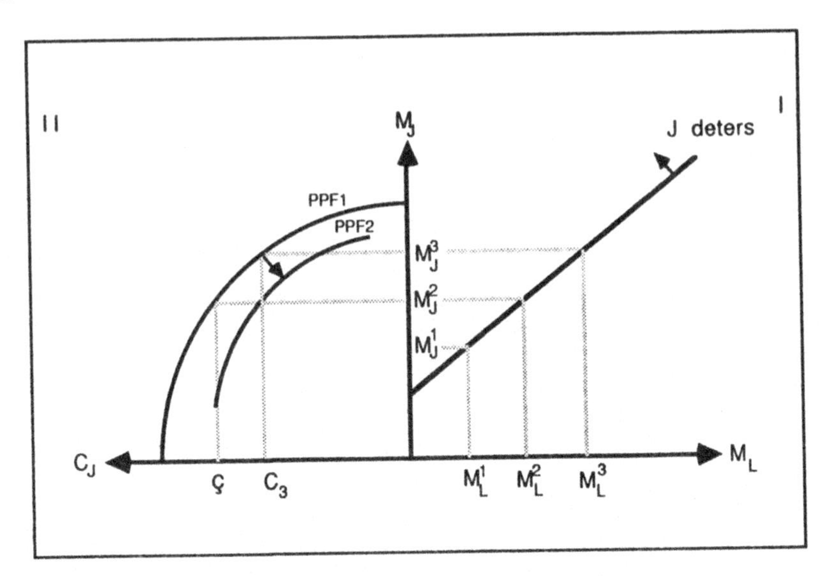

FIGURE 4.1 Arms Race Economic Warfare

Wolfson and Shabahang (1991) explore in more depth the role that the economy plays in an arms rivalry. They find, among other things, that differing rates of economic growth in an arms rivalry can lead to the breakdown of deterrence and the outbreak of war. Lambelet (1992) explains how the general bankruptcy of the Soviet economic system played an important role in the winding down of the Cold War. Many of the themes on economic growth and arms rivalry are expressed in the historical analysis of Kennedy (1987).

A Theoretical Model of Arms Rivalry and Economic Growth

The Arms Race Submodel

How weapons might be used in war significantly influences the quantities and types of weapons that military rivals acquire. This arms using motivation for weapons acquisition can be studied at a basic level with a dynamic war model such as Lanchester's. In one simple Lanchester application, L attacks J and the weapons quantities of J and L decrease in battle according to the following differential equations:

$$\dot{M}_J = -\beta_a M_L \qquad M_J(0) = M_J^0 \tag{1}$$

$$\dot{M}_L = -\alpha_d M_J \qquad M_L(0) = M_L^0 \tag{2}$$

where:

M_J, M_L - military stocks of J and L.
M_J^0,M_L^0 - initial military stocks of J and L.
β_a - effectiveness of L's military when L is an attacker.
α_d - effectiveness of J's military when J is a defender.

If J attacked L we would have:

$$\dot{M}_J = -\beta_d M_L \qquad M_J(0) = M_J^0 \tag{3}$$

$$\dot{M}_L = -\alpha_a M_J \qquad M_L(0) = M_L^0 \tag{4}$$

where β_d and α_a are the military effectivenesses of L and J when L defends and J attacks.

Define a nation's "ability to defend" as that nation's ability to prevent its adversary from disarming it without the adversary disarming itself, during a fight-to-the-finish war. Equations (1)-(4) can be used to derive the following regions where J and L can successfully defend (see Anderton 1990b):

$$M_J \geq (\beta_a/\alpha_d)^{1/2} M_L \qquad \text{J defends} \tag{5}$$

$$M_L \geq (\alpha_a/\beta_d)^{1/2} M_J \qquad \text{L defends} \tag{6}$$

A graph of equations (5) and (6) is shown in Figure 4.2. Figure 4.2 shows that at the origin, both J and L are able to minimally defend against an attack from the adversary. If L slightly increases its military goods, moving the military vector to point A, L can attack and defeat J in a fight-to-the-finish war. M_L^a is L's attack cushion at A, i.e., the amount of military goods that L has above what is needed to attack and defeat J. J's vulnerability at A is likely to induce it to acquire military goods, moving the vector to, say, point B. It seems reasonable to assume that if J and L have a roughly equal ability to acquire weapons, they will end up at some point like C where both can more than minimally defend. The distances M_J^s and M_L^s at point C in Figure 4.2 represent the security cushions of J and L, respectively; i.e., the amount of military goods that each side has above what is needed to minimally defend.

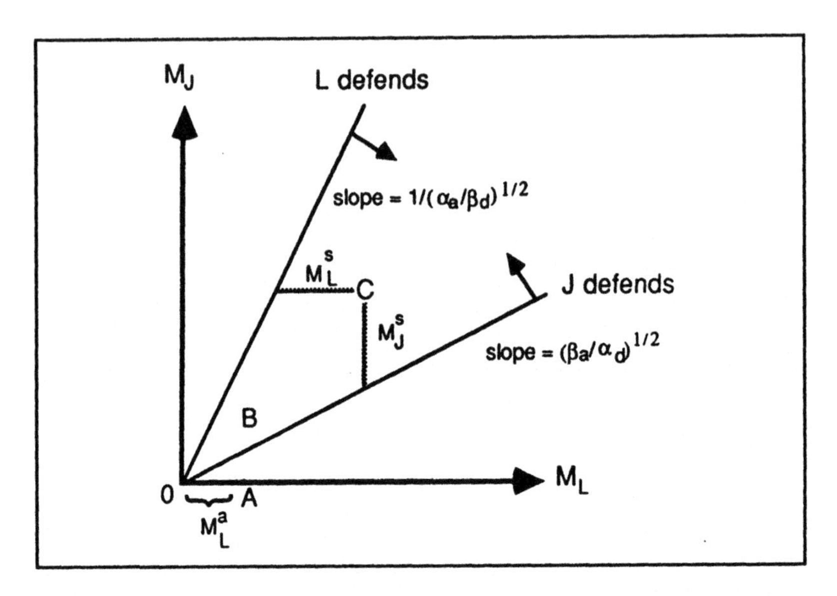

FIGURE 4.2 The "J defends" and "L defends" Regions

A simple way to represent the arms rivalry equilibrium is to assume that the parties allocate resources to achieve a given level of security or attack cushion. Remaining resources are then allocated to civilian production. For example, if J and L are both defenders, this implies the following reaction functions of J and L:

$$M_J = (\beta_a/\alpha_d)^{1/2}M_L + M_J^s \tag{7}$$

$$M_L = (\alpha_a/\beta_d)^{1/2}M_J + M_L^s \tag{8}$$

The arms rivalry equilibrium is shown in Figure 4.3 and is given by:[5]

$$M_J^* = \frac{M_J^s + (\frac{\beta_a}{\alpha_d})^{1/2} M_L^s}{1 - (\frac{\beta_a}{\alpha_d})^{1/2}(\frac{\alpha_a}{\beta_d})^{1/2}} \tag{9a}$$

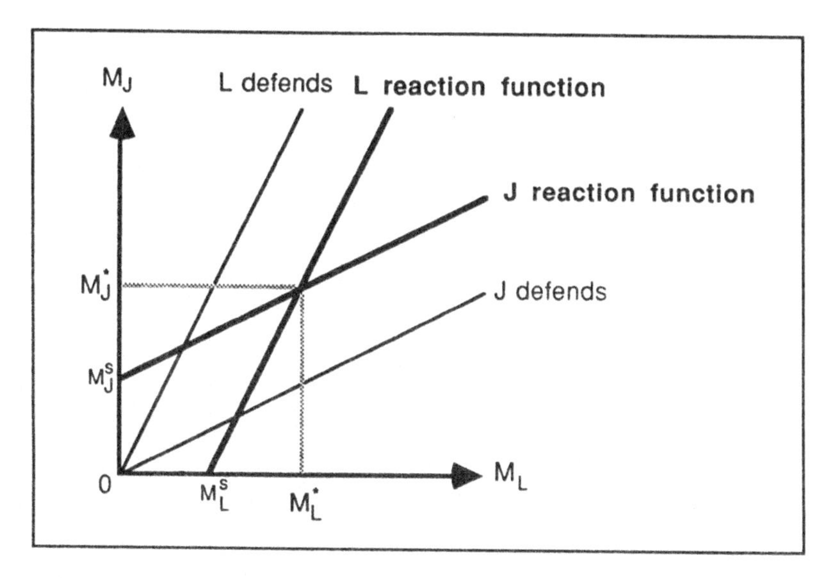

FIGURE 4.3 The Arms Rivalry Equilibrium

$$M_L^* = \frac{M_L^s + \left(\frac{\alpha_a}{\beta_d}\right)^{1/2} M_J^s}{1 - \left(\frac{\beta_a}{\alpha_d}\right)^{1/2} \left(\frac{\alpha_a}{\beta_d}\right)^{1/2}} \qquad (9b)$$

In Figure 4.4, we depict the arms rivalry equilibrium when L seeks an attack capability, but is frustrated due to resource limits.[6] In Figure 4.4, L's reaction function eventually hits the resource constraint and the arms rivalry settles at point b where J can defend and L cannot attack.

In Figure 4.5, L is assumed to have a much stronger resource base than J. J's effort to achieve defense hits its resource constraint. The arms rivalry settles at point C where L can attack J.

The Economic Growth Submodel

Assume that economic growth in nation i (i=J,L) can be described by the following differential equation:

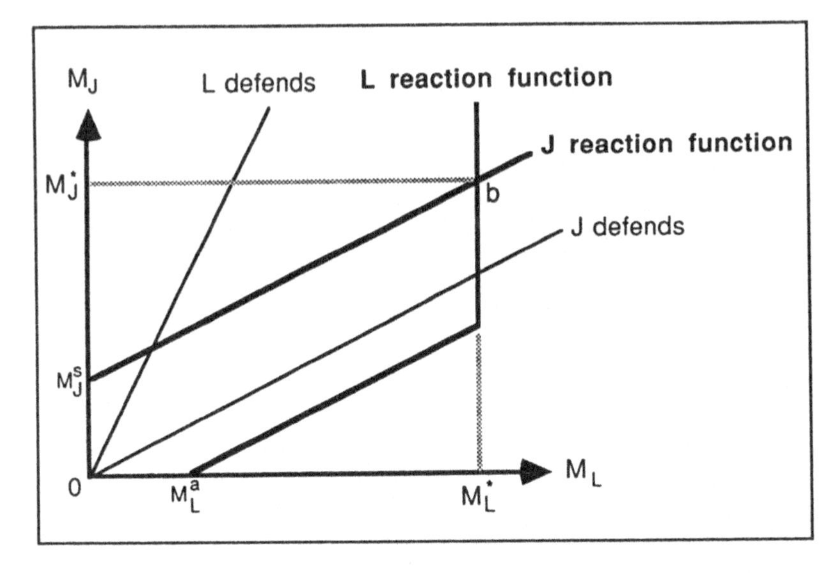

FIGURE 4.4 L's Failure to Achieve Attack Capability Due to Resource Limits

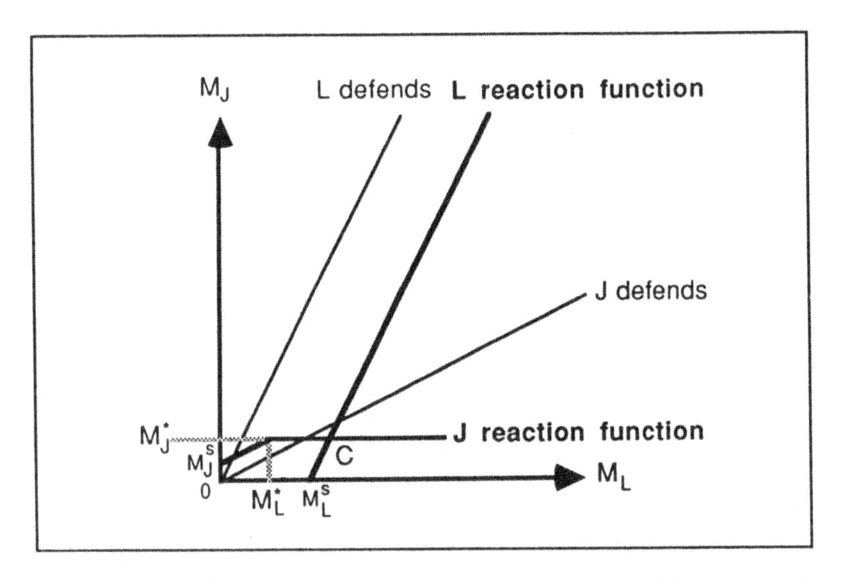

FIGURE 4.5 J's Failure to Achieve Defense Capability Due to Resource Limits

$$\dot{Y}_i = \lambda_i\left(\frac{C_i}{Y_i} - r_i\right) + b_i\frac{M_i}{Y_i} \tag{10}$$

where:

Y_i - resources available to nation i (i.e., GNP).
C_i - amount of i's resources allocated to civilian goods (including investment).
M_i - amount of i's resources allocated to military goods.
λ_i - economic growth parameter ($\lambda_i > 0$).
r_i - minimum ratio of civilian production to GNP needed to maintain a growing resource base ($0 < r_i \leq 1$). (r_i is independent of growth spillovers from military production).
b_i - economic growth parameter indicating the degree of growth spillovers from the military burden ($b_i \geq 0$).

Nation i's resource constraint is:

$$Y_i = C_i + M_i \tag{11}$$

The solution to equation (10) given the constraint of (11) is the implicit function:

$$\frac{-(b_i - \lambda_i)M_i LN[\lambda_i Y_i(1-r_i) + (b_i - \lambda_i)M_i]}{\lambda_i^2(1-r_i)^2} + \frac{Y_i}{\lambda_i(1-r_i)} - t - k = 0 \tag{12}$$

where t is time, k is the integration constant, and LN is the natural log function.

Simulations of Arms Rivalry and Economic Growth

The economic growth rates inherent in equation (12) generally follow a slow increase followed by a slow decrease. This is shown in Figure 4.6.[7] Type I nations experience increases in their growth rates. Type II nations approximate steady-state growth. Declining growth rate nations are type III. There is nothing immutable about the stage a nation is in. A type I nation might become type II or type III (and vice versa) due to economic, political or social changes.

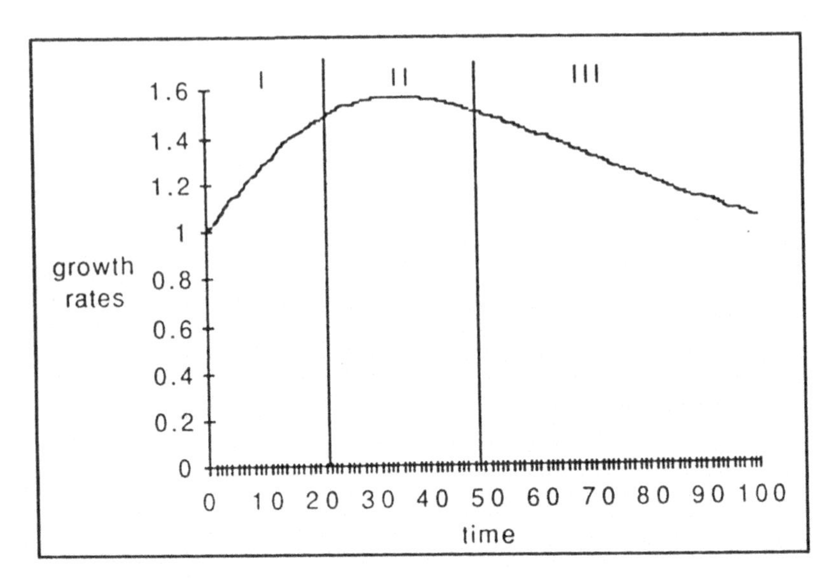

FIGURE 4.6 Economic Growth Rates Inherent in Equation 12

The Economic Burden of Defense Spending

Assume that J and L are identical type I nations involved in an arms rivalry. A reference point case is defined by the following parameters:

arms race submodel	*economic growth submodel*
$M_J^s = M_L^s = 10$	$Y_J(0) = Y_L(0) = 100$
$\alpha_d = \beta_d = 0.1$	$\lambda_J = \lambda_L = 20$
$\alpha_a = \beta_a = 0.025$	$r_J = r_L = 0.75$
	$b_J = b_L = 0$

The arms race equilibrium from equations (9a) and (9b) is $M_J^* = M_L^* = 20$. We assume that a flow of resources of 20 each period is required to maintain military goods at $M_J=M_L=20$.[8] This assumption is relaxed below.

Since J and L are identical in every respect, they have the same economic growth rates. By year 20, J and L's GNPs have grown to Y=118.38. If neither side allocated resources to defense, by year 20 their GNPs would have grown to Y=200.

The Crucial Role of Technology

A moderate advantage in weapons technology can translate into a significant advantage in economic strength. Assume that weapons technology is higher in J than in L, i.e., $\alpha_a>\beta_a$ and $\alpha_d>\beta_d$.[9] Since L's military is less effective than J's, L must allocate more of its resources to military goods to maintain its security cushion, while J can allocate less of its resources to the military. L's economic growth rate is lower than J's, decreasing L's relative economic position in the long run.

For example, assume that the parameters for the reference point case continue to hold, except for J's weapons effectiveness parameters which are now higher than L's:

$$\alpha_a = 0.03 > \beta_a = 0.025 \text{ and } \alpha_d = 0.12 > \beta_d = 0.1$$

The arms race equilibrium from (9) is $M_J^*=19.42$ and $M_L^*=20.64$. Figure 4.7 shows J and L's economic growth rates given their technological differences. J and L have roughly equal military capabilities because L's qualitative inferiority is compensated by its quantitative superiority so that the security cushions of J and L are the same. Nevertheless, the military/economic strength of J is greater than L. Although the differences between J and L's growth rates seem almost negligible, the compound effect can be substantial. By year 20, J's GNP is almost 5 per cent larger than L's, putting J in a position to increase its relative military position. If we introduced the assumption that J enjoys an economic growth spillover from the defense burden equal to, say, $b_J=5$, then by year 20, J's GNP would be over 20 percent larger than L's. (J's growth rates when $b_J=5$ are not shown in Figure 4.7).

If we go back to our assumption that J and L are identical in every respect, but now introduce a change in the offensive/defensive technology toward the offense, the growth rates of J and L are dampened relative to the reference point. For example, assume that the parameters for the reference point continue to hold, except for the attack effectiveness terms which are now:

$$\alpha_a = \beta_a = 0.03$$

The arms race equilibrium is $M_J^* = M_L^* = 22.11$. The change toward a more offensive posture in the weapons vector, causes the arms race equilibrium to move to higher levels, which dampens economic growth.

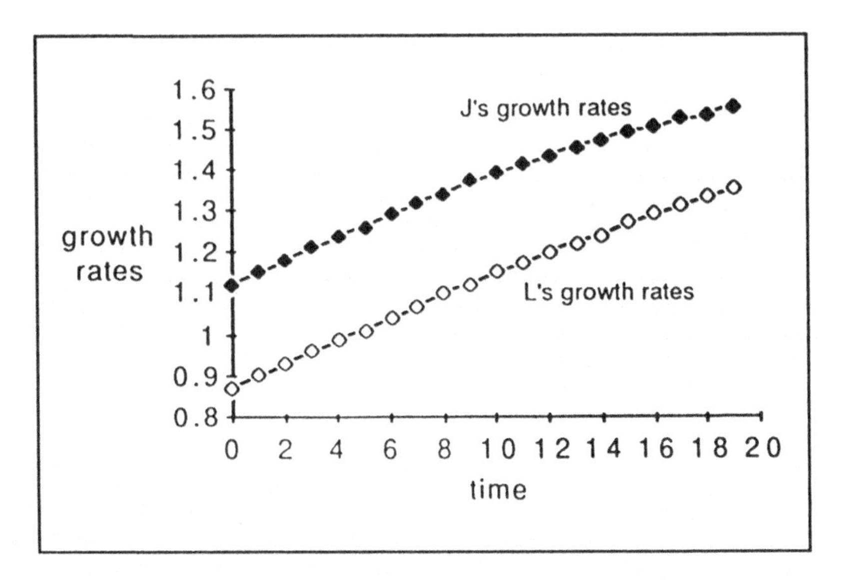

FIGURE 4.7 J and L Growth Rates Given Weapons Technology Differences

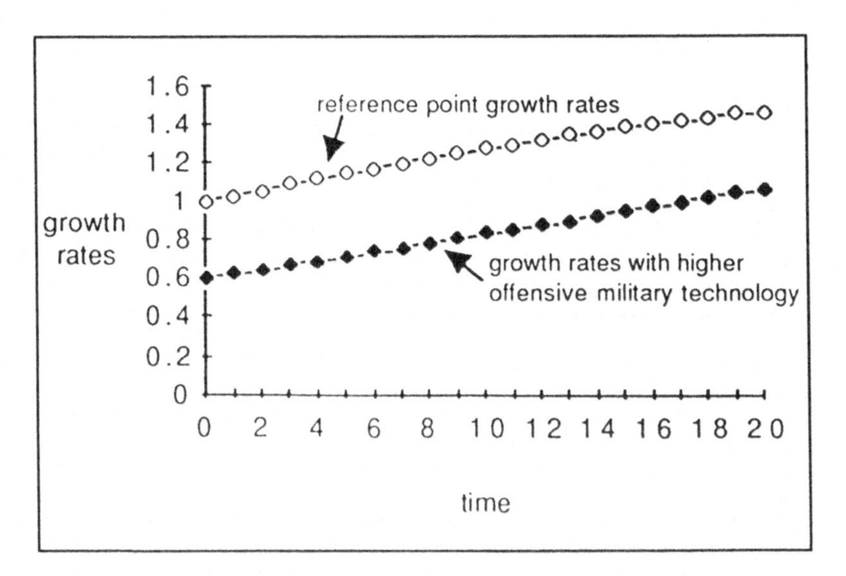

FIGURE 4.8 Offensive Weapons Technology Dampening Economic Growth

This is shown in Figure 4.8 and is consistent with Fischer's (1984) analysis.

Arms Race Economic Warfare

Suppose that J has a more vibrant, dynamic economy relative to L such that λ_J=40 and λ_L=20. All other parameter values are the same as the reference point case. After 40 years, J's resource base will grow to 306.01, while L's resource base will be only 175.19. J's superior economy puts it in a position to wage arms race economic warfare against L. Assume that in year 40, J adopts an economic warfare strategy and dramatically increases its resource allocation to military goods to M_J=70. For L to meet its security cushion of 10, it will have to increase its military allocation to M_L=45. From equation (10),

$\dot{Y}_L = 20(.743-.75)$ and $\dot{Y}_J = 40(.771-.75)$ i.e., L's economy is contracting and J's economy is expanding in year 41 (and subsequent years). J can defeat L as a rival, without firing a shot.

If L reduces its security cushion to zero, it can minimally deter J and counter J's economic warfare strategy. M_L=35 will give L minimal deterrence and a growing economy [$\dot{Y}=20(.8-.75)$ in year 41]. L's economy will now grow faster than J's and it will be able to stave off defeat from J's economic warfare strategy. Nevertheless, it is clear from these examples that L's weaker economy puts it in a weaker relative military position.

Under what conditions can J successfully wage economic warfare, even given counter-moves by L? A full exploration of this question would require an additional chapter, but we can at least lay out a preliminary analysis. Sufficient conditions for J to successfully wage economic warfare against L are:

$$M_L = (\alpha_a/\beta_d)^{1/2}M_J \quad (13)$$
$$M_L/Y_L = (1-r_L) \quad (14)$$
$$M_J/Y_J < (1-r_J) \quad (15)$$

Condition (13) shows L being pushed to a point of minimal deterrence. Conditions (14) and (15) imply that L's economy is stagnant while J's economy is still growing. Plugging (14) and (15) into (13) leads to the following sufficient condition for J to successfully wage economic warfare:

$$\frac{Y_J(1-r_J)}{Y_L(1-r_L)} > \frac{1}{(\alpha_d/\beta_d)^{1/2}} \tag{16}$$

Given the parameter values α_a=.025, β_d=0.1, and r_J=r_L=.25 from the reference point case, J's economy would have to be more than twice as large as L's for J to be able to successfully wage economic warfare, regardless of L's countermoves. For example, in the case where λ_J=40, λ_L=20 and all other parameters of the reference point hold, by year 70, Y_J=547.81 and Y_L=269.93; condition (16) is satisfied. If J forces L to produce M_L=.25(269.93) = 67.4825, L's economy will be stagnant via (14). J can force this level of M_L by producing $M_J= 1/(\alpha_a/\beta_d)^{1/2}$= 2(67.4825) = 134.965 by condition (13). J's economy will still grow by condition (15) meaning that J can increase its military capability above 134.965, putting itself in a position to attack and defeat L via the Lanchester model.

Some analysts believe that the Unted States waged arms race economic warfare against the Soviet Union (see Wolfson 1985, 1992; Lambelet 1992). The following quote attributed to Ronald Reagan seems to indicate that the U.S., at least implicitly, discussed an economic warfare strategy in the 1980s:[10]

> I do not want arms control but arms reduction. You don't achieve it through unilateral disarmament. But with a stronger economy we can outspend the Russians on defense and force them to the bargaining table.

This seems consistent with Wolfson's (1992:81) proposition that when "Ronald Reagan took office in 1980 it became apparent that he had found the ultimate weapon -- Gross National Product."

Arms Rivalry and Economic Growth During War

We model arms rivalry and economic growth during war by retaining the economic growth submodel, but modifying the Lanchester-based arms race submodel. Assume now that a Lanchester war can be described by the following differential equations:

$$\dot{M}_J = -\beta M_L + M_J^P \tag{17}$$

$$\dot{M}_L = -\alpha M_J + M_L^P \tag{18}$$

where:

M_J, M_L - military stocks of J and L at time t.
M_J^P, M_L^P - new production (re-supply) of military goods of J and L during the war.
α, β - effectiveness of J and L's weapons.

The condition for the equality of fighting strengths in a fight-to-the-finish war is (Taylor 1983: 338-343):

$$\alpha(M_J^0 - M_L^P/\alpha)^2 = \beta(M_L^0 - M_J^P/\beta)^2 \tag{19}$$

where M_J^0 and M_L^0 are the initial (pre-war) weapons stocks of J and L. It follows that J and L can defend when:

$$M_J^0 \geq (\beta_a/\alpha_d)^{1/2}M_L^0 - M_J^P/(\alpha_d\beta_a)^{1/2} + M_L^P/\alpha_d \quad \text{J defends} \tag{20}$$

$$M_L^0 \geq (\alpha_a/\beta_d)^{1/2}M_J^0 - M_L^P/(\beta_d\alpha_a)^{1/2} + M_J^P/\beta_d \quad \text{L defends} \tag{21}$$

where α_d, β_a are the weapons effectivenesses of J and L when J defends and L attacks and α_a, β_d are the weapons effectivenesses of J and L when J attacks and L defends. A pre-war arms race establishes the initial weapons stocks, M_J^0 and M_L^0. The economic potentials of J and L embodied in the economic growth submodel determine the course of the arms re-supply race during the war, M_J^P and M_L^P.

In Figure 4.9, the mutual defense region demarcated by the solid lines occurs when J and L have equal economic potentials such that $M_J^P = M_L^P$. The mutual defense region demarcated by the hatched lines occurs when J has greater economic strength and thus greater re-supply ability relative to L, i.e., $M_J^P > M_L^P$. The 45^0 line represents parity weapons vectors between J and L. If the pre-war arms race settles at point A and if $M_J^P = M_L^P$, then J and L have equal military stocks and equal military potential. When $M_J^P > M_L^P$, A still represents equal military stocks, but military potential is greater in J because of J's superior re-supply ability in the event of war. Nevertheless, J does not have the capacity to attack and defeat L because point A is in the mutual defense region.

In most if not all arms rivalries, arms control focusses on controlling weapons quantities or qualities, not military potentials. An equal reduction in weapons stocks from A to B in Figure 4.9 maintains parity, but the rivalry between J and L is dramatically different at B than at A given asymmetric economic potential. When $M_J^P > M_L^P$, point B is not associated with mutual defense. In spite of the equality in military stocks (and weapons effectivenesses) at B, J can attack and defeat L because J has a stronger ability to arm itself during war.

It is important to note that an economically weaker rival can be pushed into a lose-lose scenario. At point A in Figure 4.9, the weaker nation could try to allocate more resources to defense to move further into the mutual defense region. A greater defense burden, however, simply exacerbates the fundamental economic weakness underlying the nation's position. Disarmament to point B can take pressure off the economy of the weaker nation, but it becomes vulnerable to attack.

Some of these forces may operate in the North Korea/South Korea rivalry. North Korea's stifled, over-burdened economy is clearly weaker than South Korea's. According to the U.S. Arms Control and Disarmament Agency, South Korea's measured national output is about seven times larger than the North, while the South's population is only double the North's. In 1989, military expenditure as a percent of GNP was 20 percent in the North compared to 4.3 percent in the South. If we use soldiers per 1000 persons as a rough proxy of military goods, North Korea has a much higher stock (49.5 compared to 15.1). South Korea's stronger economy suggests that it has stronger military potential than the North, even if static comparisons of military stocks suggest otherwise. Motivation to acquire nuclear weapons by the North is driven by many factors, including leaders fears generated by falling communist regimes around the world and the threat of nuclear and conventional weapons in the South. To these we might add the perception of the North Korean leaders that nuclear weapons provide a great equalizer against the South's superior economy.

What pre-war stock of military goods would an economically weaker nation need to minimally defend against the superior arms re-supply capacity of its rival in the event of war? In actual historical settings, of course, the answer depends on many variables. Here we abstractly investigate the question with our framework.

In the economic growth submodel we assume that the growth of i's (i=J,L) resource base during war when $b_i=0$ is:

$$\dot{Y}_i = \lambda_i\{(1-r_i) - M_i^p/Y_i\} \tag{22}$$

Equation (22) is derived from equations (10) and (11) where M_i^p replaces M_i.

We now introduce a distinction between the stock and flow of military goods. We no longer assume that a continuous flow of military resources is needed to maintain a given stock of military goods. M_i^0 is the initial pre-war stock of military goods. M_i^p is the

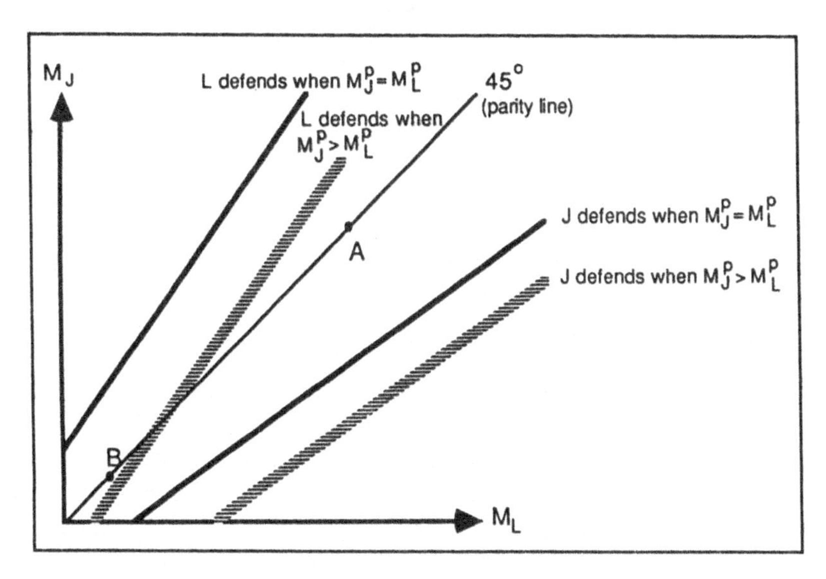

FIGURE 4.9 Differing Mutual Defense Regions Based on Different Economic Strengths

arms re-supply during war. For simplicity we ignore depreciation of military goods.

Assume that L is the economically weaker nation and the following parameters hold:

Pre-War Weapons Stocks

$M_J^0 = 50$ = weapons produced from previous years resources

M_L^0 = ? (we want to solve for the M_L^0 that gives L minimal deterrence)

During War Parameters

equations 20 and 21	*economic growth submodel*
$\alpha_d = \beta_d = 0.05$	$Y_J(0) = 1000$; $Y_L(0) = 500$
$\alpha_a = \beta_a = 0.025$	$\lambda_J = \lambda_L = 20$
	$r_J = r_L = 0.75$
	$b_J = b_L = 0$

We also assume that when war breaks out, J and L push military production to the point where economic growth is zero.[11] Given the parameters of the economic growth submodel, this implies $M_J^P = 25$ and $M_L^P = 15$. Condition (21) implies that L would need $M_L^0 = 111.1$

to minimally defend. Again we see the result that parity of pre-war weapons stocks does not necessarily imply mutual security when the economic strengths of the rivals are not at parity.

Conclusions

An arms race is fundamentally an economic competition. It is surprising that in an extensive arms race modeling literature, we find so little formal treatment of the economic struggle. Many arms race modelers incorporate resource constraints, but there is little explicit analysis of the economic rivalry underlying the arms rivalry and the interdependence between them. Murray Wolfson's work is an exception. In 1985, Wolfson published a model of the economic struggle between the U.S. and USSR in their arms rivalry. In 1987, Wolfson argued that "the course of economic warfare made it impossible for the Soviet Union to continue the arms race as it had without risking social collapse." (see Wolfson 1992:105).

Critics of Wolfson's view maintained that the U.S. and Soviet Union's defense burdens were far below World War II levels and that they were generally falling in the post World War II era. It seemed unlikely that economics would end up playing such a significant role in the winding down of the Cold War. Our simulations, however, illustrate the principle that seemingly negligible influences can be significant over the long run. Even if the defense burdens of arms rivals affect economic growth rates by a few tenths of a percentage point, the effects can be significant when compounded over a forty year period.[12]

Our simulations also point to the crucial role of technology in understanding the interdependence between arms rivalry and economic growth. Of course, if a nation has a greater degree of defense spillover to the civilian sector relative to its rival, that nation will be in a stronger economic and military position in the rivalry, everthing else the same. Less obvious is the role that military technology can play in affecting economic growth in an arms race. Our simulations indicate that a nation with a greater quality of weapons will economically outdistance its rival in the long run, even if the rival begins with an equal resource base and growth potential. We also find that when nations are identical in every respect, a change in weapons technology toward the offense raises defense burdens and dampens economic growth.

We also used simulations to study arms rivalry and economic growth during war. The simulations point to the importance of distinguishing between military stocks and military potentials. Military stocks are the quantities and qualities of weapons; military potentials are the military stocks as well as the weapons re-supply potentials of the rivals in the event of war. Rivals who fear war will be more concerned with military potentials than military stocks. Since the arms control process generally focusses on rough parity of military stocks, it might be resisted by the economically weaker rival.

Notes

1. To the best of our knowledge, no formal models of an arms race during war have been developed in the civilian literature. Harkavy (1987) writes about arms transfers after the onset of and during conflict. Wolfson and Shabahang (1991) develop a theoretical model to explore, among other things, how differences in economic growth between rivals can affect the likelihood of war.

2. Some of the material from this section is drawn from Isard and Anderton (1992:30-36).

3. The defense burden is defined as military spending as a fraction of GNP.

4. There are two Benoit theses: the strong version says that defense and economic growth are positively correlated in developing countries; the weak version says that defense and economic growth are not negatively correlated in developing countries. The distinction between the strong and weak versions of the Benoit thesis has been glossed over by some analysts. For example, Kennedy (1983:198) cites the work of Smith and Smith (1980) as evidence in favor of the weak version of the Benoit thesis while Chan (1986:29) cites the same work as evidence against the strong version of the Benoit thesis.

5. The arms race submodel is built on the assumption that $(\beta_a/\alpha_d)^{1/2}(\alpha_a/\beta_d)^{1/2} < 1$, i.e., weapons are generally more effective defending rather than attacking. The assumption guarantees the existence of a mutual defense region. There is no guarantee that $(\beta_a/\alpha_d)^{1/2}(\alpha_a/\beta_d)^{1/2}$ will be less than one. For an analysis of the arms rivalry implications of $(\beta_a/\alpha_d)^{1/2}(\alpha_a/\beta_d)^{1/2} > 1$, see Anderton (1990b, 1992).

6. The equation for L's reaction function when L is an attacker is $M_L \geq (\alpha_d/\beta_a)^{1/2} M_J + M^a_L$.

7. The parameters that gave rise to Figure 4.6 are $Y(0)=100$, $\lambda=20$, $r=0.75$, $M=20$, and $b=0$. If the military burden is equal to or greater than r, economic growth will be zero or negative.

8. In a military goods equilibrium, a flow (expenditure) of resources is needed to maintain a given stock of military capability. Our

simplifying assumption implies that the flow of resources to the military just maintains that level of military capability. For military personnel this assumption is roughly accurate (e.g., a flow of resources to pay soldiers is needed every year, so the stock of soldiers is equal to the flow of resources needed to maintain them). For military hardware, however, the assumption is roughly accurate only if the flow of resources for the military is just enough to maintain a stock of military equipment equal to that flow.

9. There are three general classes of variables that affect the weapons effectiveness terms: military technology, military organization, and geography/climate (see Anderton 1990).

10. On 12/28/89, Murray Weidenbaum gave me this quote. He said that President Reagan made a statement like this at a meeting in the early 1980s that Professor Weidenbaum attended. Since the quote is from Professor Weidenbaum's notes, it is not an exact quotation and it cannot be verified from a published source.

11. This may not be the case. A nation could produce military goods at such a high level that its economic growth becomes negative for a time. Or a nation may produce less military goods to keep economic growth positive, reaping greater military production in the future.

12. Of course, the winding down of the Cold War was driven by political, social, and ideological factors as well as economics. Even when we focus on economics, there are many influences. It seems to me that the general bankruptcy of the Soviet political, institutional, ideological and economic systems are at least as important as the defense burden for explaining the Soviet Union's economic failure.

References

Adams, G.F., Behrman, J.R., and Boldin, M. (1991), "Defense Expenditures and Economic Growth in the Less Developed Countries: Reconciling Theory and Empirical Results," *Conflict Management and Peace Science*, Vol. 11, pp. 19-35.

Anderton, C.H. (1986), *Arms Race Modeling: Systematic Analysis and Synthesis*, Ph.D. Thesis, Cornell University.

Anderton, C.H. (1990i), "Teaching Arms-race Concepts in Intermediate Microeconomics, *Journal of Economic Education*, Vol. 21, pp. 148-166.

Anderton, C.H. (1990b), "The Inherent Propensity Toward Peace or War Embodied in Weaponry," *Defence Economics*, Vol. 1, pp. 197-219.

Anderton, C.H. (1992), "Toward a Mathematical Theory of the Offensive/Defensive Balance," *International Studies Quarterly*, Vol. 36, pp. 75-100.

Ball, N. (1983), "Defense and Development: a Critique of the Benoit Study," *Economic Development and Cultural Change*, Vol. 31, pp. 507-524.

Benoit, E. (1973), *Defense and Economic Growth in Developing Countries*, Lexington: Lexington Books.

Benoit, E. (1978), "Growth and Defense in Developing Countries," *Economic Development and Cultural Change*, Vol. 26, pp. 271-280.

Bezdek, R. (1975), "The 1980 Economic Impact - Regional and Occupational -- of Compensated Shifts in Defense Spending," *Journal of Regional Science*, Vol. 15, pp. 183-197.

Biswas, B. and Ram, R. (1986), "Military Expenditures and Economic Growth in Less Developed Countries: an Augmented Model and Further Evidence," *Economic Development and Cultural Change*, Vol. 34, pp. 361-372.

Boulding, K.E. (1973), "The Impact of the Defense Industry on the Structure of the American Economy," in B. Udis (ed.), *The Economic Consequences of Reduced Military Spending*, Lexington, MA: Lexington Books.

Boulding, K.E. (1974), "Defense Spending: Burden or Boon," *War/Peace Report*, Vol. 13.

Boulding, K.E. (1978), *Stable Peace*, Austin: University of Texas Press.

Chatterji, M. (1992), "Regional Conflict and Military Spending in the Developing Countries," in W. Isard and C.H. Anderton (eds.), *Economics of Arms Reduction and the Peace Process*, Amsterdam: North-Holland, pp. 235-248.

Chan, S. (1986), "Military Expenditures and Economic Performance," in *World Military Expenditures and Arms Transfers*, U.S. Arms Control and Disarmament Agency.

Chowdhury, A.R. (1991), "Defense Spending and Economic Growth," *Journal of Conflict Resolution*, Vol. 35, pp. 80-97.

Deger, S. (1986), "Economic Development and Defense Expenditure," *Economic Development and Cultural Change*, Vol. 35, pp. 179-196.

Deger, S. and Sen, S. (1983), "Military Expenditure, Spin off and Economic Development," *Journal of Development Economics*, Vol. 13, pp. 67-83.

Deger, S. and Smith, R. (1983), "Military Expenditure and Growth in Less Developed Countries," *Journal of Conflict Resolution*, Vol. 27, pp. 335-353.

DeGrasse, R.W., Jr. (1983), *Military Expansion, Economic Decline: the Impact of Military Spending on U.S. Economic Performance*, New

York: Council on Economic Priorities/Sharpe.

Dumas, L.J. (1986), *The Overburdened Econômy*, Berkeley: University of California Press.

__________ (1989), "Economic Conversion: the Critical Link," in L.J. Dumas and M. Thee (eds.), *Making Peace Possible: The Promise of Economic Conversion*, New York: Pergamon Press, pp. 3-15.

Etzioni, A. (1971), "Federal Science as Economic Drag, not Propellent," in S. Melman (ed.), *The War Economy of the United States*, New York: St. Martin's Press, pp. 132-137.

Faini, R., Annez, P. and Taylor, L. (1984), "Defense Spending, Economic Structure, and Growth: Evidence among Countries and over Time," *Economic Development and Cultural Change*, Vol. 32, pp. 487-98.

Fischer, D. (1984), "Weapons Technology and the Intensity of Arms Races," *Conflict Management and Peace Science*, Vol. 8, pp. 49-69.

Fredriksen, P.C. and Looney, R.E. (1983), "Defense Expenditures and Economic Growth in Developing Countries," *Armed Forces and Society*, Vol. 9, pp. 633-645.

Gold, D. and Adams, G. (1990), "Defence Spending and the American Economy," *Defence Economics*, Vol. 1, pp. 275-293.

Gregory, P. (1974), "Economic Growth, U.S. Defense Expenditures and the Soviet Budget," *Soviet Studies*, Vol. 24, pp. 72-80.

Grobar, L.M. and Porter, R.C. (1989), "Benoit Revisited: Defense Spending and Economic Growth in LDCs," *Journal of Conflict Resolution*, Vol. 33, pp. 318-345.

Harkavy, R.E. (1987), "Arms Resupply During Conflict: a Framework for Analysis," in C. Schmidt (ed.), *The Economics of Military Expenditures*, London: Macmillan.

Hollenhorst, J. and Ault, G. (1971), "An Atlernative Answer to: Who Pays for Defense?," *American Political Science Review*, Vol. 65, pp. 760-63.

Isard, W. and Anderton, C.H. (eds.) (1992), *Economics of Arms Reduction and the Peace Process*, Amsterdam: North-Holland.

Kennedy, G. (1974), *The Military in the Third World*. New York: Scribners.

Kennedy, G. (1983), *Defense Economics*, New York: St. Martin's Press.

Kennedy, P. (1987), *The Rise and Fall of the Great Powers*, New York: Random House.

Lambelet, J.C. (1992), "Do Arms Races Lead to Peace?," in W. Isard and C.H. Anderton (eds.), *Economics of Arms Reduction and the Peace Process*. Amsterdam: North-Holland, pp. 249-260.

Lambelet, J.C., Luterbacher, U. with Allan, P. (1979), "Dynamics of Arms Races: Mutual Stimulation vs. Self-stimulation," *Journal of*

Peace Science, Vol. 4, pp. 49-66.
Lederman, L.L. (1971), "Introduction and General Summary," in *A Review of the Relationship Between Research and Development and Economic Growth/Productivity*, Washington: National Science Foundation.
Leontief, W.W. and Duchin, F. (1983), *Military Spending: Facts and Figures*, New York: Oxford University Press.
Lim, D. (1983), "Another Look at Growth and Defense in Less Developed Countries," *Economic Development and Cultural Change*, Vol. 31, pp. 377-384.
Luterbacher, U. (1976), "Towards a Convergence of Behavioral and Strategic Conceptions of the Arms Race: the Case of American and Soviet ICBM Build-up," *Peace Research Society (International) Papers*, Vol. 26, pp. 1-21.
Nabe, O. (1983), "Military Expenditures and Industrialization in Africa," *Journal of Economic Issues*, Vol. 17, pp. 575-587.
Nardinelli, C. and Ackerman, G. (1976), "Defense Expenditures and the Survival of American Capitalism," *Armed Forces and Society*, Vol. 13 (1), pp. 13-16.
Reppy, J. (1989), "Technology Flows Between the Military and Civilian Sectors: Theory and Evidence," Prepared for the Panel, *Defense Spending as Technology Policy for the U.S.*, American Association for the Advancement of Science, January 19, 1989.
Rosenberg, N. (1976), *Perspectives on Technology*. New York: Cambridge University Press.
Rosthchild, K.W. (1973), "Military Expenditure, Exports and Growth," *Kyklos*, Vol. 26, pp. 804-813.
Russett, B.M. (1970), *What Price Vigilance? The Burdens of National Defense*, New Haven, CT: Yale University Press.
Saris, W. and Middendorp, C. (1980), "Arms Races: External Security or Domestic Pressure?," *British Journal of Political Science*, Vol. 10, pp. 121-128.
Seiglie, C. (1988), "International Conflict and Military Expenditures," *Journal of Conflict Resolution*, Vol. 32, pp. 141-161 .
Smith, D. and Smith, R. (1980), "Military Expenditure, Resources and Development," *Birkbeck College Discussion Paper no. 87*, London, November, 1980.
Smith, R.P. (1977), "Military Expenditure and Capitalism," *Cambridge Journal of Economics*, Vol. 1, pp. 61-76.
Smith, R.P. (1980), "Military Expenditure and Investment in OECD Countries, 1954-1973," *Journal of Comparative Economics*, Vol. 4, pp. 19-32.
Solo, R.A. (1970), "Military R&D: a Drag on the Economy," in James

L. Clayton (ed.), *The Economic Impact of the Cold War: Sources and Readings*. New York: Harcourt, Brace & World, Inc., pp.157-164.

Striner, H.E. et al. (1958), *Defense Spending and the U.S. Economy*, Vol. 4, Baltimore: Johns Hopkins University, Operations Research Office.

Szymanski, A. (1973), "Military Spending and Economic Stagnation," *American Journal of Sociology*, Vol. 79, pp. 1-14.

Taylor, J.G. (1983), *Lanchester Models of Warfare*, 2 volumes. Arlington, VA: Operations Research Society of America.

Trebilcock, C. (1969), "Spin-off in British Economic History: Armaments and Industry, 1760-1914," *Economic History Review*, Vol. 22, pp. 474-490.

Weede, E. (1983), " Military Participation Ratios, Human Capital Formation, and Economic Growth: a Cross-national Analysis," *Journal of Political and Military Sociology*, Vol. 11, pp. 11-19.

Weidenbaum, M.L. (1974), *The Economics of Peacetime Defense*, New York: Praeger.

Weidenbaum, M.L. (1989), *Military Spending and the Myth of Global Overstretch*, Washington, D.C.: The Center for Strategic and International Studies.

Weidenbaum, M.L. (1990), "Defense Spending and the American Economy: How Much Change is in the Offing?," *Defence Economics*, Vol. 1, pp. 233-242.

Whynes, D.K. (1979), *The Economics of Third World Military Expenditure*, London: Macmillan

Wolfson, M. (1985), "Notes on Economic Warfare," *Conflict Mangagement and Peace Science*, Vol. 8, pp. 1-20.

Wolfson, M. (1992), *Essays on the Cold War*, London: Macmillan.

Wolfson, M. and Shabahang, H. (1991), "Economic Causation in the Breakdown of Military Equilibrium," *Journal of Conflict Resolution*, Vol. 35, pp. 43-67.

PART THREE

Effects on Industrialized Economies

5

Defense Spending and Economic Growth: Spillovers vs. Crowding Out

Laurence H. Meyer and Fredric Q. Raines

In the *Rise and Fall of Great Powers,*[1] Paul Kennedy concludes that excessive military spending often leads to economic decline. The failure of Reaganomics to spur economic growth despite implementation of much of its supply-side agenda and the slower growth of both the Soviet and U.S. economies in the last two decades relative to Japan and Germany have provided more recent historical episodes that reinforce the concern raised by Kennedy in the context of a more sweeping historical analysis.

The relation between national economic wellbeing and resources absorbed in the military sector has also been widely debated among economists. On the one hand, analysts such as Seymour Melman[2] and Lloyd Dumas[3] have long argued that massive infusion of resources into the military has weakened our technological competitiveness in civilian sectors. On the other hand, Murray Weidenbaum[4] and some earlier studies[5] failed to find any systematic evidence of a trade-off between defense and investment or defense R&D and civilian R&D. The debate seems joined but not resolved.

This paper develops some of the important interactions between defense purchases and macroeconomic performance, provides empirical evidence on the quantitative effects of projected declines in defense spending on the level and growth rate of productive capacity, and then investigates the contribution of defense and non-defense R&D to productivity growth.

There are several channels through which defense spending affects macroeconomic performance. First, there is a demand effect. Defense spending is a part of overall government purchases and thus affects aggregate demand and therefore the short-run level of production and employment. Second, there are a variety of supply effects, involving both spillover from defense technology to civilian technology and crowding out of private and public capital, of federal nondefense R&D, and even of civilian R&D. In this paper, we focus exclusively on the supply effects of defense spending.

We use two interrelated methodologies to develop empirical estimates of the macroeconomic effects of changes in defense purchases on aggregate supply. First, we use simulations of a large scale macro model to investigate the effects of a projected decline in defense spending on the level of output, capital formation, and productivity growth. The model is particularly useful at analyzing the supply effect working through a change in national saving and increase in private capital formation. The macro model employed in this study, however, assumes that technical advance in the economy is exogenous. To investigate the potential spillover effects from federal defense to productivity as well as the potential damage from crowding out of nondefense and civilian R&D and of expenditures on the public infrastructure[6] by higher defense purchases, we directly estimate the contribution of the various components of R&D and of the public capital stock to labor and multi-factor productivity and search for any causal link between federal defense purchases, spending on the public infrastructure, and non-defense R&D flows.

Simulation Analysis of a Reduction in Defense Purchases

In this section, the Washington University Macroeconometric Model of the U.S. Economy (WUMM) is used to simulate the macroeconomic effects of a projected decline in defense purchases over the coming decade.

The Base and Alternative Paths for Defense Purchases

The base case assumes that defense spending is fixed in real terms at the 1991 level in the period from 1992 through 1997 and then grows at the rate of increase in real GDP (preserving the 1997 share of defense in GDP) in the period from 1998 through 2001. This is the same base case as is employed by the Congressional Budget Office in their February 1992 study of the effects of a cut in defense spending.[7] The point of departure for the alternative path is the Administration's

Future Years Defense Program, submitted in February 1991 (hereafter referred to as "the 1991 plan"). The 1991 plan calls for a 20% cut in nominal defense purchases relative to the base by 1997 and is consistent with the spending caps incorporated in the 1990 budget agreement. The alternative path for defense purchases employed here (and corresponding to the alternative # 2 path in the CBO study) is a cut 1 1/2 times as large as the 1991 plan. After 1997, the defense spending is set to maintain its share of GDP. Table 5.1 presents the base and alternative paths for both nominal and real defense purchases.[8] Figure 5.1 plots the share of defense in GDP from 1948 to 1991 and Figure 5.2 depicts this share in both the base and alternative simulations.

The Washington University Macro Model

WUMM is a 350-equation macro model developed by Laurence H. Meyer & Associates (LHM&A) and used for forecasting and policy analysis. The model has been used extensively for analysis of fiscal policy options, including the effects of Gramm-Rudman and of the 1986 tax reform act.

The model has short run Keynesian and long run neoclassical properties. Specifically, output is demand determined in the short run. Therefore, declines in defense purchases which lower federal fiscal stimulus will lower aggregate demand and hence production and employment in the short run. The long run neoclassical properties include a tendency to adjust back toward full employment in the long run. Therefore, in the long run the effect of fiscal policy actions focuses initially on the composition rather than the level of output. However, the composition of output today, specifically the share of output devoted to business fixed investment, is an important determinant of the level of output tomorrow. Hence there will also be an important long-run effect on the level of output. In the long run, lower defense purchases allow for a transfer of resources to private investment and therefore result in an increase in the economy's level of productive capacity and hence GDP.

WUMM is able to capture the long-run effects of fiscal policy because it has a carefully articulated supply side in which the level of productive capacity in the long run is affected by labor supply and capital formation and where both input supplies in turn are affected by government policies. For the purpose of this simulation, there are two key supply side effects. First, the decline in federal employment raises the civilian labor force and provides the resources for an increase in private sector output as government output is reduced. In

TABLE 5.1
Defense Purchases in the Base and Alternative Simulations

	Nominal Values (Billions, Current Dollars)				Real Values (Billions, 1987 Dollars)			
Year	Base	Alt.	Change	%Change	Base	Alt.	Change	%Change
1992	314	304	-10	-3	269	260	-9	-3
1993	320	294	-26	-8	269	265	-4	-2
1994	328	286	-42	-13	269	234	-35	-13
1995	337	279	-58	-17	270	223	-47	-17
1996	347	273	-74	-21	270	212	-58	-22
1997	359	268	-91	-25	271	201	-70	-26
1998	375	273	-102	-27	275	199	-75	-27
1999	392	285	-107	-27	279	202	-77	-27
2000	409	297	-112	-27	284	205	-78	-28
2001	428	310	-118	-28	288	209	-80	-28

Source: Authors' calculations.

the simulation, the decline in federal employment is used directly to adjust upward the model's projections of the civilian labor force.

The second link is from government purchases to real interest rates to capital formation. The decline in government purchases reduces aggregate demand, puts downward pressure on prices and thereby raises the real money supply, in turn lowering real interest rates and stimulating investment and hence private capital formation. The increase in the private capital stock raises the economy's productive capacity. Over the period during which resources are being transferred between government purchases and private investment, the increase in the level of output and in the level of labor productivity will show up as an increase in the economy's intermediate-run rate of economic growth.

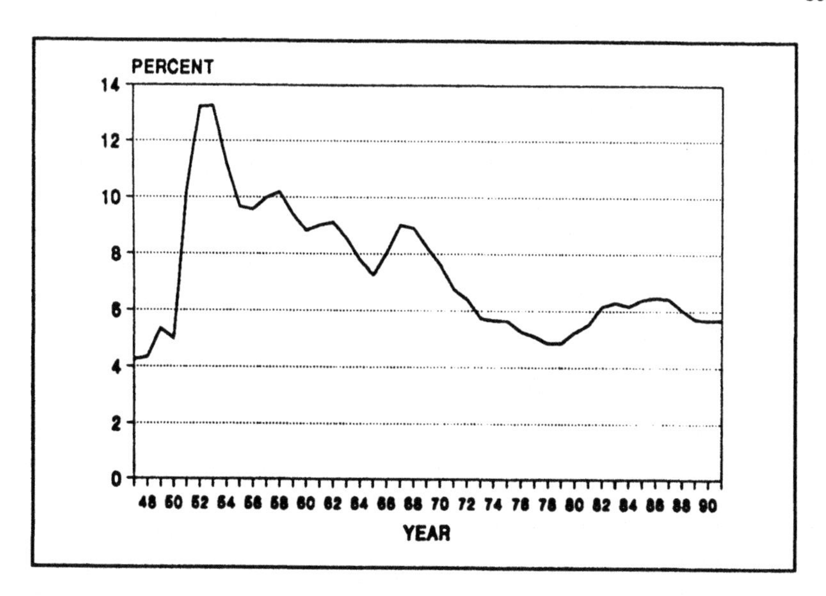

FIGURE 5.1 Share of Federal Defense Purchases in GDP

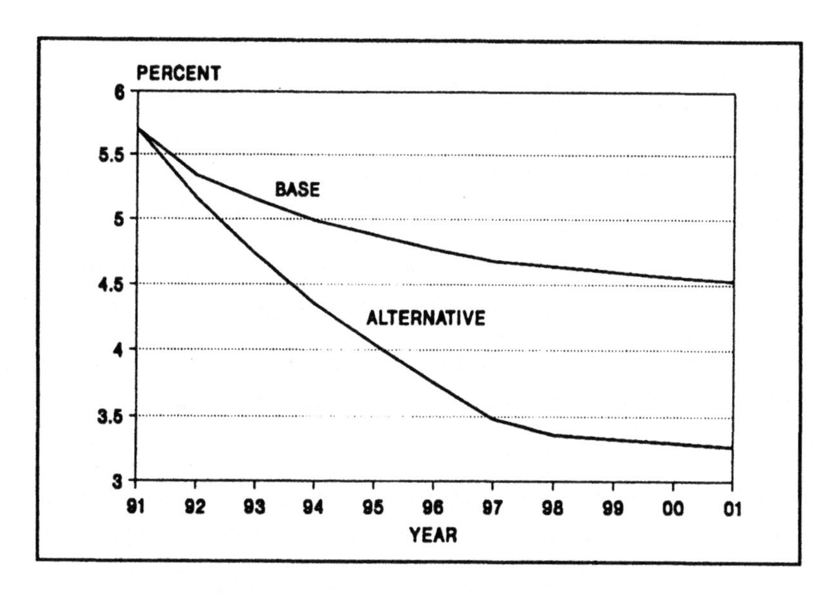

FIGURE 5.2 Share of Federal Defense Purchases in GDP in the Simulations

Technical Advance and Long-run Growth

WUMM assumes that the rate of growth in technology is exogenous. Over the historical data, the rate of technical advance is estimated in the model as part of the estimation of the demand for labor (hours worked). A series of time trends are used to estimate the rate of technical advance over subperiods. We find, for example, that there is a decline in the rate of technical advance in 1973 and an upturn in 1981. However, there is no attempt in WUMM to explain the source of the changes in the time trend.

The assumption that the rate of technical advance is exogenous means, of course, that WUMM cannot be used to simulate the effects of changes in R&D or in the public infrastructure on the level of productive capacity. To the extent that the long-run effects of lower defense spending imply increased investment in either the public capital stock or civilian or nondefense R&D, the WUMM simulations may understate the long-run benefits of lower defense purchases. We will apply a separate empirical methodology below to develop evidence on the relative contributions to technical advance of civilian R&D, federal defense and nondefense R&D, and the public non-military infrastructure.

Accommodated and Non-accommodated Runs

In simulating the effect of cuts in defense purchases, a decision must be made about the response of monetary policy. One of two extreme assumptions is usually employed. In the first case, which we call the non-accommodated case, the rate of money growth (M2 in our simulations) is assumed to be the same in the base and policy run. Monetary policy makes no attempt to adjust to the cut in defense and offset its short-run adverse effect on aggregate demand in this case. In the second alternative, which we refer to as the fully accommodated case, monetary policy becomes more stimulative as defense spending is cut so that aggregate demand is maintained. In this case, the path for the unemployment rate will be approximately the same in the base and alternative paths. The latter assumption about monetary policy is more useful in tracing the long-run response to defense cuts as it eliminates the transitional demand effect and allows us to focus exclusively on changes in the economy's productive capacity. This is the assumption we employ in the simulations reported below.

The Long-run Growth Benefits of Defense Cuts

The long-run effects are estimated using the alternative defense path and an adjusted path for M2 that maintains the unemployment rate approximately equal to its value in the base case (the accommodated case). Figures 5.3 - 5.8 depict the effects on the level of GDP, private non-farm output, the level of employment in the non-farm business sector, military employment, the real interest rate, and the private capital stock.

GDP declines in 1992 because the accommodation via easier monetary policy does not take hold immediately and therefore allows a small initial demand effect. Thereafter, however, GDP is higher in every year and the increase builds gradually over time, reaching $37 billion, a 0.6% increase relative to the base case. The source of the increase in GDP is the increase in investment and hence the private capital stock. By 2001, investment in equipment is 23% higher than in the base case and investment in plant is 15% higher. As a result, the capital stock gradually increases, rising by 2.25% by 2001.

The second important supply side effect involves the transfer of government workers to the private sector. By 1997, federal employment has declined by 580,000 and business employment has increased by about the same amount. As a result of this transfer, the increase in private sector output is greater than the increase in GDP; output in the private non-farm business sector, for example, increases by $60 billion by 2001, or by 1.3% relative to the base case.

The cumulative increase in GDP resulting from the defense cuts is $165 billion, but the increment to the compound annual growth rate of GDP over the decade is only 0.06 percentage points and the increase in the compound annual growth rate for private non-farm business output is only 0.13 percentage points. If we are looking to increase our rate of trend growth from the current level of about 2.25% per year toward even the 3% rate averaged over the 1970's, the defense cutbacks are likely to contribute only a small part of that objective.

Factors Limiting the Long-run Increase in Output

In our simulation, the effects of the defense cuts on productive capacity are attenuated in a couple of ways. First, the direct effect on national saving of cuts in defense purchases is partially offset by declines in both foreign and private saving. The decline in interest rates in the U.S. lowers the attractiveness of U.S. assets relative to those outside the U.S. and results in a depreciation of the dollar. The depreciation of the dollar in turn stimulates real net exports. The result is that some of the resources released by lower defense purchases are absorbed in production of exports and import-competing goods. Lower interest rates also stimulate residential construction, further absorbing resources. Finally, lower interest rates raise the

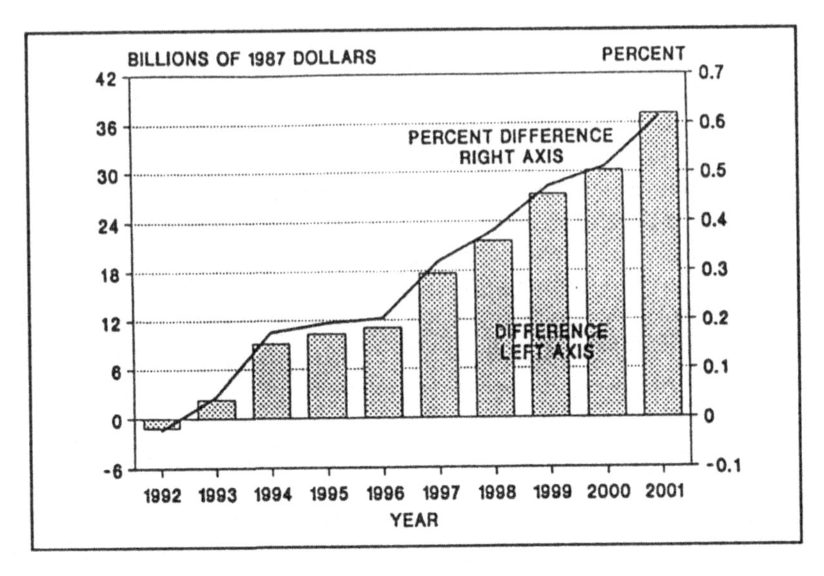

FIGURE 5.3 Real GDP: Base vs. Alternative

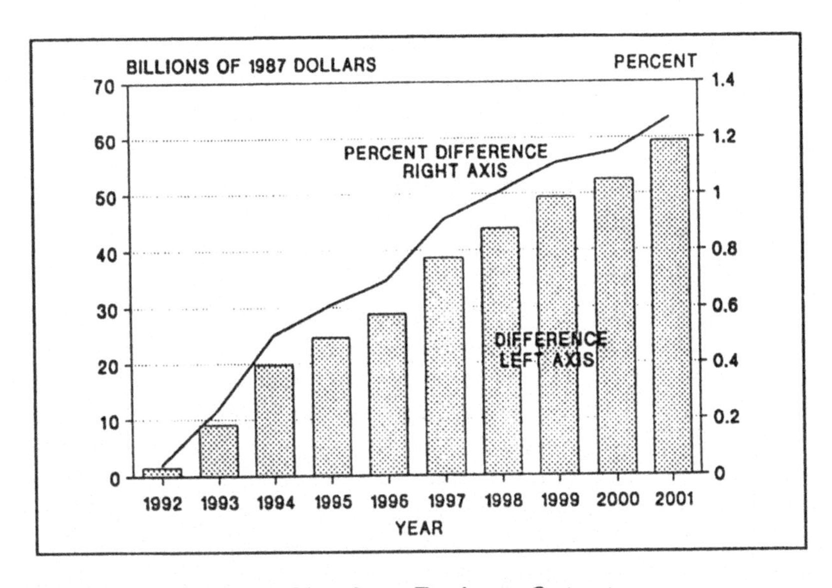

FIGURE 5.4 Private Non-farm Business Output: Base vs. Alternative

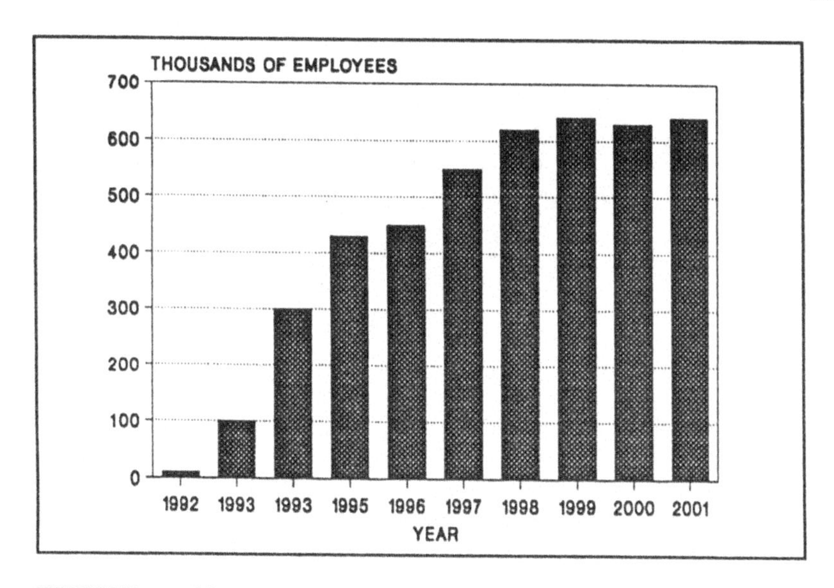

FIGURE 5.5 Non-farm Private Employment: Difference between Base & Alternative

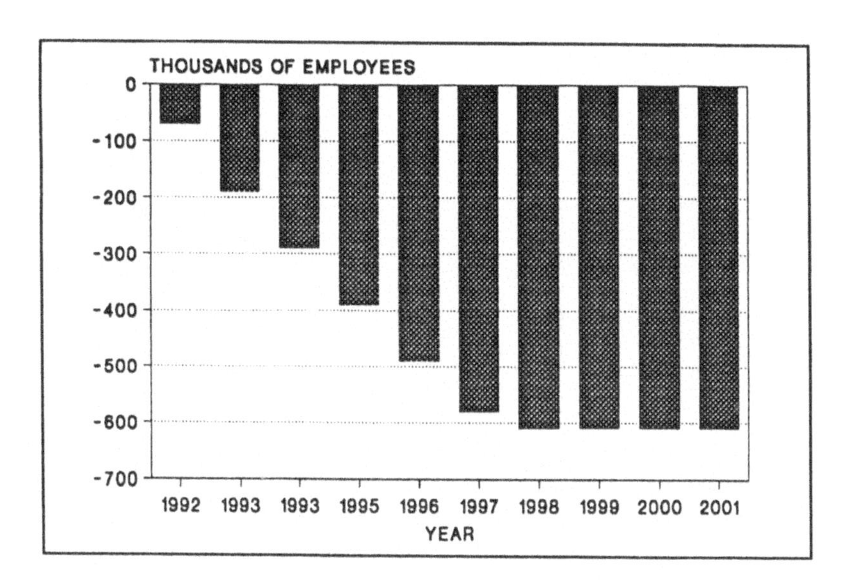

FIGURE 5.6 Military Employment: Difference between Base & Alternative

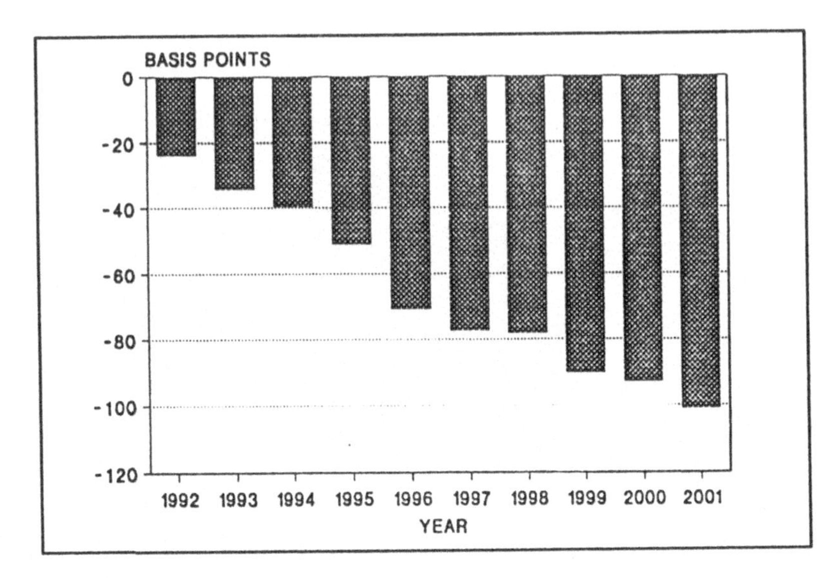

FIGURE 5.7 Real Corporate Bond Yield: Difference between Base & Alternative

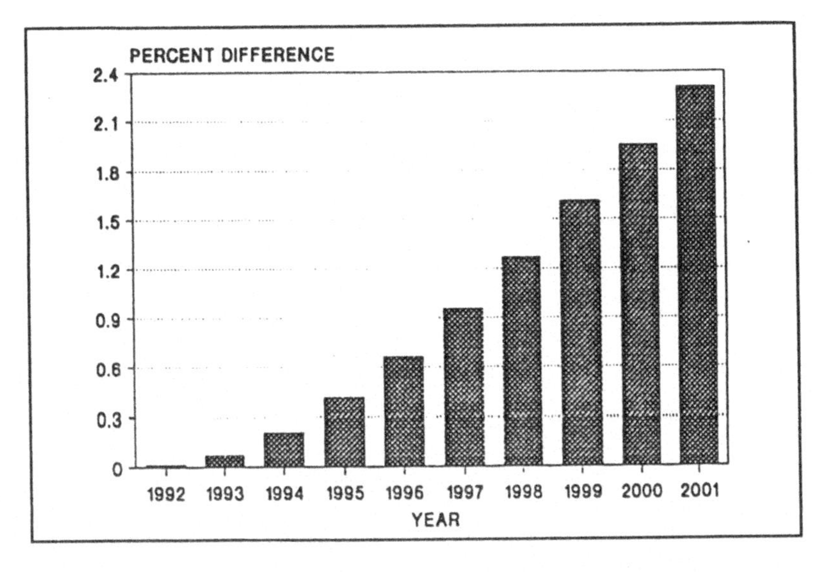

FIGURE 5.8 Stock of Equipment & Structures: Base vs. Alternative

value of equities and hence consumer net worth, stimulating consumption and lowering household saving. The net result is that only a portion of the resources flowing out of the government sector end up in private capital formation and hence provide the basis for an increase in the economy's productive capacity.

Second, the production function employed in WUMM implies that there is only a modest contribution to output from a given increment to the private capital stock. Assuming a Cobb-Douglas production function and constant returns to scale, the elasticity of output with respect to the capital stock equals the share of capital in national income, about 23% using the estimates from WUMM. This immediately implies a very small elasticity of output with respect to the capital stock. The production function in WUMM is CES rather than Cobb-Douglas, with an estimated elasticity of substitution of 0.6, implying an even smaller increase in the capital stock in response to defense cuts. Recent work by Romer[9], in contrast, suggests that the elasticity of output with respect to capital may be significantly higher than implied by its share in national income, perhaps closer to 1 than to 1/4 percentage point, reflecting increasing returns to scale arising from the endogeneity of technical change.

Third, WUMM does not allow for additional supply effects that might result from some of the defense resources flowing into spending on the public infrastructure, or from a substitution of nondefense and civilian R&D for defense R&D.

In the next section we use direct estimates of production functions to develop the relative contributions of public infrastructure and civilian, defense and government nondefense R&D to the level of productive capacity. These estimates will also allow us to develop more direct evidence on the elasticity of output with respect to the capital stock.

Sources of Growth: A Production-Function Perspective

In this section we first introduce the data employed in the production function regressions and review the important trends in the data. We focus on the decline in output and productivity growth in the 1970's and in the 1980's, and the degree to which the public capital stock and R&D stocks may have contributed to the output and productivity slowdown. Finally, we look for evidence that movements in defense purchases have influenced the growth in the public and nondefense R&D stocks.

Data Sources

The output variable is Gross Domestic Output of the non-farm business sector less housing, measured in 1987 dollars. The series is from Table 1.8 in the NIPA and the historical series was taken from the LHM&A data bank. It is the variable that best measures the output produced with the private non-farm non-residential capital stock, the measure of private capital stock employed in the regressions. The output data is available at this time only back to 1959. In order to compare our results with the recent literature on empirical production functions, generally estimated over the period from 1948 through the mid to late 1980's, we extended the business output series backward by assuming that the growth rates before 1959 in 1987 dollars would the same as they were in the unrevised series in 1982 dollars.

The capital stock data is an annual series, measured at the end of the respective years. The source is John C. Musgrave, "Fixed Reproducible Tangible Wealth in the United States, Revised Estimates."[10] To make the capital series comparable to the hours data and the output data, we take averages of the current and the previous year's values to form an average capital stock variable (KP). The labor input variable is hours worked in the non-farm business sector (LHMB). This series is from unpublished data from the Bureau of Labor Statistics ("Binder 60") and is taken from the LHM&A data bank.

We refer to two types of productivity data. Labor productivity is simply the ratio of output to hours (PROD). The growth rate for multi-factor productivity is the residual in the production function, that part of output growth that cannot be explained by the growth in labor and private capital. In deriving our series for multi-factor productivity, we assume the production function is Cobb-Douglas with constant returns to scale over labor and private capital. The share of capital assumed in deriving this series was .23, based on estimation of the investment equations in WUMM and consistent with the national income data.

Public capital and various components of R&D used to explain the trends in labor and multi-factor productivity. The data on the stock of public non-military infrastructure also is from the Musgrave article referenced above. As in the case of the private capital stock, the public capital stock is measured at the end of the respective years and is therefore averaged with the previous year to construct a measure of the average public non-military capital stock (KG). Data on the civilian R&D flows and stock for 1948 - 1981 are from U.S. Bureau of

Labor Statistics, *The Impact of Research and Development on Productivity Growth*[11] and for 1982 - 1990 are from John E. Jankowski, Jr., *National Patterns in R&D Resources: 1990*.[12] The deflators for the 1982 - 1990 period were calculated consistent with the methodology employed by the BLS for 1948 - 1981. Data for the federal R&D flows and stocks are based on R&D data provided by Mark Wasserman. The methodology underlying these series is developed in *Budget of the United Sates Government, Fiscal Year 1992*.[13] These were converted into stocks using the same methodology as was used in deriving the civilian R&D stock: basic flows are assumed to enter the stock with a 5-year lag, and applied and development R&D flows with a 2-year lag. Zero depreciation is assumed for the basic R&D stock and a 10% rate of depreciation is assumed for applied R&D stock. The share of defense purchases in GDP is the ratio of nominal federal defense purchases to nominal GDP, both taken from the LHM&A data bank.

Trends in the Data

Table 5.2 presents the compound annual growth rates of key variables over the 1950's, 1960's, 1970's and 1980's and the average share of defense in GDP over each decade. The growth rate of private non-farm business output is about 4% over both the 1950's and the 1960's, but declines to 3% over the 1970's and to 2.6% over the 1980's. The decline in the growth rate of output has virtually nothing to do with the pattern in the growth in hours worked. Indeed, hours worked grows slightly more rapidly in the last two decades as the growth of output slows. As a result, the trend in labor productivity growth mirrors the trend in output growth.

The trend in private capital formation contributes to the decline in output growth over the 1970's and the 1980's, but only marginally, particularly in light of the usual assumption of a low elasticity of output with respect to the capital stock. The limited contribution from labor and capital growth to the slowdown in output growth leaves most of the explanation in the residual, multi-factory productivity growth.

The deceleration of growth in the 1970's is clearly dominated by the slowdown in the growth of multi-factor productivity. Output growth slows by 1.09 percentage points and multi-factor productivity by .93 percentage points. A slowdown in the growth of capital accounts for the rest of the slowdown in output growth in the 1970's. The further slowing in output growth over the 1980's is associated with a slowing in the growth of private capital and a further slowing in multi-factor productivity growth.

TABLE 5.2
Trends in Output Growth and Sources of Output Growth

	1950s	1960s	1970s	1980s
Private non-farm business output	3.99	4.09	3.00	2.63
Pvt. non-farm bus. productivity	2.68	2.39	1.30	0.82
Pvt. non-residential capital stock	3.75	4.35	3.85	3.23
Private non-farm hours	1.28	1.66	1.68	1.80
Capital/labor ratio	2.44	2.65	2.14	1.40
Multi-factor productivity	2.11	1.75	0.82	0.52
Public non-military capital stock	3.81	4.66	2.20	1.25
Civilian R&D stock	8.67	7.68	4.84	4.97
Federal defense R&D stock	16.31	10.95	1.48	2.16
Federal non-defense R&D stock	2.89	20.50	5.70	1.80
Defense share of GDP	10.20	8.50	5.80	6.10

Source: Authors' calculations.

Table 5.2 also presents growth rates for four factors that might help to explain multi-factor productivity growth: the public non-military infrastructure and three components of the stock of R&D. The growth of the stock of public non-military infrastructure accelerates in the 1960's and then slows dramatically in the 1970's and further in the 1980's. Not surprisingly, this variable will perform very well in production function regressions as a complement to labor and the private capital stock.

The growth in the civilian stock of R&D also slows sharply in the 1970's and 1980's, relative to the 1950's and 1960's. It too should perform well in production function regressions. The federal defense R&D stock slows progressively over the 1960's and 1970's, then accelerates modestly in the 1980's. The growth of federal nondefense R&D stock accelerates sharply in the 1960's, then decelerates sharply in the 1970's, and further in the 1980's. The pattern in these variables does not suggest as large a role in the explanation for the productivity slowdown as for the public capital stock or civilian R&D stock (see Figure 5.9).

The share of defense spending in GDP declines in the 1960's and the 1970's and rises slightly in the 1980's. This pattern does not suggest that the percentage of the nation's resources absorbed in defense contributed to the slowdown in output growth in either the 1970's or the 1980's. Indeed, we can find little direct evidence that

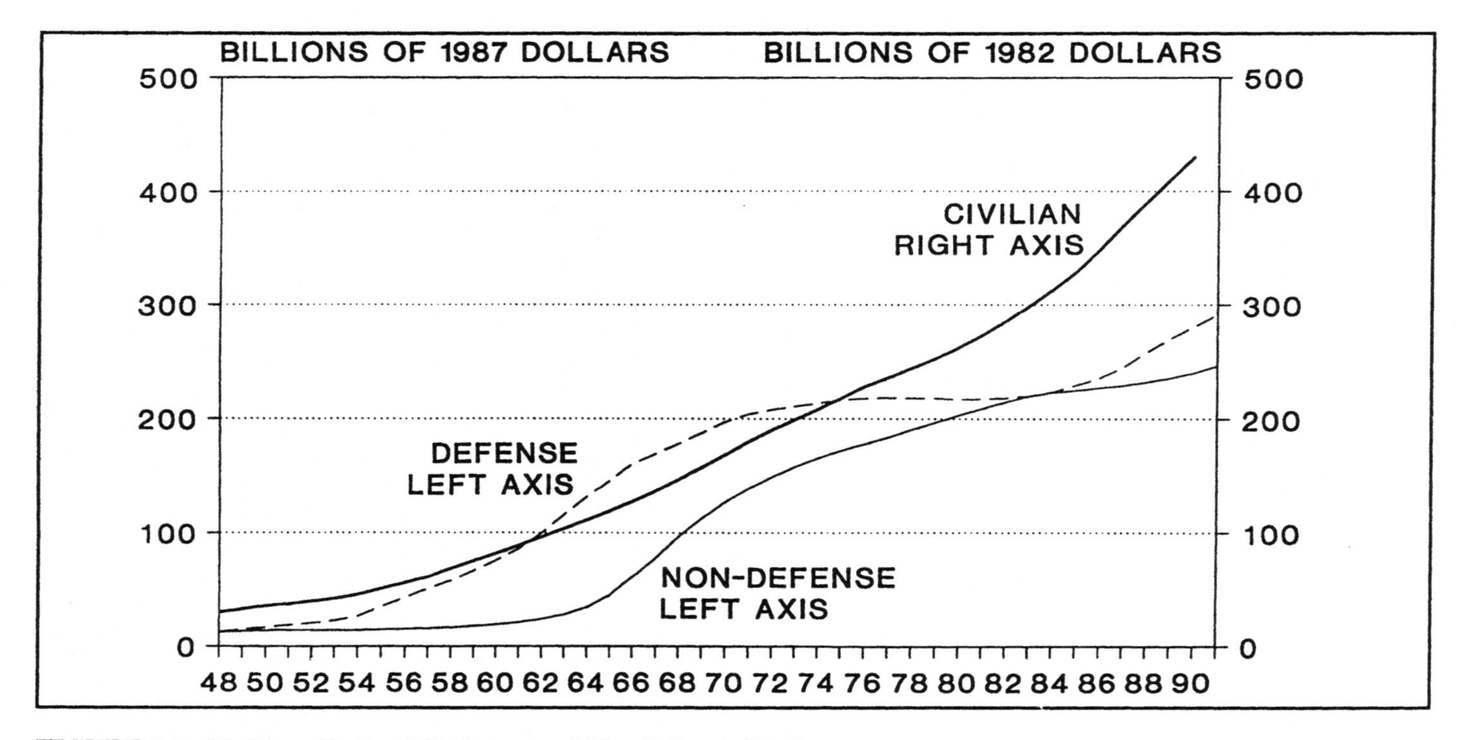

FIGURE 5.9 Civilian, Federal Defense and Nondefense Stocks

defense purchases in general or defense R&D flows crowd out either public infrastructure spending, or civilian or federal non-defense R&D flows. Nevertheless, it is certainly true that reducing resources flowing into defense spending would free resources which policy could then redirect into either public infrastructure or non-defense R&D.

Defense R&D, Technology Transfers and Economic Growth: Results from Productivity Regressions

Significance of Defense R&D

Throughout the postwar period federal funding of defense related R&D has constituted a large fraction of all R&D spending in the U.S. During most of this period, the fraction of total R&D allocated to defense followed an irregular downward trend, from a high of over 50% during the late 1950's, to 33% in the mid-1960's, to 25% by 1980. The share going to defense then rose during the 1980's, peaking at 30% during 1985-6. It has since started to decline again.

During the 1979-87 defense build-up, virtually 100% of the increase in defense R&D occurred in applied research and development, funding a broad range of exotic, expensive weapons systems. Basic defense research was generally stagnant at around $800 million (1987$) during the 1980's, dropping to less than 3% of total federal defense R&D. At the same time, more than 100% of the decrease in federal nondefense R&D over the 1979-87 period was due to the decline in applied R&D, as basic nondefense research actually increased by 37% over this period.

At the level of overall productivity, the issue of the contribution of defense R&D has tended to be subsumed under two other issues: what are the relative contributions to productivity of civilian vs. federal R&D; and, how important is R&D in general in the explanation of the slowdown in productivity growth. After reviewing the empirical evidence, Griliches[14], and separately Jorgenson[15], both conclude that company funded R&D contributes more than federally funded R&D to productivity growth, but that R&D itself has not been a major contributor to the productivity slowdown. Our aim in this section is to narrow the focus of investigation and address the empirical role of defense R&D more directly. Working from a standard production function model, and making use of direct measures of the stocks of R&D as well the stocks of private and public capital, we estimate the relative contributions to productivity trends of civilian, defense and nondefense R&D stocks, as well as the stock of public capital. Due to limitations of space and the imposed scope of analysis, a number of pertinent issues have been left unaddressed, or at least unresolved. These issues form the basis for future research.

Methodological Issues

Labor and Multi-factor Productivity. We investigate two different productivity measures. The first is labor productivity (LPROD), defined as the natural log of the ratio of output to total hours over the non-farm business sector. The second is multi-factor productivity (LMFP), defined as the natural log of output minus a weighted average of the natural logs of private capital and labor where the weights are based on factor shares and sum to 1.0. The weights used are based on factor shares in the WUMM model, and are equal to .23 for capital and .77 for labor.[16]

Explanatory Variables. The key explanatory variables are all in logarithm form. These include the private non-farm non-residential capital stock, LKP; total hours in the non-farm business sector, LL; the stock of public non-military capital, LKG; the stock of company-financed R&D, LCRD, and its basic research and applied research plus development components, LCRDB and LCRDA; the stock of federally funded defense R&D, LFDRD, and its basic and applied components, LFDRDB and LFDRDA; and the stock of federally funded non-defense R&D, LFNRD, and its basic and applied components, LFNRDB and LFNRDA. Data sources for the public capital and R&D variables were presented earlier. Attempt was made to control for cyclical fluctuations in productivity by means of the capacity utilization rate in manufacturing, CU.

First-difference vs. Level Regressions. Much of the recent work on productivity equations, including Aschauer and Munnell, have employed log level specifications of productivity equations. First differencing may, however, be a preferred technique, both because of collinearity among the levels of key explanatory variables and because of common trends in the explanatory and dependent variables. The correlation between the stocks of private capital and civilian R&D, for example, is .9899, and that between civilian R&D and public capital is .9948. In these circumstances it is difficult for regression estimation to apportion partial effects with a high degree of precision, particularly given a limited number of time series observations.

We also investigated the appropriateness of the level vs first difference specification by means of the Augmented Dickey-Fuller test.[17] We reject at the 10% (or higher) significance level that LPROD and LMFP have no unit roots where the tests allowed for a constant term or constant plus trend terms. Similar tests on the first differences of these variables, significant at the 1% level for LMFP and the 10% level for LPROD, indicated that there is at most a single unit root. These tests imply that a first difference model is appropriate and this specification is therefore consistently applied below. The first-differenced variables are denoted by the prefix D (hence, LPROD becomes DLPROD and LMFP becomes DLMFP).

The Use of Deterministic Trend Variables. In level specifications, time trends are employed to capture the residual component of productivity growth, i.e., that portion that cannot be explained by the alleged causal variables. Often, multiple time trends are included to allow for breaks in the time trend. However there exists a high degree of collinearity between the trend variables and the capital and R&D variables. The correlation between TREND and LKP, for example, is .9985. Confounding the issue is the fact that deterministic trend variables will frequently be better proxies of technological effects than specific technology variables measured with error. In the first difference specification, the time trend becomes the constant term. A dummy variable with zeros up to 1973 and ones thereafter, denoted DUM73, is used to capture a break in the trend beginning in 1973.

Returns to Scale

We investigate returns to scale in the regressions for labor productivity. Regression results for DLPROD are presented in Table 5.3. Alternative specifications are listed by column. Included in each specification, although not reported, is the change in manufacturing capacity utilization, DCU, which is always significant.

Column 1 of Table 5.3 presents the basic model that includes first differences of private and public capital and labor, DLKP, DLKG and DLL. The R^2 for this sparse specification is .563, respectable for a first difference regression. The elasticity of private capital is more than twice that of public capital, while the sum of the estimated elasticities over all three inputs in this unrestricted version is precisely equal to 1.00, identical with CRS. Constant returns to scale is imposed in column 2 by means of the variables DLKPL (DLKP - DLL) and DLKGL (DLKG - DLL), a restriction that cannot be rejected at virtually any level of significance. The coefficients of private and public capital are unchanged by the CRS restriction.

Next we test the effects of introducing deterministic time trends which, as noted, become the constant term C and the dummy variable DUM73 in the first-difference specification. In column 3 of Table 5.3,

TABLE 5.3
Dependent Variable: Change in Log of Labor Productivity (DLPROD)

Independent Var.	(1)	(2)	(3)	(4)	(5)	(6)	(7)	(8)	(9)	(10)	(11)	(12)
DLL	-0.81**		-0.69**		-0.47*							
DLKP	0.55**		-0.0044									
DLKPL		0.55**		0.25	0.075	0.35	0.32	0.36	0.53**	0.30	0.54**	0.27
DLKG	0.26											
DLKGL		0.26*		0.37*	0.27	0.26*	0.25*	0.26*	0.23	0.19	0.24	0.35**
DLCRD						0.082						
DLCRDB							0.096					
DLCRDA								0.078				
DLFDRD									0.013			
DLFDRDB										0.064*		
DLFDRDA											0.011	
DLFNRDB												0.046
Constant, C			0.032**	0.006	0.018*							
DUM73			-0.011**									
R^2	0.56	0.56	0.66	0.59	0.63	0.58	0.59	0.58	0.56	0.61	0.56	0.60
S.E.	0.011	0.011	0.0099	0.011	0.010	0.011	0.011	0.011	0.011	0.010	0.011	0.011
DW	1.99	1.99	2.16	1.94	2.02	1.97	1.98	1.97	1.99	2.09	1.99	2.00

*denotes significant at 5% level
**denotes significant at 1% level

Source: Authors' calculations.

C and DUM73 replace DLKG. Both C and DUM73 are significant, and the R^2 has increased to .663. However, the coefficient of private capital has been driven to zero. The trend variables thus act as proxies for technological factors that otherwise are reflected in private capital.

The initial specification for DLPROD, without either time trends or R&D stock variables, exhibits CRS over private and public capital and labor. However, when either the deterministic time trends (constant and DUM73) or significant R&D stocks are included, CRS will generally be rejected, and decreasing returns over the three basic inputs will be indicated. This is demonstrated in column 5 of Table 5.3, where DLL has been added to the specification that includes C in column 4, thus relaxing the restriction of CRS, which is rejected at the 5% level.

The question then arises, when, if ever, should CRS be imposed? While any approach involves a degree of arbitrariness, it appears that comparability of R&D stock comparisons across alternative specifications is improved if CRS over private and public capital and labor is assumed throughout. Hence, this is the procedure we follow.

The Contribution of Public Capital to Private Productivity

We focus on the role of the public non-military capital stock because Aschauer among others has called attention to its powerful contribution to private productivity. In addition, this variable has a special importance in discussions about the effect of defense spending on macroeconomic performance, because resources now consumed in defense might be reallocated to the public infrastructure as defense spending is significantly reduced.

Shown in columns 1 and 2 of Table 5.4 are results for public capital, DLKG, based on regressions for DLMFP. As with Table 5.3 for DLPROD, the first difference in capacity utilization, DCU, is not shown, but is always included and is always significant at the 1% level. The constant term is shown only when included in the specification. Alone, public capital is highly significant. Including a constant (trend) term, DLKG remains significant, though its coefficient falls off somewhat. Including the trend break, DUM73, in addition to C, renders public capital insignificant. Column 3 presents the deterministic version of the model. It is interpreted as saying that MFP in the non-farm business sector grew at an average annual rate of 1.8% over the 1950-72 period, but only at a 0.5% rate during the 1973-90 period. These systematic determinants, together with capacity utilization, explain 62.2% of the variation in DLMFP, compared to 55.5% for public capital (with DCU) alone. At this point, it appears

TABLE 5.4
Dependent Variable: Change in Log of Multi-factor Productivity (DLMFP)

Independent Var.	(1)	(2)	(3)	(4)	(5)	(6)	(7)	(8)	(9)	(10)	(11)	(12)
DLKG	0.39**	0.32*										
DLKGL												
DLCRD				0.16*	0.20**							
DLCRDB						0.19**						
DLCRDA							0.20**					
DLFDRD				0.017								
DLFDRDB								0.11**				
DLFDRDA												
DLFNRD									0.085*			
DLFNRDB				0.013						0.10**		
DLCOMB											0.27**	0.32*
Constant, C		0.027	0.018**									-0.002
DUM73			-0.013**									-0.002
R^2	0.55	0.56	0.62	0.60	0.59	0.62	0.59	0.66	0.45	0.54	0.65	0.66
S.E.	0.012	0.012	0.011	0.012	0.012	0.011	0.012	0.011	0.014	0.013	0.011	0.011
DW	1.75	1.75	1.999	1.79	1.76	1.90	1.72	2.10	2.04	1.84	1.97	2.03

*denotes significant at 5% level
**denotes significant at 1% level

Source: Authors' calculations.

that the public capital stock does make a significant contribution to private productivity, but its contribution is difficult to disentangle from other factors that are captured in trend terms. We will return to this issue once we have included R&D stocks in the regressions.

Relative Contributions of Civilian, Defense and Nondefense R&D

We investigate the relative contributions of alternative R&D sources by means of the DLPROD regressions. Columns 6 through 12 in Table 5.3 present results of including alternative R&D stocks in the CRS constrained model. Columns 6-8 present the results for the total stock of civilian R&D and its basic and applied components. In each case the coefficient of private capital is reduced to the .32 - .36 range, a loss of about 40% from its value where there are no competing factors. The coefficient of public capital is remarkably stable. Despite their influence on private capital, none of the coefficients of civilian R&D stocks are significant.

Results of including defense R&D in the DLPROD specification are given in columns 9-11 of Table 5.3. The total defense stock is insignificant, and the coefficients of the private and public capital stocks are essentially unchanged from the basic model. The same story holds for the stock of defense applied research and development, shown in column 11 of Table 5.3. Finally, the stock of basic defense research is significant at the 5% level (column 10). As would be expected, inclusion of the significant basic defense stock reduces the estimated elasticity of private capital.

The relative significance of basic civilan and defense research must be viewed as tentative given the high degree of collinearity between the basic stocks of civilian and military R&D. The correlation between the *changes* in these two variables is 0.86. There is little reason to believe that the contribution to productivity would substantially differ between basic civilian and defense research. This proposition was tested with the DLPROD model. Equality of coefficients between the basic defense and civilian stocks could not be rejected at an arbitrarily high significance level.

The final column of Table 5.3 presents results for basic nondefense research. The estimated coefficient, .046, is somewhat lower than that for basic civilian or basic defense research, but is significant at the 6% level. However, neither total nor applied nondefense R&D is significant in explaining DLPROD.

Turning to the regressions for the growth of multi-factor productivity in Table 5.4, column 4 presents the results when all three total R&D stocks are included. Only the civilian stock is significant, the federal defense and nondefense stocks proving highly insignificant. When a regression is run using all three stocks of basic research, the story changes somewhat. Only the stock of basic defense proves significant. However, the hypothesis that the coefficients of basic defense and civilian research are equal cannot be rejected at a very high significance level. Thus, equality of basic research coefficients is confirmed for both productivity variants.

The importance of civilian R&D for multi-factor productivity is demonstrated in columns 5 - 7 in Table 5.4. The total stocks of civilian R&D, and its basic and applied R&D components, are all highly significant and remain so when a constant (trend term) is included. Moreover, the elasticities of civilian R&D and its components are relatively large (substantially in excess of federally funded R&D) and of equal magnitude. The key role of civilian R&D for private productivity seems clearly established.

Results presented in column 8 in Table 5.4 suggest that federally funded basic defense research also strongly contributes to multi-factor productivity. The addition of a constant (trend) term has little effect on either the significance level or the coefficient of DLFDRDB. The stock of defense applied R&D also proves to be significant, even after including a constant term, in contrast to the results in the DLPROD regressions. However, the significance of defense applied R&D appears suspect based on other grounds. When basic and applied components are entered together, the basic stock remains significant with an unchanged elasticity, while the applied stock becomes insignificant, consistent with the findings in the DLPROD regressions.

Columns 9 and 10 in Table 5.4 present the results for the stocks of total and basic nondefense R&D. The total stock is significant at the 1.5% level and the basic stock at better than the 1% level. However, the R^2s are relatively low, and introducing a constant (trend) term reduces the significance level of both stocks below 10%.

Due to collinearity, it is not possible to obtain any precision in the estimates of public capital together with a given R&D stock when both are included in the same DLMFP regression. One or the other, or both, will be insignificant. To overcome this problem, we experimented with a combination variable constructed from a weighted average of the changes in the logs of public capital and the more significant R&D stocks. Two different variables were constructed, one that excluded basic nondefense R&D, and a second that included this stock. Based on performance we prefer the latter variable, which is defined as follows.

DLCOMB = .39*DLKG +.20*DLCRD +.11*DLFDRDB
+.10*DLFNRDB.

The weights are equal to the coefficients of the corresponding variables when entered alone in basic regressions explaining DLMFP. Results of this experiment are presented in columns 11 and 12 of Table 5.4. The coefficient of DLCOMB reflects the extent to which the weights of the component variables must be shrunk due to collinearity. Note the relatively high R^2s, exceeded by only one other regression in Table 5.4 (that for the basic defense stock alone). Note also that DLCOMB retains significance at the 5% level when the two trend variables are introduced, and that these variables have essentially zero coefficients. In effect, the combination variable leaves a zero trend residual to be explained.

Technology Spillovers onto Private Capital

As noted above in the discussion of returns to scale in the labor productivity model, the coefficient of private capital in the basic model with CRS imposed over private and public capital and labor (column 2 of Table 5.3) is equal to .55, substantially in excess of typical estimates of capital's share of output. However, on the theory of endogenous technical change, a coefficient for private capital this large, or even larger, is to be expected. According to the theory of endogenous productivity growth as developed by Paul Romer[18], technological change drives economic growth because while technology is available to all (in Romer's terminology, it is a "nonrival input"), technological improvements can be imbedded in new investment by the firm so that the benefits are at least partially appropriable (they are "excludable"). This process generates both the inducement to invest and the mechanism by which investment reflects technological change. Explicitly including a variable that reflects this accumulated technology, i.e., an R&D stock, in a productivity regression will reduce the coefficient of capital by an amount that reflects the technology embedded in capital due to that R&D stock.[19]

All three basic stocks make a substantial contribution to the productivity of private capital. It is perhaps not surprising that these returns are approximately the same magnitude, given that the source of funding for basic research, unlike applied research and development, may not be very critical to their ultimate application. In contrast, only civilian applied R&D is relevant for private capital: federally funded defense and nondefense R&D appear to have no measurable impact. Most defense applied R&D may be too specialized for civilian application, while much nondefense applied R&D may be directed to "quality of life" outputs whose effect on private capital is likely to be quite tenuous and indirect.

Issue of Defense R&D Crowding Out of Other R&D or Public Capital

A number of useful stylized facts have emerged from the analysis of this section. First, basic defense R&D, currently around $1 billion per year, while only a very small part of total defense R&D, appears to have a highly significant impact on both labor and total factor productivity. Second, applied defense R&D, approaching $40 billion per year, appears to have little impact on productivity growth in the private sector after allowance is made for collinearity. The evidence here is stronger for labor productivity than for multi-factor productivity, but appears to hold for both. Third, we find that both basic and applied civilian R&D make a significant contribution to productivity, both directly and through their technological transfer to private capital. Fourth, basic nondefense research, by far the largest component of total outlays for basic research from all sources (more than twice the combined total of civilian plus defense), was estimated to be significant for multi-factor productivity, and possibly significant for labor productivity. However, there is little evidence that applied nondefense R&D makes a significant contribution to private productivity. Finally, this study adds to the evidence that the public capital stock plays a significant role in explaining productivity trends.

Given these findings one can proceed in two alternative ways. The first is to ask whether and to what extent defense R&D has crowded out a productivity-enhancing factor, based on past evidence. Because of such factors as time lags, collinearity with time trends, and controlling for the external environment, the issue turns out to be a complex one, deserving an extended separate treatment. Thus, we offer at this point no definitive conclusions. Focusing on civilian R&D, a number of alternative models were estimated relating the flow of civilian R&D expenditures to current and lagged flows of defense R&D. The approaches included working with ratios to total private output or otherwise controlling for scale effects, including a measure of the share of overall defense spending, exploring alternative lag structures by means of polynomial distributed lags, and employing Granger causality tests. While the results were not clear-cut, and a number of issues remain unresolved, the evidence on balance did not indicate a negative impact of either total defense R&D, or its applied component, on civilian R&D.

A second way to proceed is to inquire what the impact would be on productivity of reallocating defense R&D outlays to a nondefense productive input. This is not to say that part of the existing stock of applied defense R&D can simply be transferred to the stock of civilian R&D or public capital. However, it is assumed that there is sufficient potential supply of technical resources in the sector receiving the additional funding to use the funds efficiently. We illustrate the potential for multi-factor productivity gain by making use of the estimates for the combination variable regression, column 11 of Table 5.4. Given the construction of DLCOMB and its estimated elasticity of .273, the net elasticities with respect to the stocks of civilian R&D, public capital, and nondefense basic research are .055, .107, and .027 respectively. Suppose that during the 1980's the stock of applied defense R&D, instead of increasing by 36.9% or 3.2% per year, had remained constant in real terms. Such an assumption is not entirely without foundation, since this is almost precisely what occurred during the decade of the 1970's. The result for the 1980's would have been that the stock of applied defense R&D would have increased by $73.3 billion less (1987 dollars). Adding this amount in turn to the stocks of civilian R&D, public capital, and nondefense basic research would have increased their growth over the 1980's by 28%, 4%, and 110% respectively. Working with changes in the logs, and multiplying by the respective net elasticities, yields increases in the growth of multi-factor productivity over the ten year period of 0.9%, 0.4%, and 1.3%, respectively. While the magnitudes involved are relatively small in absolute terms, they represent significant fractions of the overall increase in multi-factor productivity over the decade.

Conclusion

If the reduction in federal defense purchases leads to a decline in overall federal spending and in the federal budget deficit, the resulting decline in real interest rates will encourage a reallocation of national resources toward private capital formation, and, as a result, the level of the economy's productive capacity will increase. Simulations reported here provide confirmation of this expectation, but also suggest that the resulting increase in productivity will be modest, certainly small relative to the productivity slowdown that occurred after the early 1970's.

We have also found, however, that there are other important linkages between defense spending and private productivity that are not captured in the WUMM simulations. If the defense cutback translates into significant reductions in expenditures in applied defense R&D and these resources are re-directed into some combination of civilian R&D and public infrastructure, a substantial further increment to private productivity could result. While there are spillovers from basic R&D to private productivity, in 1990 less than $1 billion was spent on basic defense research, compared to $33 billion on applied defense R&D (1987 dollars). Since there is little evidence that applied R&D contributes to private productivity, these funds would constitute a massive transfusion to productivity enhancing public capital and civilian R&D.

However, we must be careful not to overstate the potential gains. An increase in resources flowing into public infrastructure or civilian R&D could reduce the increase in private capital formation associated with lower defense purchases. Thus, one cannot simply add together the increases in private productivity from higher private capital formation from the model simulation and the potential increase from public capital formation and R&D from the productivity regressions.

Notes

1. Paul Kennedy, *The Rise and Fall of Great Powers*, New York: Random House, 1987.

2. Seymour Melman, *The Permanent War Economy*, New York: Simon & Schuster, 1985.

3. Lloyd Dumas, *The Overburdened Economy*, University of California Press, 1986.

4. Murray Weidenbaum, "Defense Spending and the U.S. Economy: How Much Change is in the Offing?" *Defence Economics*, Vol. I, 1990: pp. 233 - 242.

5. See, for instance, Bruce Russett, *What Price Vigilance? The Burdens of National Defense*, Yale University Press, 1970; and Alan Mintz, "Guns vs. Butter: A Disaggregated Analysis," *American Political Science Review*, December 1989.

6. See David Aschauer, "Is Public Expenditure Productive?" *Journal of Monetary Economics*, Vol 23, 1989: pp. 177 - 200 for a discussion of the contribution of the public capital stock to private sector productivity.

7. Congressional Budget Office, *The Economic Effects of Reduced Defense Spending*, Washington, D.C.: U.S. Government Printing Office, February 1992.

8. There are some differences in the base and alternative paths employed here, compared to the CBO study. First, in the CBO study,

the base level of defense spending is smaller in 1991 than in either of the alternatives and is also smaller in 1992 compared to their alternative # 1. In our analysis, the base and alternative are identical in 1991 and the alternative is smaller than the base in every year thereafter. Second, in setting up our base and alternative simulations, we began by making similar assumptions about real defense purchases, specifically constant real levels followed by constant share. However, we applied this assumption directly to outlays, while CBO allowed for constant real authority in 1992 and 1993, but declining real outlays, reflecting a declining trend in authority from 1985 through 1991. Also, because our inflation forecasts differ somewhat from CBO's, our resulting path of nominal defense purchases also differs from theirs.

9. Paul Romer, "Endogenous Technical Change," *Journal of Political Economy*." Vol. 98, 1990, pp. S71-S102.

10. John C. Musgrave, "Fixed Tangible Wealth in the United States, Revised Estimates," *Survey of Current Business*, January 1992.

11. U.S. Bureau of Labor Statistics, *The Impact of Research and Development on Productivity Growth*, Washington, D.C.: U.S. Government Printing Office, September 1989.

12. John E. Jankowski, Jr., *National Patterns in R&D Resources: 1990*, National Science Foundation, May 1990.

13. *Budget of the United States Government*, Fiscal Year 1992, Washington, D.C.: U.S. Government Printing Office, 1991, pp. 35-49.

14. Zvi Griliches, "Productivity Puzzles and R&D: Another Nonexplanation," *Journal of Economic Perspectives*, Fall 1988, pp. 9-22.

15. Dale Jorgenson, "Productivity and Postwar U.S. Economic Growth," *Journal of Economic Perspectives*, Fall 1988, pp. 23-42.

16. Other researchers have constructed measures of MFP using different weights. For instance, in a study of the effect of public capital on productivity, Munnell employs a weight of .35 for capital and .65 for labor. See Alicia Munnell, "Why Has Productivity Growth Declined? Productivity and Public Investment." *New England Economic Review*, Jan./Feb. 1990. Some experimentation with a MFP variable constructed with these wights suggested that there were no qualitative differences in findings and only minor quantitative ones.

17. D.A. Dickey and W.A. Fuller, "Distribution of the Estimators for Autoregressive Time Series with Unit Root," *Journal of the American Statistical Association*, Vol. 74 (1979), pp. 427-431.

18. Paul Romer, "Endogenous Technical Change."

19. This is simply an application of the formula for the bias in the coefficient of an included variable (private capital), due to the omission of a relevant variable (R&D stock).

References

Aschauer, David (1989), "Is Public Expenditure Productive?" *Journal of Monetary Economics*, Vol 23: 177-200.

Budget of the United States Government, Fiscal Year 1992. 1991. 35-49. Washington, D.C.: U.S. Government Printing Office.

Congressional Budget Office, (1992), *The Economic Effects of Reduced Defense Spending*, Washington, D.C.: U.S. Government Printing Office.

Dickey, D.A. and W.A. Fuller (1979), "Distribution of the Estimators for Autoregressive Time Series with Unit Root," *Journal of the American Statistical Association*, Vol. 74, pp. 427-431.

Dumas, Lloyd (1986), *The Overburdened Economy*, Berkeley: University of California Press.

Griliches, Zvi. (1988), "Productivity Puzzles and R&D: Another Nonexplanation," *Journal of Economic Perspectives*, Vol. 2, pp. 9-22.

Jorgenson, Dale (1988), "Productivity and Postwar U.S. Economic Growth," *Journal of Economic Perspectives*, Vol. 2, pp. 23-42.

Jankowski, John E. Jr. (May 1990), *National Patterns in R&D Resources: 1990*, Washington, D.C.: National Science Foundation.

Kennedy, Paul (1987), *The Rise and Fall of Great Powers*, New York: Random House.

Melman, Seymour (1985), *The Permanent War Economy*, New York: Simon & Schuster.

Mintz, Alex (1989), "Guns vs. Butter: A Disaggregated Analysis," *American Political Science Review*, Vol. 83, pp. 1285-1293.

Munnell, Alicia (1990), "Why Has Productivity Growth Declined? Productivity and Public Investment," *New England Economic Review*, Jan/Feb 1990, pp. 3-22

Musgrave, John C. (1992), "Fixed Tangible Wealth in the United States, Revised Estimates," *Survey of Current Business*, Vol. 72, pp. 106-131.

Romer, Paul (1990), "Endogenous Technical Change." *Journal of Political Economy*," Vol. 98, pp. S71-S102.

Russett, Bruce (1970), *What Price Vigilance? The Burdens of National Defense*, Yale University Press.

U.S. Bureau of Labor Statistics (1989), *The Impact of Research and Development on Productivity Growth*, Washington, D.C.: U.S. Government Printing Office.

Weidenbaum, Murray (1990), "Defense Spending and the U.S. Economy: How Much Change is in the Offing?" *Defence Economics*, Vol. I, pp. 233-242.

6

Military Expenditure and Employment

J. Paul Dunne

The end of the Cold War promises a more secure European military environment. This has prompted considerable speculation about the possibility of major cuts in military expenditure and the distribution of a "Peace Dividend" as the resources currently absorbed by defence are transferred to other uses such as higher consumption, investment or net exports.

While the unilateral actions of a number of countries in cutting their defence budgets reflects an understanding that military expenditures impose a substantial burden on economic development, there is still considerable debate in the literature. A recent example is the contribution by Gold (1990) arguing that there is no evidence that military spending has been an economic burden on the US, and the critical response by Dumas (1990).

In addition, the Gulf crisis has presented the vested interests within the defence sector with an opportunity for arguing against defence cuts. The military arguing the need for continued development of advanced weapons systems to deal with future threats and the industrialists emphasizing the importance of military production to the economy.

It is important that these arguments meet opposition. Apart from the damaging social effects of militarism there is considerable evidence to suggest that military spending is an economic burden and that reducing military spending can be an opportunity rather than a cost. This is not to say that a move to lower levels of military spending is without its problems. There will be considerable structural adjustments required within economies and these may not be painless. It is, therefore, important that the likely impacts of these changes are understood and any economic disruption minimized.

This paper is intended as a contribution to that task. It focuses on the relation between military spending and employment and considers what the evidence suggests would be the effect of cuts in military spending. Section 1 considers the magnitude of military expenditure and present trends. Any analysis of the relation between military expenditure and economic development will be contingent on a theoretical understanding of the role of military spending in the economy and, indeed whether it has a specific role which differs from other forms of government expenditure. Section 2 therefore surveys briefly the different approaches.

In providing an empirical analysis of the employment effects of military spending, it is necessary to work at different levels of abstraction to answer different types of questions. Starting from the most aggregate level, Section 3 considers the relationship between military burden and aggregate unemployment in the OECD. Section 4 then moves on to consider the problems involved in measuring the employment supported by military expenditures, providing some comparative results. Section 5 considers the problems of attempting to measure the likely effects of changes in military spending. Finally, some general conclusions are drawn.

The Magnitude of Military Spending

The relative importance of defence spending in the OECD is presented in Table 6.1 which gives the military expenditures of the OECD countries as a percentage of their GDP, the usual measure of military burden, for selected years from 1975 to 1988. This shows that there is a wide dispersion of military burden across the OECD countries, with the US, Greece and the UK having the largest. It also shows that while total military expenditure increased over the period the mean share has declined steadily, though the experiences of some individual countries differ. The UK's military burden was 8.1% in 1955, in the aftermath of the Korean War rearmament, it then fell to 5.2% by 1975 and was the same in 1985.

It would appear that there has been a general tendency towards reductions in the military share of output from the mid 1950s in the OECD. This means that the changes in defence spending should be seen in the context of a generally declining defence burden in the

TABLE 6.1
OECD Military Expenditure (as $ of GDP)[a,b]

Country	1955	1965	1975	1985	1988[c]
Australia	3.8	3.0	2.3	3.0	2.4
Austria	0.2	1.2	1.0	1.3	1.1
Belgium	3.8	3.0	3.1	2.9	2.7
Canada	6.3	2.9	1.9	2.2	2.0
Denmark	3.2	2.8	2.5	2.2	2.2
Finland	1.6	1.7	1.2	1.4	1.9
France	6.4	5.2	3.8	4.1	3.8
Germany	4.1	4.3	3.7	3.2	2.9
Greece	5.1	3.5	6.8	7.1	6.4
Italy	2.4	3.1	2.5	2.7	2.5
Japan	-	1.0	0.9	1.0	1.0
Luxembourg	3.2	1.4	0.9	0.9	1.1
Netherlands	5.7	4.0	3.2	3.1	3.0
New Zealand	2.4	2.0	1.6	2.1	2.1
Norway	3.9	3.8	3.2	3.1	3.2
Portugal	4.2	6.2	5.3	3.2	3.2
Spain	1.1	1.4	2.1	2.2	2.1
Sweden	4.5	4.2	3.2	3.0	2.5
Switzerland	2.8	2.5	2.0	2.3	1.7
Turkey	5.6	5.0	6.3	4.5	3.8
UK	8.1	5.8	5.2	5.2	4.3
US	10.0	7.4	5.8	6.9	6.1
Yugoslavia	8.9	5.4	5.9	3.9	3.6
All OECD countries					
Mean share	4.2	3.5	3.2	3.1	2.9
Standard Deviation	2.5	1.7	1.8	1.6	1.4
Total Expenditure	195.9	233.9	266.2	364.1	
Mean Expenditure	8.5	10.2	11.6	15.8	

[a]Military expenditure is based on NATO definition.
[b]Expenditures are in USD 1,000 million 1980.
[c]SIPRI figures, only Finland shows noticeable discrepancy in 1985.

Source: International Institute for Strategic Studies (Annual), SIPRI Yearbook (1990).

OECD. Thus any transitional costs to lower levels of military spending are likely to be less marked than would otherwise be the case. Indeed the experience of the early fifties military expenditure reductions, after the Korean war, show that it is possible for considerable changes to be accommodated without serious economic problems.

Nevertheless, it is important to recognize that there have been differences in the experiences of the OECD countries over this period, in the average burden its relative speed of its decline, and in the differing structural impact of military expenditure. It is, therefore, important to consider the particular features of the individual economies. There are likely to be differences not only in aggregate measures of military burden, but also in specific localized effects on the economy, at the regional, industrial and local community level.

It is also worth noting that despite the reduction in the military burden, the figures for the constant price military spending are not so pronounced. As shown in Table 6.1 the growth of expenditures in the early 80s has tailed off for most countries, though there are exceptions. In particular there has been a marked increase in the level of Japanese defence spending. This is likely to increase further as the commitment to Japanese military spending remaining under 1% of GDP is no longer relevant.

Theoretical Approaches: Military Expenditure and the Economy

The magnitude of military spending does not provide a measure of its overall importance to the global economy. It is necessary to consider its impact on the pace and character of economic development. This requires an understanding of the specific role of military expenditure in the economy and in society and this can differ depending on the theoretical approach used. While it is difficult to draw the boundaries between the approaches of different schools of thought, they do have certain characteristics which distinguish them. (Dunne, 1990).

In fact few schools of thought deal with military expenditure explicitly and fundamentally. The Neoclassical approach to military expenditure is based upon the notion of a state, reflecting some form of social democratic consensus, recognizing some well defined national interest, and threatened by some potential enemy. Given the external potential enemy it is necessary to deter aggression and this is done by developing a particular level of capability which is derived from some optimization procedure. Game theoretic models reflecting, in a limited way, inter-state behavior have become more prevalent. High military spending is then the result of technology, rising costs and arms races and the industrial effects of military expenditure are simply the impact of moving the industries from some competitive ideal. These models are discussed in Gleditsch and Njostad (1990). Military expenditure is also seen as important for New Classical economics, in a dynamic context, in that it provides shocks to the system. Though these are exogenous rather than endogenous shocks, as for example in Barro (1981).

The critical liberal approach hinges on the nature of the 'military industrial complex' with its conflicting interest groups which lead to internal pressures for military spending, external threats are simply a way of justifying these. For this approach there is still some national interest but it is distorted by vested interests. (Melman, 1985, Dumas 1986).

None of these schools of thought provide an understanding of the role of military spending and militarism in economic development that is other than a partial understanding in a comparative static framework, or a phenomena which has an impact on the economy to knock it away from some well defined ideal. While they can provide valuable insights, they provide little basis for examining the relation between military spending and economic development as a historic and dynamic process.

In contrast the marxist approach sees the role of military expenditure in the development of capitalism as a much wider and pervasive process, with the military industrial complex constrained by the laws of motion of the capitalist system. Within the marxist approach there are a number of strands which differ in their treatment of crisis and in the extent to which they see military expenditure as necessary for capital accumulation. Military expenditures can act as a countervailing tendency to the falling rate of profit by slowing the increase in the organic composition of capital by diverting capital from accumulation, can cheapen constant capital and increase relative surplus value through spin-off; the military can be used to coerce workers, military expenditures can be used to overcome realization crises either caused by overproduction or underconsumption. Military expenditure may lead to a search for control of raw materials sources and the development of international hegemony. This tendency for the expansion of capitalism via imperialism has stirred debate since Lenin. (Brewer, 1990).

The only theoretical development in which military spending is both important in itself and integral to the analysis, has followed from the work of Baran and Sweezy (1966). In this 'underconsumptionist' approach military spending is important in preventing realization crises as it allows the absorption of surplus without increasing wages, so maintaining profits. Other forms of state expenditure do not do this. From this approach Kidron (1970) developed the permanent arms economy approach which bore some similarities to the underconsumptionists, but focused on the threat of overproduction.

The underconsumptionists approach has been the subject of considerable debate. At a concrete level the underconsumptionists' arguments imply that there should be a relation between the share of military spending in national income and the level of prosperity and that military expenditure is used in stabilizing the economy. Smith (1977, 1978) found its empirical predictions were not consistent with the data. Recent studies by Abell (1990) and Dunne and Smith (1990) fail to find evidence that military expenditure has been used to maintain levels of unemployment and find no support for the further implication is that nations with a high level of military expenditure should have higher levels of utilization and lower levels of unemployment than states with lower levels of military spending. Pivetti (1989) provides a recent contribution supportive of the underconsumptionists approach.

The failure of the underconsumptionists approach to be consistent with the data led Smith (1977) to argue that it was necessary to analyze the relation between military expenditure and accumulation more concretely, as a complex historical process, which is a contingent, rather than a deterministic relationship. A complex process of dialectical interaction, which plays a contradictory role in being important to capitalism but imposing economic costs. Since then the issue of hegemony and the potentially contradictory role of the military has been the subject of considerable debate in recent years, particularly within the international political economy literature, for instance Kennedy (1987), Strange (1988).

If one accepts this approach then the economic costs of military expenditure become important, especially in the medium run. It is possible for military expenditure to play a long run role, for example maintaining US hegemony and allowing the 'Golden Age' of the post WWII period, but also to have clear economic costs on individual economies. The positive role of military spending is also unlikely to continue because of the dialectical nature of economic processes, which implies that change will be brought about through inherent contradictions.

The analysis of the effects of military spending will be contingent on other economic and social variables and on historical conditions. This contingency means that it is difficult to make general statements on the basis of empirical work and it is necessary to undertake the analysis at different levels of abstraction. One can consider the relationship at a purely macroeconomic level or at a more detailed level, namely regions, industries, local communities and the individual. All of these levels will provide different information. For instance an aggregate analysis may imply that reduction in military spending will have little impact on the macroeconomy, but this may well hide serious and painful problems of adjustment within the economy.

The next section deals with the macroeconomic relations providing a comparative analysis of the relationship between military spending and the unemployment rate in a number of OECD countries.

Military Expenditure and Unemployment

The approach we adopt to the analysis of the relationship between the share of military expenditure and unemployment follows Dunne and Smith (1990). There are 14 OECD countries for which we have adequate data for our statistical analysis[1], the creation of which is described in the notes. Table 6.2 presents the means and standard deviations for the unemployment rate and the share of military expenditure in output, together with the correlation coefficients. There are considerable country differences in the average unemployment rate over the period, from an average of 1.72 for Japan to 6.74 for Spain. These two countries both have the lowest shares of military expenditure and are, with Belgium, the only countries to show a positive correlation between the two variables over time. Most of the countries show negative correlations. If we average over all countries the mean unemployment rate is 4.21 and the mean share of military expenditure is 3.3 percent, with the correlation coefficient of 0.21. This simple correlation analysis thus implies a negative correlation between the two variables for most countries but a positive one across countries. To investigate the relationship further we move to a more general dynamic model.

We begin by assuming that the evolution of unemployment is described by a second order autoregression:[2]

$$du_t = a_0 + a_1u_{t-1} + a_2du_{t-1} + b_1m_{t-1} + b_2dm_{t-1} + e_t$$

where u is the unemployment rate and m is the share of military expenditure in output. This gives a number of interesting hypotheses. If $a_1 = 0$, unemployment has a unit root, it shows infinite persistence, and employment and labor force, labor demand and labor supply, are

TABLE 6.2
Military Expenditure and Unemployment 1962-85: Summary Statistics and Correlations

Country	Unemployment Mean	Unemployment SD	Military Exp. Mean	Military Exp. SD	Correlation
Australia	4.17	2.61	2.79	0.39	-0.51
Belgium	5.52	3.97	3.19	0.22	0.43
Canada	6.65	2.46	2.34	0.64	-0.51
Denmark	0.54	0.40	2.49	0.25	-0.39
France	4.30	2.75	4.33	0.67	-0.53
Germany	2.66	2.41	3.71	0.55	-0.57
Italy	6.54	1.90	2.32	0.23	-0.51
Japan	1.72	0.54	0.89	0.06	0.70
Netherlands	4.54	3.78	3.40	0.37	-0.58
Norway	2.01	0.52	3.26	0.26	-0.27
Spain	6.74	6.26	1.85	0.26	0.90
Sweden	2.13	0.61	3.52	0.37	-0.62
UK	5.40	3.34	5.19	0.50	-0.23
US	5.98	1.76	6.82	1.43	-0.62
Pooled	4.21	3.44	3.29	1.51	0.06
Max	6.74		6.82		
Min	0.54		0.89		
Mean	4.21		3.29		
SD	2.06		1.47		
CV	0.49		0.45		
Correlation	0.21				

Source: OECD Databank, SIPRI Yearbook (1990).

not cointegrated (Engle and Granger, 1987). We would expect $a_1 < 0$, though the Dickey-Fuller critical value on the t-statistic is about -3.1 rather than -2. If $b_1 = b_2 = 0$, m is Granger non-causal with respect to u. In other words past values of military expenditure and unemployment are no better for predicting future values of unemployment than past values of unemployment on their own. This can be tested by an F-test between the equations with and without m. Such a concept of causality is, of course, purely statistical and should not be interpreted as anything more substantive.

Table 6.3 presents the regression results for the different countries

TABLE 6.3
Individual Country and Pooled Results 1962-85

Country	a	b	Long Run Coefficients	Granger Causality F-test: M on U	Granger Causality F-test: U on M
Australia	-0.06	-0.46	- 7.67	0.39	2.98
Belgium	-0.01	-0.69	-69.00	1.82	0.54
Canada	-0.22	-0.67	- 3.04	3.88	0.88
Denmark	-0.09	-0.25	- 2.78	4.36*	0.15
France	0.09	-0.10	1.11	2.33	0.92
Germany	-0.09	-0.48	- 5.33	0.95	1.38
Italy	-0.07	-0.73	-10.43	1.54	0.71
Japan	-0.00	-0.31	-15.50	3.67	1.97
Netherlands	-0.12	-0.88	- 7.33	1.35	0.05
Norway	-0.52	-0.84	- 1.62	3.49	1.85
Spain	0.13	-2.02	15.54	2.46	5.08*
Sweden	-0.49	-0.47	- 0.96	1.97	2.98
UK	-0.12	-0.46	- 3.38	1.80	0.77
US	-0.48	-0.42	- 0.88	3.97	1.60
Pooled with:					
No dummies	0.01	-0.03	3.00	2.97	6.69*
Country dummies	-0.01	-0.18	-18.0	5.90*	7.56*
Time dummies	0.02	-0.01	0.5	0.69	4.37*
Time and country	-0.01	0.06	6.0	0.70	4.90*

[a]the coefficient of the lagged unemployment rate.
[b]the coefficient of the lagged military expenditure share.
*significant at 5 %

Source: OECD Databank, SIPRI Yearbook (1990).

using all of the time series available for each country. Our null hypothesis is that there is no significant effect of the share of military expenditure on unemployment in the post-world war capitalist economies and this was supported by a previous study (Dunne and Smith, 1990). The results in Table 6.3, using different military expenditure data and a larger sample of countries, do not appear to support the null hypothesis. There is evidence of Granger causality from the share of military expenditure to unemployment for a number of countries, although there is evidence of significant causality the other way for Spain.The results for the pooled equation when dummies for country and year specific effects were included were:

$$du_t = -0.79 - \underset{(0.5)}{0.01u_{t-1}} + \underset{(3.6)}{0.23du_{t-1}} + \underset{(0.7)}{0.06m_{t-1}} + \underset{(0.8)}{0.15dm_{t-1}} + \text{dummies}$$
$$(1.2)$$

$R^2 = 0.46$ SER = 0.61 SSR = 108.65

where positive values of t-statistics are in brackets. Neither of the military expenditure share terms are significant.

One concern with the specification of the relation estimated above might be its failure to consider possible effects of output on unemployment. To take account of this we introduce lagged values of the log of constant price GDP and the growth of GDP, together with a time-trend into the individual country equations. The effect of this specification change, shown in Table 6.4 is to remove the evidence of Granger causality. In this case, the null hypothesis is rejected only for Norway.

The results in Table 6.4 for the pooled data show that when all the dummies are included there is no evidence of Granger causality from military expenditure to unemployment, but there is some evidence the other way round. For the pooled data the results including lagged values of the log of constant price GDP and the growth of GDP were:

$$du_t = \underset{(0.6)}{-3.71} - \underset{(0.3)}{0.01u_{t-1}} + \underset{(2.3)}{0.15du1_{t-1}} + \underset{(0.1)}{0.01m_{t-1}} - \underset{(0.4)}{0.74dm_{t-1}}$$

$$- \underset{(0.6)}{0.26q_{t-1}} - \underset{(3.2)}{0.07dq_{t-1}} + \text{dummies}$$

$R^2 = 0.48$ SER = 0.60 SSR = 104.65

where q is the log of output and dq is thus the annual rate of growth of output, as measured by constant price GDP. Both time and country dummies were included. Using the time specific dummies rather than the time trend means that the individual country relationships and the pooled one are not nested.

The coefficients on the lagged levels of unemployment rate do not change much with the introduction of the output terms and the military expenditure share terms are insignificant, with the lagged growth of output significant. There is little evidence of Granger causality from unemployment to military spending for the pooled results when time dummies are included, in contrast to the previous results.

Overall, the results presented here suggest that there is little evidence that military expenditure influences unemployment at the

TABLE 6.4
Individual Country and Pooled Results 1962-85 with Output Term and Time Trend Included

Country	a	b	Long Run Coefficients	Granger Causality F-test M on U	Granger Causality F-test U on M
Australia	-1.13	-0.88	-0.78	1.58	2.25
Belgium	-0.48	3.52	7.33	2.72	0.83
Canada	-0.89	1.37	1.54	0.85	0.04
Denmark	-0.12	-0.33	-2.75	2.32	1.78
France	-1.93	-0.04	-0.02	0.83	0.88
Germany	-1.06	-0.17	-0.16	0.06	0.50
Italy	-0.67	0.96	1.43	0.74	0.00
Japan	-0.87	0.88	1.01	1.76	1.35
Netherlands	-0.98	-0.71	-0.72	0.12	0.83
Norway	-0.61	-1.30	-2.13	4.13*	1.45
Spain	-0.49	0.20	0.41	0.22	1.03
Sweden	-0.66	0.62	0.94	0.37	1.85
UK	-1.46	0.66	0.45	0.59	3.45
US	-1.37	-0.44	-0.32	1.85	0.94
Pooled with:					
No dummies	0.01	-0.03	25.00	1.95	5.94*
Country dummies	-0.01	-0.18	-1.4	0.95	5.62*
Time dummies	0.02	-0.01	1.0	0.30	2.30
Time and country	-0.01	0.07	8.0	0.08	3.71

[a]the coefficient of the lagged unemployment rate.
[b]the coefficient of the lagged military expenditure share.
*significant at 5 %

Source: OECD Databank, SIPRI Yearbook (1990).

macroeconomic level. This implies that the fear that reductions in the share of military expenditure will be associated with higher average unemployment levels is misplaced. Such a conclusion is, of course, subject to the inevitable qualifications about the quality of the data, the sensitivity of the results to specification, and the possibility of structural change. This does not mean that there will not be problems of adjustment, but these will need to be analyzed at a more detailed level than that of macroeconomic aggregates.The next section considers a more detailed analysis of military spending and employment and provides some comparative results.

Measuring the Employment Generated by Military Expenditure

In principle one should be able to estimate the employment supported by military spending but in practice there are considerable difficulties of definition, theory and measurement in calculating such estimates. The most immediate problem is defining military expenditure. The armed forces in different countries can reflect different institutions and their roles can be differently perceived. In some countries the distinction between police and army duties is blurred (eg the French Gendarmerie). The existence of conscription can change the perception of the forces and their relation to the state, and can act as a tax in kind. The treatment of social services for the military forces such as health, education of their children and pensions, and of dual-use activities such as space, nuclear research, meteorology also raises difficulties of measurement. It is also possible for expenditures to be hidden in other categories of government expenditure, as in the case of Chevaline in the UK.

Information on the direct employment in the armed forces and civil service supported by military expenditure is normally readily available, but the estimates of industry output and employment generated by procurement are more problematic. Surveys can be used to estimate direct industrial employment but have the problems that they are open to misrepresentation or misunderstanding and in many firms where both non-military and military production takes place it is difficult to allocate employment between the two. It is also difficult to trace through the indirect employment generated by inputs and subcontracted work through such surveys. For these reasons industrial employment, both direct and indirect, is often estimated using an input-output model, with Leontief and co-authors (1961, 1965, 1983) undertaking the pioneering studies.

There are a large number of individual country studies which are surveyed in Dunne (1986). The input-output model may be static using the average labor coefficient, suited to providing an estimate of the level of employment supported by military expenditure, or dynamic using the marginal labor coefficients, more suited to estimating the effects of changes in military expenditure. The econometric estimates of the marginal output-employment elasticities will reflect such factors as labor hoarding, so if there is underutilized labor the average elasticity would overestimate of the employment effect of a change in military expenditure. In comparing the various estimates it is difficult to distinguish real differences, whether between countries or time periods, from those which arise from differences in method, initial conditions, scenarios, and assumptions about compensatory policies on the demand and supply sides.

Different types of models would be used to answer different questions. Thus a Canadian study, CSDRM (1983), sponsored by the Ministry of National Defence used three different models: a standard input-output model to analyze the 1981 level of defence expenditure; a neoclassical model which assumed fixed supplies of labor, full employment and profit maximization to estimate the effects of changes in defence expenditure in a comparative static framework; and a dynamic model, (CANDIDE) to explore the impact of alternative growth rates of defence spending.

National studies tend to produce the results in terms of expenditure in local currency per person employed. International comparisons of such measures may be unrevealing because of presence or absence of conscription, differences in general wage rates, and productivity between countries. Converting them to a common currency may also introduce errors since exchange rates can be volatile, do not necessarily reflect purchasing power parity, and are affected by the prevailing regime, whether gold-standard, Bretton-Woods, or the European Monetary System.

Table 6.5 presents some of the results of the international comparisons attempted in Dunne (1986). The studies were based upon various forms of static input-output model, except for Sweden which used the survey techniques discussed above. To provide a basis for comparison the figures for military expenditure, in each study, were translated into US dollars and then deflated by the US GDP deflator for 1980. The fairly large differences, for some countries, between the IISS figures for military expenditure and those of the studies, probably reflect definitional differences. The figures show a wide dispersion in the number of jobs supported by military expenditure. The number of jobs per one billion US dollars being highest in France and lowest in Sweden. Care is needed in interpretation, however, as the differences might reflect the success of the studies in measuring indirect employment, rather than any fundamental differences across countries. It appears from the studies that military expenditures support around 4 per cent of the labor force. While this is not a particularly high proportion the studies also show that the effects are generally concentrated around particular industries and regions. As expected, the higher the burden of military expenditure, as measured by its share in output, the higher the share of the labor force dependent on it. In addition, the countries with the highest burdens also have employment shares higher than their expenditure shares, possibly reflecting changes in the nature of military expenditure as it increases.

TABLE 6.5
Comparison of the Effects of Military Expenditure in Seven Industrialized Countries

	Canada	France	FRG	Norway	Sweden	UK	USA
IISS military expenditure figures (USD 000 m)	5.2	23.9	15.5	1.3	3.9	23.9	122.3
Years of study	1981	1981	1976	1978	1980	1981	1979
Military expenditure from studies (1980 USD 000 m)	4.6	17.5	18.4	1.6	5.9	22.8	133.5
Industrial employment (thousand)							
Direct	105.8[a]	-	837.0[b]	46[e]	18.0	330.0	-
Indirect	120.5	-	121.0	35	18.0	270.0	-
Total employment		451.0		81			1844.2[c]
Total overall	226.3	1105.0[d]	959.0	1442	138.0	1134.0	4810.3
Jobs per USD 1,000 m	48.8	63.1	52.2	50.6	23.3	49.7	36.0
Jobs as percent of labor force	1.9	4.6	3.5	5.6	3.4	4.3	4.5
Military expenditure as percent of GDP	1.8	4.0	3.3	2.9	3.3	5.0	5.6

[a]Total direct employment.

[b]Total direct employment composed of 152,000 direct industrial and 685,000 public sector employment.

[c]Private sector employment.

[d]Total including conscripts and gendarmerie (896,000 if they are excluded).

[e]Total direct employment (no. of person years) including officers and conscripts.

Source: Dunne (1986), based on individual country studies. A summary and references are included in a chapter in Paukert and Richards (1991) which also contains comparative information.

At its 67th session in 1981 the ILO adopted a resolution concerning the economic and social consequences of disarmament, urging member states to provide the relevant available information. The ILO attempted to glean information on military expenditure and employment by means of a questionnaire. The results of this study reported in Paukert and Richards (1991) are a valuable source of information, though not without problems. As they admit they were rather over ambitious in the form of the questions asked which led to poor response to certain questions, but nevertheless they gathered some important information on military expenditure and employment creation; on the employment and manpower structure of the armaments industry and related services personnel engaged in military research and development; and the conversion of manpower from military to civilian use, though there was little response to this last one. They also produced a range of papers analyzing the employment effects of military expenditure, including comparative work, and individual country and industry studies commissioned from researchers in the particular countries. Despite being somewhat overtaken by events these studies are still useful.

Evaluating the Effects of Changes in Military Spending

Although measuring the employment effect of military spending is not straightforward it is much simpler than attempting to evaluate the impact of a change in military spending. The factual estimates, which can be thought of as average or static estimates are often used to answer a counterfactual question: "How would employment change if military expenditure changed?" However, this may not be valid, since the counterfactual involves marginal, dynamic estimates, and will involve specification of other conditioning variables, since the effect of military expenditure on employment is unlikely to be linear and independent of other circumstances and thus will be scenario dependent. Dunne (1986) attempts to compare some estimates of the effects of changes in military expenditures from the models mentioned above, but there is little one can conclude from such an exercise.

Any individual country study will require some form of model plus some policy scenarios, to determine how the savings are to be used, for example. Some consideration will need to be given of the likely responses to policy changes of the major actors such as companies, allies, organized labor, even if only at a qualitative level. When compensating polices are considered the evidence suggests that reductions in military spending with reallocations to other forms of government expenditure lead to improved economic performance. In general the alternative scenarios for reallocating expenditures are not intended to represent practical policy options. The technical studies are limited by what the model can handle and what changes it is responsive to. They do, however, provide a base for comparison and the evaluation of more realistic and richer policy scenarios can be undertaken as a more qualitative, off model, analysis. Paukert and Richards (1991) survey a number of studies, and Barker, Dunne and Smith (1991) provide a recent study for the UK.

The specific nature of the problems of structural adjustment and policy response for different countries makes comparative assessments difficult, but the basic concerns will be similar. At the level of industry there will be concern over the effects of military spending on industrial structure, companies, and organized labor. This can concern manufacturing as a whole, depending on the importance of the defense sector, as well as specific companies. Within companies one has to consider the influence on defense spending on the enterprise as well as at the level of individual establishments. Some companies separate defense and non-defense work in recognition of the different relations of production in defense production that result from the relationship between defense counterfactors and the state. The regional distribution of defense spending, is also of importance. In many countries there is an inequitable distribution of defense spending to wealthier regions. A further consideration is the specific impact on local communities who may be dependent upon defense installation, factories or shipyards. (Dunne and Smith, 1984, Lovering 1990).

Recently there has been some concern in the literature that the economic approach to problems of conversion is too limited and that a more general political economy approach which takes account of the environmental impact of economic development and recognizes the importance of breaking both with the relations of production inherent in weapons production and with the dominant materialist ideology. (Willet, 1990).

Overall, the evidence suggests that with political will large cuts in defense spending can be undertaken. There will be problems of structural adjustment, but these are little different to those presented by any declining industry. The availability of the resources released by the cuts in military spending mean that it is possible to ease adjustments. Certainly with compensatory policies reductions in military expenditure would appear to be an opportunity rather than a cost.

Conclusion

The end of the Cold War has provided the opportunity for substantial cuts in military spending. While some countries have made cuts in the belief that military expenditure is a burden there is still considerable debate over whether this is in fact the case. This paper has provided a contribution to the debate. It considered the complex nature of the relationship between military expenditure and economic development and then considered some empirical evidence.

The evidence presented in this paper suggests that the fears that cuts in military spending are likely to lead to an increase in unemployment are unjustified. This does not mean that there are not problems of adjustment but the evidence suggests that with compensatory policies the pain of adjustment can be minimized.

Simple macroeconomic studies of the economic effects of military expenditure are useful but rather limited. More disaggregate analyses, however, needs a clear framework and this requires the use of some form of disaggregated model, formal or informal. The almost unanimous conclusion of disaggregate studies is that in economic terms disarmament is an opportunity not a problem.

Notes

This paper was prepared for an international seminar on the conversion of the military industry to civilian production, FUHEM, Madrid, January 1991 and has benefitted from the comments of the participants to whom I am grateful. I am also grateful to the ESRC for financial support under award R000231266 and to Ron Smith for comments and suggestions.

1. In any exercise of this nature a major problem is finding data which are in fact comparable. In the cross country exercise two main sources were used. The unemployment data is the standardized unemployment rate from the OECD databank, created and maintained by the Center for Labor Economics at the London School of Economics. See Bean, et. al. (1986), for details. This source also provided the GPD series used to compute the share of military expenditure in output. The military expenditure figures themselves are from SIPRI Yearbooks.

2. This can either be regarded as a parsimonious times-series description or as the reduced form of an insider-outsider model of the labor market, where workers face a partial adjustment labor demand schedule. See Dunne and Smith (1990) for more detail.

References

Abell, J.D. (1990), "Defense Spending and Unemployment Rates: An Empirical Analysis Disaggregated by Race," *Cambridge Journal of Economics*, Vol. 14, No. 4, pp. 405-420.

Ball, N. (1989), *Security and Development in the Third World*, London: Adamantine.

Baran, P. and Sweezy, P. (1966), *Monopoly Capital*, London: Monthly Review Press.

Barker, T., Dunne, P. and Smith, R. (1991), "Measuring the Peace Dividend in the United Kingdom," *Journal of Peach Research*, Vol. 28, No. 4, pp. 345 - 358.

Barro, R.J. (1981), "Output Effects of Government Purchases," *Journal of Political Economy*,Vol. 89, pp. 1086-1121.

Bean, C., Layard, R. and Nickell, S. (eds) (1986), *Unemployment Economica*, Vol. 53, supplement.

Brewer, A.A. (1990), *Marxist Theories of Imperialism: A Critical Survey, Routledge.*

Chans, S. (1986), "Military Expenditures and Economic Performance," in *World Military Expenditure and Arms Transfers*, US Arms Control and Disarmament Agency, US Government Printing Office, 1987.

CSDRM (1983), *The Economic Impact of Canadian Defense Expenditures and Arms Transfers*. Center for Studies in Defense Resources Management, Summer, Kingston, Canada.

Dumas, L. (1986), *The Overburdened Economy*, University of California Press.

______ (1990), "Making Sense Out of Nonsense," Mimeo, University of Texas. Paper distributed at the *UN Conference on Conversion*, Moscow, August 1990.

Dunne, P. (1986), "The Employment Consequences of Military Expenditure: A Comparative Assessment," ILO Disarmament and Employment Programme, Working paper No. 6, International Labor Office, Geneva.

______ (1990), "The Political Economy of Military Expenditure: An Introduction," *Cambridge Journal of Economics*, Vol.14, no. 4, pp. 395-404.

Dunne, P. and Smith, R.P. (1984), "The Economic Consequences of Reduced UK Military Expenditure," *Cambridge Journal of Economics*, Vol. 8, No. 3, pp. 297-310.

_______(ed) (1991), *Quantitative Marxism*, Cambridge (UK): Polity press.

______ (1990)," Military Expenditure and Unemployment in the OECD," *Defence Economics*, Vol. 1, pp. 57-73.

Engle, L.F. and Granger, C.W.F.J. (1987),"Cointegration and Error Correction: Representation, Estimation and Testing," *Econometrica*, Vol. 55, pp. 297-310.

Gleditsch, N. and Njolstad, O. (eds) (1990), "Arms Races: Technological and Political Dynamics," Sage.

Gold, A. (1990),"The Impact of Defense Spending on Investment, Productivity and Economic Growth," *Defense Budget Project*, February.

International Institute for Strategic Studies (various) "The Military Balance," IISS, London.

Kennedy, P. (1987), *The Rise and Fall of the Great Powers*, Unwin.

Kidron, M. (1968), *Western Capitalism Since the War*, Weidenfeld and Nicolson.

Leontief, W. and Hoffenburg, M. (1961),"The Economic Effects of Disarmament," *Scientific American*, Vol. 204, No. 4.

Leontief, W., Morgan, A. Polenska, K. Simpson, D. and Turner, E. (1965), " The Economic Impact-Industrial and Regional- of an Arms Cut," *Review of Economics and Statistics*, Vol. 47, No. 3.

Leontief, W. and Duchin, F. (1983), *Military Spending*, Oxford: Oxford University Press.

Lovering, J. (1990), " Military Industry and the Restructuring of Capitalism: The Military Industry in Britain," *Cambridge Journal of Economics*, Vol. 14, No. 4, pp. 453-468.

Melman, S. (1985), *The Permanent War Economy*, New York: Simon and Schuster.

Paukert, L. and Richards, P.(eds) (1991), *Defense Expenditure, Industrial Conversion and Local Employment*, International Labor Office, Geneva.

Pivetti (1989), "Military Expenditure and Economic Analysis: A Review Article," *Contributions to Political Economy*, Vol. 8, pp. 55-68.

SIPRI (various) World Armaments and Disarmament. SIPRI Yearbook, Taylor and Francis, London for Stockholm International Peace Research Institute.

Smith, D. and Smith, R. (1983), *The Economics of Militarism*, London: Pluto Press.

Smith, R. (1977), "Military Expenditure and Capitalism," *Cambridge Journal of Economics*, Vol. 1, pp. 61-76.

Smith, R. (1978), "Military Expenditure and Capitalism: A reply," *Cambridge Journal of Economics*,Vol. 2, pp. 299-304.

Strange, S. (1988), *States and Markets*, Pinter Publishers.
Willet, S. (1990), "Conversion Policy in the UK," *Cambridge Journal of Economics*, Vol. 14, No. 4, pp. 469-482.

7

Defense Versus Nondefense Spending: A Macroeconomic Comparison

James E. Payne, Kevin L. Ross and Edward A. Olszewski

In light of the rapid military buildup under the Reagan administration during the 1980's and the more recent proposals for cuts in the U.S. defense budget due to the massive reforms in Eastern Europe this paper wishes to pose the question what are the macroeconomic ramifications of defense spending? In comparison, what are the macroeconomic effects of nondefense expenditures? This simple dichotomy has often been posed in the context of the "guns or butter" trade-off. The task of this study is a rather straightforward one: of undertaking an explicit comparison of the impact of defense versus nondefense expenditures upon the U.S. economy. Though comparative studies have been done along the lines of analyzing productivity and growth differences between the civilian and military sectors (for a more detailed discussion see Aschauer, 1989) this study examines the short-run dynamics via a vector autoregressive model.

Section II discusses the macroeconomic effects of defense and nondefense spending. Section III sets forth the methodology while section IV provides the empirical results. Section V presents the concluding remarks. We find that both defense and nondefense spending have no significant impact upon real output, interest rates, inflation, and the money supply. However, there is some evidence to suggest that prices have a statistically significant but minor effect on both defense and nondefense spending.

Defense and Nondefense Spending

According to traditional Keynesian macroeconmic theory, nondefense or government spending would have aggregate demand or output effects either through direct channels on spending or indirectly through consumers who view the increase in government debt as increases in their wealth. The proposal that government spending, that is financed through debt issuance has no effects on the macroeconomy, is one of the main tenants of the Ricardian Equivalence theory that has been fiercely debated through the 1980's. Barro (1974) re-established the importance of this idea with his theory that debt financed government spending is no more expansionary than tax financed government spending because of the intergenerational transfers of deficit burdens. Thus, any new debt financed government spending results in reductions in present consumption and associated increases in savings to pay for higher future tax burdens where output, interest rates and inflation remain unaffected. In this study, we do not attempt to ascertain how government spending is financed, or to break down these government spending effects into consumption, savings or investment components. Rather, our work is an attempt simply to compare or isolate within a vector autoregressive framework the defense spending and nondefense spending effects on certain macroeconomic variables.

Barro (1981) finds that defense spending associated with wars is transitory while other changes in defense spending yield permanent effects. Smith (1977, 1978) in a study of 15 industrialized economies found military expenditures to undermine the stabilizing aspects of defense initially sought via fiscal policy. The empirical results on employment effects are indeed mixed, Greenberg (1967) finds defense spending to have a positive impact upon employment levels. More recent research by Abell (1990) as well as Dunne and Smith (1990) find that cuts in defense spending have no long run discernible impact upon employment. The analysis by Smith (1980) of the relationship between defense spending and private investment expenditures suggests the possible presence of "crowding out". With respect to the foreign sector, early work by Dudley and Passell (1968) found a negative impact of an increase in military burden upon the U.S. balance of payments. Work by Ayanian (1988), Grilli and Beltratti (1989), as well as Olszewski, Payne, and Ross (1992) investigate the effects of defense spending upon the U.S. real exchange rate. Both Ayanian (1988) as well as Grilli and Beltratti (1989) find a positive association between defense spending and the exchange rate. On the other hand, Olszewski, Payne, and Ross (1992) find the U.S. real exchange rate simply follow a random walk with defense spending having no significant effect.

Does defense spending have positive or negative effects upon capital accumulation and economic growth? The empirical evidence on this issue is mixed. Melman (1988), Garner (1989) and Payne (1990) argue that defense expenditures divert resources from more productive uses in the civilian sector, and thus have a negative impact upon economic growth. In comparing military versus non-military public capital, Aschauer (1989) finds that military capital contributes little to overall productivity in comparison to non-military capital. On the other hand, Atesoglu and Mueller (1990) find defense spending to have a positive and significant effect upon economic growth.

Does defense spending generate inflationary pressures? Defense spending can affect the overall price level via changes in aggregate demand and/or aggregate supply. With respect to the effects upon aggregate demand, rapid growth in defense spending contributes to the increase in nominal demand growth, which could accelerate inflation if such growth is not counterbalanced by tax increases or restrictive monetary policy actions. With respect to the effects upon aggregate supply, capacity constraints could stimulate cost increases within the defense industry that are potentially inflationary given this industry's monopolistic and monopsonistic pricing practices. The empirical results are mixed with respect to the inflationary impact of defense spending. Vitaliano (1984), Payne (1990), as well as Sahu, Payne, and Kleiman (1992) do not find defense spending to have inflationary effects while Nourzad (1987) does.

Given the preceding discussion we turn our attention to examining the macroeconomic ramifications of defense and nondefense spending using an unrestricted vector autoregressive model. Previous work by Kinsella (1990, 1991), Baek (1991), as well as Payne and Ross (1992a,b) within a VAR framework analyze the macroeconomic effects of defense spending. They find no significant macroeconomic relationships. Unlike these previous studies, we undertake an explicit comparison between defense and nondefense spending in the United States.

Methodology

The empirical methodology used in this study is that of an unrestricted vector autoregressive model. Two VAR models are examined with respect to defense spending and nondefense spending, respectively. A quarterly time frame from 1960:1 to 1990:4 is used as provided by CITIBASE databank. The respective models include the following variables:

Defense:	log of real defense spending
Nondefense:	log of real nondefense spending
Output:	log of real gross national product
Prices:	log of GNP implicit price deflator
Money:	log of real money supply based on M2
Interest:	3 month Treasury bill rate

Each VAR model will contain a five variable system. In general, each VAR model can be expressed as

$$\mathbf{X}_t = \mathbf{C} + \sum_{i=1}^{n} \phi\,(\mathbf{l})\mathbf{X}_{t-i} + \varepsilon_t \qquad (1)$$

where **C** is a n x 1 vector of constants; $\mathbf{X}_t$ is a n x 1 vector of variables specified for each model; ϕ **(l)** is a n x n time invariant matrix of autoregressive coefficients; and ε_t is a n x 1 vector of white noise residuals that are independently and identically distributed as multivariate normal with mean vector equal to zero and covariance denoted Σ. The appealing aspect of estimating a VAR system is that no a priori assumptions concerning the exogeneity of policy variables are placed on the model. Moreover, the VAR model provides a convenient means to summarize the empirical channels with respect to economic relationships as well as provides evidence on the Granger-causal relations among the variables of the system. The estimated systems can be utilized to estimate the strength of these relations based upon variance decompositions.

Variance decompositions originate from the moving average representation of the VAR model. Often called innovation accounting, variance decompositions show the portion of the forecast error variance for each variable that is attributable to its own innovations and to shocks with respect to the other system variables. Since no contemporaneous terms enter the VAR system, any contemporaneous correlations are reflected in the cross-equation residual correlation. The Choleski factorization eliminates the cross-equation residual correlations among any given innovation series and those series that appear prior in the ordering. Thus, estimation of the forecast error variance decompositions are based on the Choleski factorization of the variance-covariance matrix of the estimated variables.

Before implementing the VAR models the respective time series were analyzed to determine the existence of stationarity. We implement Dickey-Fuller (DF) and Augmented Dickey-Fuller (ADF) tests for each time series. The simple Dickey-Fuller (DF) test used appears as follows:

$$\Delta x_t = \alpha + \rho x_{t-1} + v_t \tag{2}$$

where the null hypothesis is $\rho = 0$. The augmented Dickey-Fuller (ADF) test appears as follows:

$$x_t = \alpha + \rho x_{t-1} + \beta t + \sum_{i=1}^{8} \phi_i \Delta x_{t-i} + v_t \tag{3}$$

where t denotes a time trend variable. The above ADF test allows one to differentiate between trend and difference stationary series. If $\rho = 1$, $ß = 0$ then the time series follows a difference stationary process, on the other hand, if $|\rho| < 1$ and $ß \neq 0$ then the time series follows a trend stationary process (see Nelson and Plosser, 1982; Mills, 1990). Eight lags were chosen to ensure serially uncorrelated residuals.

In addition to testing for unit roots, a co-integration test following Granger (1986), Engle and Granger (1987), as well as Engle and Yoo (1987) was undertaken. In general, if two time series, x_t and y_t are nonstationary but some linear combination of them is a stationary process then x_t and y_t are said to be cointegrated. If cointegration exists then the VAR model needs to incorporate an equilibrium error-correction term. In order to test for the possibility of cointegration the following cointegrating regression is implemented:

$$y_t = \beta_0 + \beta_1 x_t + u_t \tag{4}$$

where x_t is a vector of independent variables. The residuals then undergo an augmented Dickey-Fuller test as follows:

$$\Delta u_t = \rho u_{t-1} + \sum_{i=1}^{8} \gamma_i \Delta u_{t-i} + e_t \tag{5}$$

where the null hypothesis is $\rho = 0$. The critical values for higher-order systems are from Engle and Yoo (1987: Table 3, p.158.).

Tables 7.1A and 7.1B present the unit root and cointegration tests for both defense and nondefense spending. All the time series fail to reject the null hypothesis suggesting that each time series is

TABLE 7.1A
Defense Spending

Variable	Unit Root Tests DF	ADF	Cointegration Tests E-Y
Defense	-0.197	-1.57	-2.14
Output	-1.62	-2.58	-2.60
Prices	-2.10	-2.49	-3.60
Money	-0.819	-1.18	-3.59
Interest	-2.66	-2.88	-3.14

TABLE 7.1B
Nondefense Spending

Variable	Unit Root Tests DF	ADF	Cointegration Tests E-Y
Nondefense	-1.77	-1.92	-3.73
Output	-1.62	-2.58	-2.47
Prices	-2.11	-2.49	-3.52
Money	-0.819	-1.18	-3.73
Interest	-2.66	-2.88	-1.57
Critical	-2.89*	-3.45*	-4.36*
values	-3.51**	-4.04**	-4.98**

*5 percent significance level
**1 percent significance level

TABLE 7.1C
Tests for Lag Length*

	4 vs. 5 lags	5 vs. 6 lags
Defense:	25.56 (1.00)	27.37 (.00)
Nondefense:	25.47 (1.00)	34.13 (.00)

*Statistics are modified log-likelihood ratios for restrictions on the longer lag of all variables in all equations. Significance levels are in parentheses.

Source: Authors' calculations

nonstationary in levels which requires first-order differencing to render stationarity. The cointegration tests following Engle and Yoo (E-Y) fail to reject the null hypothesis of no cointegration. Thus, all variables are estimated using first-differences. Moreover, given the absence of cointegration the VAR models will not incorporate an error correction term. Before we estimate the VAR system we need to determine the appropriate lag lengths for the variables. Lag lengths will be determined via modified log-likelihood ratios. The test statistic follows a chi-square distribution as follows:

$$\chi^2 = (T-K)(\log|\textstyle\sum_R| - \log|\textstyle\sum_U|) \tag{6}$$

where T is the sample size, k is the number of coefficients in each unrestricted equation, and Σ_R and Σ_U are the restricted and unrestricted residual covariance matrices, respectively. The Sims-type VAR differs from the popular estimation of VARs based on Hsiao (1981) and the use of Akaike's final prediction error (FPE) criterion for determining lag lengths. Implementation of the FPE criterion imposes a structure in the estimation of the VAR system whereas we wish to experiment with the response of the VAR model to changes in the ordering of the variables. Thus, the estimation of the Sims-type system using common lag lengths parallels recent work by McMillin (1990) in using Akaike's AIC criterion to determine common lag lengths for the VAR system[1]. Table 7.1C tests for lag length using modified log-likelihood ratios. Both defense and nondefense VAR's will incorporate 5 lags in the rest of the analysis.

Empirical Results

Tables 7.2 and 7.3 provide Granger-causality tests for defense and nondefense spending, respectively. Tables 7.2A and 7.3A illustrate that both defense and nondefense spending have virtually no significant impact upon the economic performance variables. Moreover, Tables 7.2B and 7.3B show that the economic performance variables have no discernable effect upon either defense or nondefense spending[2]. We next analyze the variance decompositions for alternative orderings as shown in Tables 7.4 and 7.5[3]. Ordering 1 has either defense or nondefense spending preceding output, money, prices, interest. The rationale is simply that changes in either defense or nondefense spending affects output via the multiplier. Money

TABLE 7.2A
Causality Tests for Defense Spending

Defense as cause of:	F-statistics	Significance Level
Output	0.9434	.46
Prices	1.0590	.39
Money	0.1222	.99
Interest	0.7196	.61
ALL*	13.1700	.87

*Log-likelihood test of block exogeneity

TABLE 7.2B
Causality Tests for Economic Performance

Defense as effect of:	F-statistics	Significance Level
Output	0.2446	.94
Prices	0.3962	.85
Money	1.7160	.14
Interest	0.6293	.68

Source: Authors' calculations

accommodates the fiscal changes by influencing prices and interest. Ordering 2 places either defense or nondefense last focusing upon the influence of the monetary sector. Changes in the money supply affect interest rates which influence investment expenditures and thus output. In turn, aggregate demand pressures can affect prices.

Tables 7.4A and 7.5A display the forecast error variance decompositions in the economic performance variables attributable to defense and nondefense spending, respectively. To determine the standard errors associated with the forecast error variance decompositions to infer significance, a Monte Carlo integration technique of five hundred draws was used to generate estimates of the standard errors for the forecast error variance decompositions. Following McMillin (1990) if the value of the variance decomposition

TABLE 7.3A
Causality Tests for Nondefense Spending

Nondefense as cause of:	F-statistics	Significance Level
Output	0.4472	.81
Prices	0.6192	.69
Money	1.1430	.34
Interest	1.6290	.16
ALL*	16.6500	.68

*Log-likelihood test of block exogeneity

TABLE 7.3B
Causality Tests for Economic Performance

Nondefense as effect of:	F-statistics	Significance Level
Output	0.9423	.46
Prices	1.1150	.36
Money	1.1400	.34
Interest	0.6489	.66

Source: Authors' calculations

is at least two standard deviations larger than the estimated standard error we consider the variance decomposition statistically significant. With respect to orderings 1 and 2 in Tables 7.4A and 7.5A neither defense or nondefense spending have an impact upon the economic performance variables. As for orderings 1 and 2 in Tables 7.4B and 7.5B prices seem to have a minor, though statistically significant, effect upon both defense and nondefense spending. Our finding that prices influence defense and nondefense spending parallels the finding by Baek (1991) that prices affect defense spending. Aside from the impact of prices upon the two spending components, the point to emphasize is the absence of either defense or nondefense spending having a significant impact upon macroeconomic aggregates.

TABLE 7.4A
Percentage of Forecast Error Variance in Economic Performance Variables Attributed to Defense Spending Innovations

Ordering 1: Defense, output, money, prices, interest				
Quarter	Output	Prices	Money	Interest
4	1.56	1.05	1.42	0.29
8	1.85	1.21	2.02	1.39
12	1.90	1.26	2.30	1.81
16	2.00	1.33	2.30	1.91
20	2.01	1.51	2.30	1.91
24	2.03	1.68	2.30	1.93
Ordering 2: Money, interest, output, prices, defense				
Quarter	Output	Prices	Money	Interest
4	3.96	1.07	2.15	0.74
8	4.12	1.32	2.64	2.01
12	4.06	1.38	2.83	2.52
16	4.06	1.47	2.82	2.66
20	4.06	1.64	2.81	2.68
24	4.05	1.78	2.82	2.74

Source: Authors' calculations

Concluding Remarks

The task of this paper has been to compare the macroeconomic effects of defense and nondefense spending using a vector autoregressive framework. In the process of this comparison, we perform unit root and cointegration tests, finding the absence of cointegration. Without the presence of cointegration we proceed to implement our VAR models. Granger-causality tests for both defense and nondefense spending reveal no significant impact of these variables upon the economic performance variables. Likewise, Granger-causality tests of the respective economic performance variables show no significant impact upon either defense or nondefense

TABLE 7.4B
Percentage of Forecast Error Variance in Defense Spending Attributed to Economic Performance Innovations

Ordering 1: Defense, output, money, prices, interest				
Quarter	Output	Prices	Money	Interest
4	5.00	1.22	0.41	0.88
8	4.58	4.84*	0.77	1.71
12	4.91	6.59*	1.21	2.09
16	4.95	7.36*	2.10	2.17
20	4.94	7.71*	2.62	2.17
24	4.95	7.90	2.77	2.17
Ordering 2: Money, interest, output, prices, defense				
Quarter	Output	Prices	Money	Interest
4	2.52	0.50	0.21	1.31
8	2.63	3.78	0.64	1.67
12	3.08	5.23	0.99	2.03
16	3.10	5.83	1.86	2.10
20	3.10	6.12	2.31	2.10
24	3.10	6.28	2.42	2.10

*denotes that the value of the forecast error variance decomposition is at least two standard deviations larger than the estimated standard error.

Source: Authors' calculations

spending. Further analysis with the forecast error variance decompositions substantiate the Granger-causality tests with the exception of prices influencing both defense and nondefense spending. The finding that prices influence both defense and nondefense spending parallels in some degree the finding by Baek (1991) that prices affect defense spending. In any event, we find that total defense spending and total nondefense spending to be autoregressive in nature. The empirical work presented is tentative at best. Further research in evaluating the potential differential impacts of these two types of federal government expenditures is justified. Finally, our results also point to the nonexistent effect that variations in defense spending have on the U.S. economy.

TABLE 7.5A
Percentage of Forecast Error Variance in Economic Performance Variables Attributed to Nondefense Spending Innovations

Ordering 1: Defense, output, money, prices, interest				
Quarter	Output	Prices	Money	Interest
4	1.74	1.02	4.06	0.93
8	1.68	1.20	4.30	2.82
12	1.86	1.19	4.42	3.41
16	1.89	1.36	4.41	3.46
20	1.90	1.73	4.41	3.46
24	1.92	2.04	4.42	3.48
Ordering 2: Money, interest, output, prices, defense				
Quarter	Output	Prices	Money	Interest
4	1.24	1.35	4.26	1.41
8	1.80	1.40	4.38	2.84
12	1.89	1.38	4.42	3.51
16	1.91	1.54	4.41	3.54
20	1.91	1.87	4.40	3.58
24	1.90	2.15	4.42	3.65

Source: Authors' calculations

TABLE 7.5B
Percentage of Forecast Error Variance in Nondefense Spending Attributed to Economic Performance Innovations

Ordering 1: Nondefense, output, money, prices, interest				
Quarter	Output	Prices	Money	Interest
4	4.85	1.96	1.95	3.58
8	4.57	5.51	2.15	5.25
12	4.99	7.55*	2.40	5.54
16	5.09	8.83*	2.98	5.59
20	5.11	9.60*	3.50	5.59
24	5.13	10.05*	3.75	5.59
Ordering 2: Money, interest, output, prices, nondefense				
Quarter	Output	Prices	Money	Interest
4	4.31	1.19	0.95	2.86
8	4.13	4.23	1.23	4.73
12	4.46	5.92	1.51	5.03
16	4.53	7.02*	2.06	5.08
20	4.54	7.71*	2.50	5.08
24	4.57	8.11*	2.72	5.08

*same as in Table 7.4

Source: Authors' calculations

Notes

1. The authors realize the potential degrees of freedom problem when estimating Sims-type systems in an attempt to avoid bias introduced by underspecifying the lag length. Furthermore, following the work of Hafer and Sheehan (1991) on the various decision rules used in VAR models, we estimated *ad hoc* systems with various lag lengths. This experiment resulted in significant differences in our findings.

2. To examine the possibility that our lag length decision rule biased our results toward rejection, we also ran Granger causality tests over *ad hoc* lag lengths. We found no lag specification capable of detecting Granger causality.

3. Note the variance decompositions are sensitive to alternative orderings.

References

Abell, John D. (1990), "Defense Spending and Unemployment Rates: An Empirical Analysis Disaggregated by Race," *Cambridge Journal of Economics*, Vol. 14, No. 4, pp. 405-420.

Aschauer, David Alan (1989), "Is Public Expenditure Productive?," *Journal of Monetary Economics*, Vol. 23, pp. 177-200.

Atesoglu, H. Sonmez and Michael J. Mueller (1990), "Defense Spending and Economic Growth," *Defence Economics*, Vol. 2, No. 3, pp. 19-27.

Ayanian, Robert (1988), "Political Risk, National Defense, and the Dollar," *Economic Inquiry*, Vol. 26, pp. 345-351.

Baek, Ehung Gi (1991), "Defense Spending and Economic Performance in the United States: Some Structural VAR Evidence," *Defence Economics*, Vol. 2, No. 3, pp. 251-264.

Barro, Robert J. (1974), "Are Government Bonds Net Wealth?," *Journal of Political Economy*, December, pp. 1161-1176.

Barro, Robert J. (1981), "Output Effects of Government Purchases," *Journal of Political Economy*, Vol. 89(6), pp. 1086-1121.

Dickey, David A. and Wayne A. Fuller (1979), "Distribution of the Estimators for Autoregressive Time Series with a Unit Root," *Journal of the American Statistical Association*, Vol.74, pp. 427-431.

Dunne, Paul and Ronald P. Smith (1990), "Military Expenditure and Unemployment in the OECD," *Defence Economics*, Vol. 1, No. 1, pp. 57-73.

Engle, Robert F. and C.W.J. Granger (1987), "Co-Integration and Error Correction: Representation, Estimation, and Testing," *Econometrica*, Vol. 55, pp. 251-276.

Engle, Robert F. and Byung Sam Yoo (1987), "Forecasting and Testing in Co-Integrated Systems," *Journal of Econometrics*, Vol. 35. pp. 143-159.

Garner, Alan (1991), "The Effect of U.S. Defense Cuts on the Standard of Living," *Economic Review, Federal Reserve Bank of Kansas City*, Jan/Feb, pp. 33-47.

Granger, C.W.J. (1986), "Developments in the Study of Cointegrated Economic Variables," *Oxford Bulletin of Economics and Statistics*, Vol. 48, No. 3, pp. 213-228.

Greenberg, Edward (1967), "Employment Impacts of Defense Expenditures and Obligations," *Review of Economics and Statistics*, Vol. 49, No. 2, pp. 186-198.

Grilli, Vittorio and Andrea Beltratti (1989), "U.S. Military Expenditure and the Dollar," *Economic Inquiry*, Vol. 27, pp. 737-744.
Hafer, R. W. and Richard G. Sheehan (1991), "Policy Inference Using VAR Models," *Economic Inquiry*, Vol. 29, No. 1, pp. 44-52.
Hsiao, C. (1981), "Autoregressive Modelling and Money Income Causality Detection," *Journal of Monetary Economics*, Vol. 9, pp. 85-10.
Kinsella, David (1990), "Defense Spending and the Economic Performance in the United States: A Casual Analysis," *Defence Economics*, Vol. 2, No. 2, pp. 295-309.
Kinsella, David (1991), "Defense and the Economy: A Reply," *Defence Economics*, Vol. 2, No. 3, pp. 265-267.
McMillin, W. Douglas (1990), "The Velocity of M1 in the 1980's: Evidence from a Multivariate Time Series Model," *Southern Economic Journal*, Vol. 56, pp. 634-648.
Melman, Seymour (1988), "Economic Consequences of the Arms Race: The Second Rate Economy," *American Economic Review*, Vol. 78, No. 2, pp. 55-59.
Mills, Terrence C. (1990), *Time Series Techniques for Economists*, Cambridge University Press, NY.
Nelson, Charles R. and Charles I. Plosser (1982), "Trends and Random Walks in Macroeconomic Time Series: Some Evidence and Implications", *Journal of Monetary Economics*, Vol. 10, pp. 139-162.
Nourzad, Farrokh (1987), "A Re-examination of the Effect of Rapid Military Spending on Expected Inflation," *Quarterly Journal of Business and Economics*, Vol. 26, pp. 57-66.
Olszewski, Edward A., James E. Payne, and Kevin L. Ross (1992), "U.S.Military Expenditure and the Dollar: Another Look," *mimeo.*
Payne, James E. (1990), "Granger Causality Between Inflation and Defense Spending: An Empirical Note," *Kentucky Journal of Economics and Business*, Vol. 10, pp. 38-41.
Payne, James E. (1990), "Military Burden, Savings and Growth: A Note on the U.S.," *Journal of Business and Economic Perspectives*, Vol. 16, No. 1, pp. 47-49.
Payne, James E. and Kevin L. Ross (1992a), "Defense Spending and the Macroeconomy," *Defence Economics*, Vol. 3, No. 2, pp. 161-168.
Payne, James E. and Kevin L. Ross (1992b), "The Macroeconomic Effects of Defense Spending: Some Further Evidence," *mimeo.*
Sahu, Anandi P., James E. Payne, and Robert T. Kleiman (1992), "Defense, Nondefense Expenditures, and Inflation: An Empirical Analysis," *mimeo.*
Schultze, Charles L. (1981), "Economic Effects of the Defense Budget," *The Brookings Bulletin*, Vol. 18, No. 2, pp. 1-5.

Sims, Christopher A. (1980), "Macroeconomics and Reality," *Econometrica*, Vol. 48, No. 1, pp. 1-48.

Smith, Ronald P. (1977), "Military Expenditure and Capitalism," *Cambridge Journal of Economics*, Vol. 1, pp. 61-76.

Smith, Ronald P. (1978), "Military Expenditure and Capitalism: A Reply," *Cambridge Journal of Economics*, Vol. 2, pp. 299-304.

Smith, Ronald P. (1980), "Military Expenditure and Investment in OECD Countries," *Journal of Comparative Economics*, Vol. 4, pp. 19-32.

Vitaliano, Donald F. (1984), "Defense Spending and Inflation: An Empirical Analysis," *Quarterly Review of Economics and Business*, Vol. 24, pp. 22-32.

8

Some Economic Effects of Unilateral and Multilateral Reductions in Military Expenditures in the Major Industrialized and Developing Countries

Jon D. Haveman, Alan V. Deardorff, and Robert M. Stern

The original impetus for our research was to analyze some of the possible economic effects of a "peace dividend." While events in the Persian Gulf have diverted attention away from the idea of a peace dividend, there is reason to believe that there will be continuing pressure to reduce and to restructure defense spending. The purpose of our paper is to investigate the possible sectoral impacts on trade and employment in the United States that might be experienced as a result of an across-the-board reduction in military spending.[1] We do not address the effects of a restructuring of military expenditures.

Using the computational general equilibrium (CGE) Michigan Model of World Production and Trade, we first investigate the impact of a 25% unilateral reduction in military spending for the United States alone, and subsequently a 25% multilateral reduction in military spending in all of the major Western industrialized and developing countries. An important advantage in using the Michigan Model is the sectoral detail that it provides. In what follows, we

This chapter was reprinted from *Conflict Management and Peace Science* 12(1), 1992, with permission from the editor.

perform a variety of computational experiments that take into account different compensating macroeconomic policies and that enable us to compare the sectoral effects involved. Further, the Michigan Model allows us to extend previous studies by incorporating the effects of international trade and by allowing for price and exchange rate responses as well as primary input substitution possibilities. It is hoped that these additional elements will provide a richer insight into the sectoral effects stemming from possible reductions in military expenditures than has been provided by earlier research.[2]

Previous work has generally compensated for changes in military expenditures by changing nonmilitary government purchases. However, as discussed below, prior episodes of substantial reductions in U.S. military expenditures did not follow this path. We therefore assume that reductions in government military spending will be compensated by shifting expenditures to various components of final demand, including: nondefense government spending; private consumption; investment; and a *pro rata* reallocation across all nondefense sectors.

We proceed as follows. In Section II we briefly review previous research. Section III presents a brief description of the Michigan Model and discussion of elements of it that are of particular importance to our study. Section IV contains the results for the unilateral reductions for the United States and Section V the results for the multilateral experiments. Our conclusions and implications of the results are discussed in Section VI.

Previous Research

Over the past 30 years, there have been a number of studies assessing the impact of defense spending on a nation's economy. The pioneer work was done by Leontief and associates in the early 1960s. The results of these studies have been fairly consistent, even though there has been a great deal of variation in methodology and country of analysis. Most studies find that reductions in military expenditures have a positive effect on an economy, in terms of increased employment and, where modelled, increased GNP. The rest of this section will discuss several representative studies.

Leontief and Hoffenberg (1961) used input-output analysis to estimate the impact of a change in military expenditures on employment in 58 broad sectors of the U.S. economy. They analyzed a 20% reduction in military expenditures coupled with a compensating increase in nonmilitary forms of government spending. The net result was an increase of 288,040 workers in "business employment." This increase stemmed from a transfer of spending, but no reduction in military personnel. The same experiment including a cut in personnel of 20% yielded a net reduction in employment of 120,758 workers. They, as do we, also provided results to facilitate the analysis of a shift towards other sectors of final demand, including consumption and investment among others. However, their study was performed in a framework with no modelling of international effects, price changes, or substitution possibilities.

Leontief et al. (1965) was an analysis of the regional impact of a 20% reduction in military expenditures. This model assumed that final demand adjusts to maintain a constant level of employment in the aggregate U.S. economy. It therefore concentrated on the changing industrial and regional composition of employment.

Dunne and Smith (1984) used the econometrically based Cambridge Growth Project to calculate the impact of military spending on the U.K. economy. Their experiments involved a cut in military expenditures from 5% of GDP to 3.5% of GDP, the European average. These cuts were accompanied by matching increases in other forms of government spending. Their general conclusion was that this reduction in military expenditures would increase total employment by approximately 100,000 jobs.

There have been other studies like our own that have employed CGE methods in an international framework. Liew (1985) used the ORANI model of Australia to assess the impact on international trade, prices, and GNP of a 10% increase in military expenditures. This increase was assumed to be compensated by a reduction in one of three other categories of government spending (i.e., health, education, or welfare), thereby holding total government expenditure constant. Although the results of these three experiments differed somewhat in direction and magnitude, the general message, although quantitatively small in each case, was that an increase in military expenditure would tend to reduce GNP and employment, and create a small merchandise trade deficit. The experiments were consistent in suggesting increased imports, and two of the three experiments suggested a reduction in exports. Liew's results are in line with the other studies mentioned, given the direction of change in military spending.

Overview of the Michigan Model

The theoretical structure and equations of the Michigan Model are described in detail in Deardorff and Stern (1986, pp. 9-36 and 235-47; 1990, pp. 9-35). For our purposes here, we present a brief overview of the model and call attention to some of its features that are pertinent to the present analysis.

In designing the Michigan Model, the objective was to take into account as many of the microeconomic interconnections among industries and countries as possible. This disaggregated general equilibrium framework enables us to examine a variety of economic issues that most other computational models cannot address, either because they are too highly aggregated, or because they are specified only in partial equilibrium terms.

Data and Parameters

The version of the model used here includes 22 tradable and 7 nontradable industries in 18 industrialized and 16 developing countries, plus an aggregate sector representing the rest of the world.[3] We use a base of 1980 data on trade, production, and employment for all 34 countries, plus constructed measures of the coverage of nontariff barriers (NTBs) for the 18 industrialized countries.

Trade, Production, and Employment. The import and export data are adapted from United Nations trade tapes, with concordances that relate the Standard International Trade Classification (SITC) to our version of the International Standard Industrial Classification (ISIC) categories. Information on the gross value of production and employment by ISIC sector is directly calculated or estimated from United Nations, *Yearbook of Industrial Statistics*, Organization for Economic Cooperation and Development (OECD) publications on national accounts and labor statistics, and various national statistical sources.

Nontariff Barriers. NTBs in the model are represented in two forms: as coverage indices and as tariff equivalents. However, only the coverage indices play a role in the current analysis. These indices measure the degree to which imports are subject to nontariff restrictions. They serve to reflect the role of existing NTBs in dampening the quantitative response of trade when other changes in the economies take place.

Exchange Rates. In an effort to approximate the functioning of foreign exchange markets, exchange rates are modelled in several different ways. We model the industrialized countries in terms of a flexible exchange rate regime in which exchange rates are determined by the requirement that a country's balance of trade plus an exogenous capital flow be equal to zero. Thus, when an exogenous shock alters the trade balance, the exchange rate is used to restore the trade balance to its initial level. In contrast, most developing countries in the model are assumed to have a system of import licensing with exchange rate pegging. The import licensing scheme in countries with pegged exchange rates is assumed to function in such a way as to assure approximate balance-of-payments equilibrium through a mechanism of proportional rationing of imports.

Input-Output Tables. Our input-output coverage currently includes national tables for all of the industrialized countries of the model except Switzerland. They are taken from various years ranging from 1975 for Japan and members of the EEC to 1982 for Finland. The 1977 table for the United States is applied to Switzerland. For the developing countries our coverage currently includes separate tables for Brazil (1975), Chile (1977), Israel (1977), Korea (1980), Portugal (1981), and Spain (1980). The Brazilian table is applied to the remaining developing countries. The use of national tables allows for differences in technology among the countries included in the model.[4]

Coefficients and Elasticities. In general, the coefficients of explanatory variables that appear in the model are calculated from data on production, trade, and employment by sector in each country, from the input-output matrices, and from relevant published estimates of demand and substitution elasticities. The import-demand elasticities used in the model, for all countries, are constructed from the "best guesstimates" of U.S. import-demand elasticities calculated by Stern et al. (1976). Using the import-demand elasticities together with data on trade, we first calculate the implied elasticities of substitution in demand between imported and home-produced goods in each industry of the United States, and we assume that these same substitution elasticities are valid for all other countries. The implicit import-demand elasticities in the other countries are then derived from these common elasticities of substitution, and they differ across countries due to their differences in shares of trade.[5]

On the supply side of the model, we use elasticities of substitution between capital and labor in each sector, based upon Zarembka and Chernicoff (1973). These were estimated from U.S. data, but, due to a dearth of estimates for other countries, are assumed to apply for all countries.

The Model Structure

The model is best thought of as composed of two parts: the country system and the world system. The country system contains separate blocks of equations for the individual tradable and nontradable sectors for each country, and the world system contains a single set of equations for individual tradable sectors for the world as a whole. The country blocks are used first to determine each country's supplies and demands for goods and currencies on world markets, as functions of exogenous variables, world prices and exchange rates. The supply and demand functions for each country are then combined to provide the input to the world system that permits world prices and exchange rates to be determined.

The world system is the less complicated of the two systems. We start with the export supply and import demand functions from the country equations, which depend on world prices and exchange rates. To get world prices we add these supplies and demands across all countries and set the difference equal to net demand from the rest of the world. To obtain exchange rates, where these are flexible, we add the value of excess supply across all of the industries in a country and equate the resulting trade balance to an exogenously given capital flow. Once we obtain the world prices for each tradable industry and the exchange rate for each country, we enter them back into the separate country blocks in order to determine the rest of the relevant country-specific variables.

Description of the Exogenous Change Variables

The Michigan Model can be used to analyze price and quantity responses to a number of exogenous changes in the world trading environment. These changes can be represented through the use of some 18 exogenous variables, each referring to a different change in the trading environment. These variables include, for example, changes in import tariffs, changes in export taxes, changes in exchange rates where they are exogenous, and changes in the aforementioned capital flows.

For the current analysis, however, we use only two exogenous change variables, both representing particular kinds of shifts in demand. One is an inter-industry shift variable, denoted $e\alpha$, that describes a reallocation of final demand across industries. The other is an intra-industry shift variable, denoted $e\beta$, that captures a shift of demand within an industry from home- produced goods to imports. A formal statement of the role that these two shift parameters play in the Michigan Model is available from the authors on request.

U.S. Unilateral Reductions in Military Expenditures

In this section, we consider the effects of a 25% unilateral reduction in military expenditures in the United States and discuss the implications of different assumptions regarding the macroeconomic policies accompanying such a reduction. The effects of a multilateral 25% reduction in military expenditures simultaneously in all of the major Western industrialized and developing countries included in the Michigan Model are considered in the following section. The results presented in this section are intended to facilitate the analysis of a broad spectrum of scenarios concerning the macroeconomic policies accompanying a reduction in U.S. military expenditures. We first provide some background of previous periods of reduced defense spending and then a description of the assumptions and theoretical implementation of the scenarios within the Michigan Model. The results of the various scenarios are presented at the end of this section.

Substantial reductions in defense spending are not new to the United States (Steuerle and Wiener, 1990). The periods immediately following World War II, the Korean conflict, and the Vietnam War each saw a substantial de-emphasis of defense spending within the government budget and as a share of GNP. The immediate post-WWII years represent the largest decline, when defense spending fell from 39.1% to 3.7% of GNP between 1945 and 1948. The five years following the Korean and Vietnam wars each saw defense spending decline, but by the more modest amount, in both cases, of approximately 4% of GNP.

In periods of substantial restructuring of government spending, the question naturally arising is what happens to nonmilitary expenditures when military expenditures are reduced. There are principally three macroeconomic policies that could accompany a reduction in military expenditures: (1) increase other spending; (2) reduce taxes; or (3) reduce government borrowing. That is, first, policy makers could redistribute the expenditure to other forms of government spending, for example on human or physical resources. Second, the reduction in expenditure could be matched by a reduction in government receipts, thus increasing civilian consumption. Finally, the reduced expenditure could be used to reduce (increase) a budget deficit (surplus), reducing interest rates, and thereby stimulating investment. The three postwar periods experienced each of these policies, but in rather different combinations.

Table 8.1 provides a detailed account of the macroeconomic policies accompanying the demilitarization in each of the three periods noted above and the present period of reduced defense expenditures.

TABLE 8.1
Changes in the Composition of Postwar Government Spending

	Change in Percent of GNP			
Period	Military Expenditures (1)	Human Resources Spending (2)	Government Receipts (3)	Government Deficit (4)
WWII (1945-48)	-35.4	3.1	-4.5	-27.1
Korean War(1953-58)	-4.0	1.7	-1.4	-1.2
Vietnam War(1968-73)	-3.6	2.3	0.0	-1.8
Recent(1986-89)	-0.6	-0.5	0.8	-2.3

Source: Steuerle and Wiener (1990).

Column 1 shows the change in defense spending, while columns 2-4 display the accompanying changes in the other major components of the government budget. From column 4, it can be seen that each period is associated with falling budget deficits. In each of the postwar periods, 30% or more of the reduction in military spending was used to reduce the budget deficit. In the current period, the decline in the deficit exceeds the reduction in military spending.

In the immediate post-WWII and post-Korean conflict years, a significant portion of the reduced defense spending was used to offset federal government receipts, as displayed in column 3. The latter two time periods have, however, been associated respectively with a zero and positive change in receipts, as a percent of GNP. The propensity for shifting expenditure from defense to human resources increased throughout the first three periods, while the current demilitarization is accompanied by a fall in human resources spending.[6]

As Steuerle and Wiener note, the late-Reagan-early-Bush era of reduced defense spending is rather uncharacteristic. The period from 1986 to 1989 witnessed a reduction in defense spending, as a percent of GNP, a reduction in spending on human resources, an increase in total revenue, and a reduction in the deficit of almost four times the reduction in defense spending. The uncharacteristic nature of this period is not surprising given that this is the first large-scale peace-time demilitarization.

It is evident from these experiences that there have been a variety of macroeconomic responses to reductions in military expenditures. This makes it difficult to determine what the appropriate strategy should be in modelling such expenditure reductions. The effect on the sectoral composition of trade and employment due to a reduction in defense spending depends crucially on the assumptions one makes about the accompanying macroeconomic policies. Since the Michigan Model does not formally allow for changes in interest rates or domestic taxes, the individual scenarios are implemented by exogenously altering the composition of final demand. In what follows, we make allowances accordingly for shifts in defense spending to several categories of final demand, including consumption, investment, nonmilitary government spending, and a *pro rata* shift across all sectors of nonmilitary final demand. We then examine separately the results of each shift.

Computational Experiments and Assumptions

We shall concentrate on the four scenarios just mentioned. Each scenario is based on an alternative redistribution of $64.8 billion in military expenditures, or 25% of the 1985 U.S. national defense budget.[7] This reduction is taken as a uniform percentage of the defense budget allocated to each of the 29 sectors being modelled. In the first scenario, the reduction in military spending is assumed to be absorbed proportionally by all three sectors of final demand: consumption; investment; and nonmilitary government expenditure. The second scenario redistributes spending from defense to other forms of government expenditure, maintaining constant levels of consumption and investment. The third scenario redistributes the spending across consumption while keeping other sources of final demand constant, and the fourth redistributes the spending across investment[8] while, again, maintaining a constant level of consumption and nonmilitary government purchases. In all runs, the $64.8 billion is allocated to each sector according to that sector's share in demand.[9] While we do not suggest that any one of these experiments captures exactly what is likely to happen, the linear nature of the model allows one to approximate any in-between cases.

In interpreting the results to follow, it is important to note the assumptions that are common to all scenarios:

(1) The level of aggregate expenditure is constant.
(2) Capital stocks are fixed for each industry, on the grounds that the time period under investigation is too short for changes in

investment to be realized as additions to the capital stock.

(3) Real wages are assumed to be flexible, i.e., labor markets are permitted to clear.

(4) The U.S. Department of Defense is assumed to follow a "buy American" policy. All defense expenditure is assumed to have been allocated to domestic industry.

(5) Exchange rates are modeled as flexible, except for a number of developing countries.

Some of these assumptions are in need of further explanation or justification. First, the assumption that aggregate expenditure is held constant is necessary because the microeconomic orientation of the Michigan Model makes it inappropriate for discussing macroeconomic phenomena such as the determination of aggregate expenditure or employment. Implicit within this assumption, and the form of each scenario, is that a dollar-for-dollar transfer is made. For example, with a reduction in the budget deficit it is assumed that investment changes by exactly the amount of the change in the deficit. Further effects of the changed interest rate would likely be changes in consumers' savings-consumption choices. Such effects are not represented explicitly in the Michigan Model.

A further consequence of the microeconomic nature of the model is assumption (3). Our results are all dependent on constant aggregate employment, which is assured by allowing for flexibility in real wages. There are alternative methods of maintaining constant employment, such as allowing the composition of final demand to adjust appropriately, but these adjustments would de-emphasize the role played by the differences in the distribution of military spending and the distribution of other sources of final demand.

Assumption (4), representing the "buy American" or "buy domestic" policy of the U.S. Department of Defense (DOD), is designed to reflect the preference given to domestic manufacturers and suppliers when contracts are signed and purchases are made. Given this preference, we believe that the average propensity of the DOD to import is significantly less than that of final and intermediate demand in the aggregate. Zero imports are thus assumed to be a more accurate representation of reality than is the aggregate average propensity to import.

Implementation of the policy experiments is conceptualized as a shift in the final demand for the output of each of the 29 sectors. The first step in each of the scenarios is to redistribute the reduction in military spending appropriately. Using the actual 1985 final demand (input-output) levels of consumption, investment, government

TABLE 8.2
Sectoral Changes in Demand Resulting from Reduced Military Spending (millions of $, 1985)

		Total Civilian Demand		Nondefense Government		Consumption		Investment	
Industry	(ISIC)	$ Value	%	$ Value	%	$ Value	%	$ Value	%
Traded Goods									
Agr., For., & Fishing	(1)	558	1.68	1378	4.15	524	1.58	- 3	-0.01
Food, Bev., & Tobacco	(310)	3489	1.67	775	0.37	4973	2.37	-45	-0.02
Textiles	(321)	127	1.53	35	0.42	143	1.72	140	1.69
Wearing Apparel	(322)	887	1.35	-89	-0.14	1375	2.10	-205	-0.31
Leather Products	(323)	51	1.56	0	0.00	76	2.32	-4	-0.12
Footwear	(324)	143	1.63	0	0.00	211	2.41	-4	-0.05
Wood Products	(331)	9	0.84	9	0.84	13	1.21	-7	0.65
Furniture & Fixtures	(332)	517	1.64	216	0.69	400	1.27	1232	3.92
Paper & Paper Products	(341)	220	1.49	305	2.07	265	1.80	-26	-0.18
Printing & Publishing	(342)	428	1.41	795	2.62	478	1.57	-79	-0.26
Chemicals	(35A)	216	0.44	194	0.40	401	0.82	-495	-1.01
Petrol. & Rel. Prod.	(35B)	160	0.19	10	0.01	526	0.64	-1149	-1.40
Rubber Products	(355)	62	0.50	30	0.24	117	0.95	-127	-1.03
Nonmettalic Min. Prod.	(36A)	23	1.05	14	0.64	34	1.55	-13	-0.59
Glass & Glass Products	(362)	26	1.42	74	4.04	24	1.31	-4	-0.22
Iron & Steel	(371)	-49	-14.80	-40	-12.08	-51	-15.41	-49	-14.80
Nonferrous Metals	(372)	-78	-9.42	-47	-5.68	-85	-10.27	-78	-9.42

TABLE 8.2 (contd.)
Sectoral Changes in Demand Resulting from Reduced Military Spending (millions of $, 1985)

Industry	(ISIC)	Total Civilian Demand		Nondefense Government		Consumption		Investment	
		$ Value	%	$ Value	%	$ Value	%	$ Value	%
Metal Products	(381)	-752	-4.62	-823	-5.05	-842	-5.17	-342	-2.10
Nonelectric Machinery	(382)	-786	-0.61	-2160	-1.68	-2567	-2.00	7366	5.74
Electric Machinery	(383)	-4517	-4.10	-5505	-5.00	-5169	-4.70	-1122	-1.02
Transportation Equip.	(384)	-11093	-4.60	-13269	-5.51	-11772	-4.89	-6587	-2.73
Miscellaneous Manufac.	(38A)	-1144	-1.55	-1436	-1.95	-1404	-1.91	124	0.17
Total Traded		-11503		-19534		-12330		-1477	
Nontraded Goods									
Mining & Quarrying	(2)	32	1.14	162	5.78	-7	-0.25	75	2.68
Electric, Gas & Water	(4)	1361	1.17	1069	0.92	1912	1.65	-559	-0.48
Construction	(5)	3364	0.81	6738	1.62	-3438	-0.83	27228	6.54
Wholesale & Ret. Trade	(6)	9757	1.40	-1356	-0.19	13949	2.00	2683	0.39
Transp., Stor., & Com.	(7)	297	0.21	-418	-0.30	825	0.59	-1176	-0.84
Fin., Ins. & Real Est.	(8)	7631	1.16	1408	0.21	11314	1.73	-1575	-0.24
Comm., Soc. & Pers. Serv.	(9)	-10937	-1.16	11930	1.26	-12226	-1.29	-25197	-2.67
Total Nontraded		11505		19533		12329		1479	

Source: Authors' computations based on the 1985 U.S. input-output table reported in the *Survey of Current Business*, January 1990.

nondefense, and defense spending that are reported in the January 1990 *Survey of Current Business*, we show in Table 8.2 the sectoral changes in demand brought about by each of the above scenarios. These redistributions of final demand are represented in the Michigan Model as changes in the demand share parameters of the consumers' utility function. In what follows, α_j will be used to represent the share of final demand attributable to purchases from sector j. Given the nature of the model, the proportional change in these parameters is needed to reflect the shift in final demand. The proportional change variable is obtained by calculating the actual share of each sector in final demand (α_{0j}, j = 1,...,29) and the final demand share of each sector once the defense spending has been redistributed (α_{1j}, j = 1,...,29). The proportional change is then calculated as:

$$e\alpha_j = \frac{d\alpha}{\alpha} = \frac{\alpha_{1j} - \alpha_{0j}}{\alpha_{0j}} \qquad j = 1...29 \qquad (1)$$

As noted above, defense purchases are assumed to be made entirely from domestic production. The shift of expenditure away from defense will therefore be accompanied by an exogenous increase in imports. As a result, we need to adjust the fraction of new expenditure that now goes towards the purchase of imported goods. We assume that each category of total demand in an industry purchases imports in the same percentages as that of final demand in that industry as a whole. More precise estimates could be made if a breakdown of imports by consumption, investment, and government purchases could be used, but unfortunately, such data are not available.

Tables 8.3a and 8.3b present a simple hypothetical example that is intended to clarify the process outlined above. Columns 1 and 2 represent the part of final demand made up of defense and all other final demand respectively. Column 3 is total final demand, and column 4 is the α, or share of each sector in total final demand, from equation 1. Table 8.3b shows what happens to final demand and demand shares when $150 million, or 25%, of defense spending is shifted to other final demand.

The process begins by reducing the value of defense in each cell by 25%. Thus, column 1 in Table 8.3b is 75% of column 1 in Table 8.3a. This $150 million is then redistributed across other final demand in proportion to each sector's share in total other demand. For example, other final demand in sector 1 is 50% of total other demand and, therefore, increases by $75 million, 50% of the reduction in military spending. As can be seen from column 4 of each table, the

TABLE 8.3
Assumed Redistribution of $150 Million from Defense to Other Spending

a. Original Distribution

Sector	Defense	Other	Total Final Demand	α
1.	100	300	400	.33
2.	300	100	400	.33
3.	200	200	400	.33
Total	600	600	1200	1.00

b. After Redistribution

Sector	Defense	Other	Total Final Demand	α	eα
1.	75	375	450	.38	.15
2.	225	125	350	.29	-.12
3.	150	250	400	.33	.00
Total	450	750	1200	1.00	

Source: Authors' assumptions.

redistribution causes the αs to change significantly. As discussed above, the proportional changes, eαs, are needed for carrying out the experiments. For sector 1, we have:

$$e\alpha = \frac{.38 - .33}{.33} = .15 \tag{2}$$

The other changes in shares are calculated analogously.

It is also convenient to use Table 8.3 to illustrate the exogenous change in imports discussed above. In sector 1, for example, other final demand increases by $75 million. If 10% of all demand, both intermediate and final, in sector 1 is imported, the imports of sector 1 commodities are assumed to increase by 10% of the increase in other final demand, which is $7.5 million in this case. Similarly, in sector 2, nonmilitary final demand increases by $25 million. If 20% of all demand in sector 2 is imported, imports of sector 2 commodities increase exogenously by $5 million.

Some Theoretical Considerations

Before looking at the computational results of our experiments, it is useful to examine what one would expect in terms of a simple theoretical model that captures some, though by no means all, of the interactions that are present in the Michigan Model. This can be done with the aid of the (partial equilibrium) supply and demand diagrams shown in Figure 8.1.

The top panel of Figure 8.1 shows the market for home-produced goods in a representative industry. Supply and demand in such a home market depend of course on the home price, but the positions of the supply and demand curves also depend on various prices of imports. This dependence is only shown in the figure for the price of the imported good in the same industry. This matters for demand because of consumer substitution, and it matters for supply because of the use of imports as inputs into production.

The bottom panel shows the markets for exports and imports within the same industry. Here the prices and quantities of exports and imports are drawn for convenience on the same axis, because in the model they are viewed as identical products in the world market. However, within the country imports of an industry are viewed as distinct from exports, and there is no reason in general to compare them. Nonetheless, we show them being equal initially, partly for convenience and partly to enable us, even though inappropriately, to represent the process of exchange rate adjustment in this single market context.

For both exports and imports the world price in the industry, P_W, is translated into domestic currency by multiplying by the exchange rate, R. In the absence of any export taxes or subsidies, this gives the export price, P_X. The supply of exports depends upon this price, as well as the price in the home market, again because of the use of home market goods as inputs into production for export.[10]

The price facing importers, P_M, is also given by RP_W, except that it is augmented by t, representing the ad valorem tariff together with the tariff equivalent of any nontariff barrier that may be present. Thus the demand curve is drawn as a function of P_M, as well as, again, having its position depend on the home price from the other panel.

A cut in defense expenditure has two effects, as already noted. First, depending upon where defense expenditure was concentrated compared to the pattern of expenditure in the category of final demand

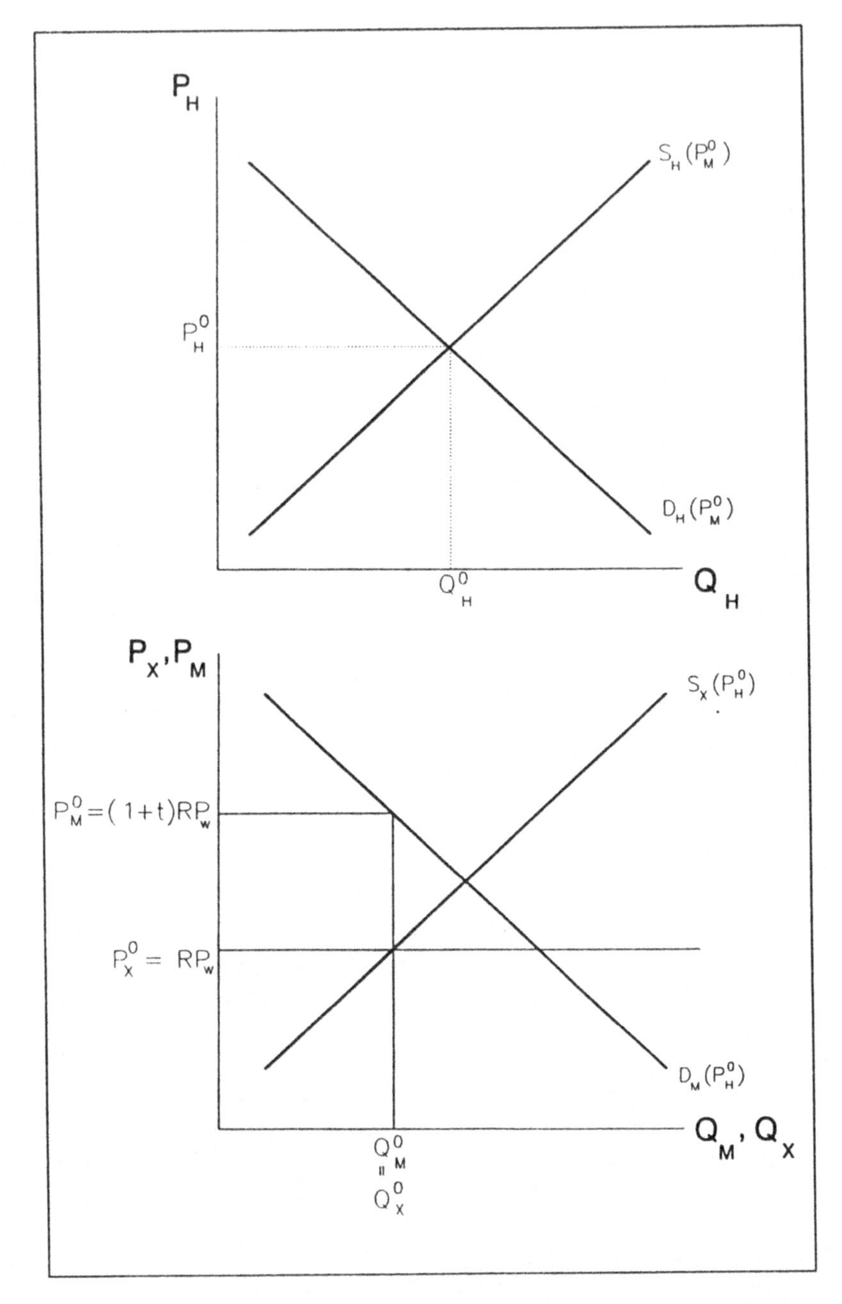

FIGURE 8.1 Partial Equilibrium Determination of Home-Sector Prices and Quantities and of Exports and Imports

to which that expenditure is shifted, total demand in some industries will rise and in other industries will fall. We will look at both cases in turn. Second, even in industries where total demand declines, and certainly in ones where demand expands, there is a shift from defense spending, which was devoted exclusively to home goods, to other demand that is spent partly on imports. This means that there is an additional leftward shift of the home-sector demand curve and a rightward shift of the import demand curve.

Consider, then, an industry in which there has been no defense spending. The cut in defense spending will therefore, at initial prices, unambiguously increase total demand in that industry, as well as increasing demands for both imported and home produced goods there. This is shown in Figure 8.2 by the shifts of the two demand curves to $D^1_H(P^0_M)$ and $D^1_M(P^0_H)$. As long as the world price and the exchange rate do not change, the prices of exports and imports in the sector will remain constant. However, the shift in demand in the home sector requires a price increase there, to P^1_H, and this induces a further shift in both supply and demand for exports and imports. The demand for imports shifts further to the right, to $D^1_M(P^1_H)$, due to substitution away from higher priced home goods. And the supply of exports shifts to the left, to $S_X(P^1_H)$, due to the higher prices of inputs from the home sector. Thus the result at this point is a rise in output in the home sector, a fall in exports, and a rise in imports.

These results could change somewhat, however, if there is a change in prices of exports and imports, though this is not shown in the diagram. If the country is large in the world market, then its increased net demand for imports will raise the world price, P_W. In addition, if the increase in net imports here applies to other industries as well, then the worsening of the trade balance will lead to a depreciation of the currency, that is a rise in R, which will also raise the domestic currency prices of traded goods. On the export side, a price increase for either of these reasons will tend to offset the decline in exports shown in Figure 8.2, and may even lead exports in certain sectors to increase overall.

On the import side, the possible price increase for these two reasons may in addition be enhanced by still another possibility. If the industry being considered is covered by a nontariff barrier, then the attempt to increase imports will lead to a rise in the tariff equivalent of the barrier, and thus to a rise in t, raising the price of imports still further. Thus for three reasons P_M may rise, and if it does the changes in Figure 8.2 will be further complicated. Such a rise in P_M will lead to a further upward shift in D_H, plus an upward shift in S_H, possibly changing the quantity in the home market from that shown in Figure

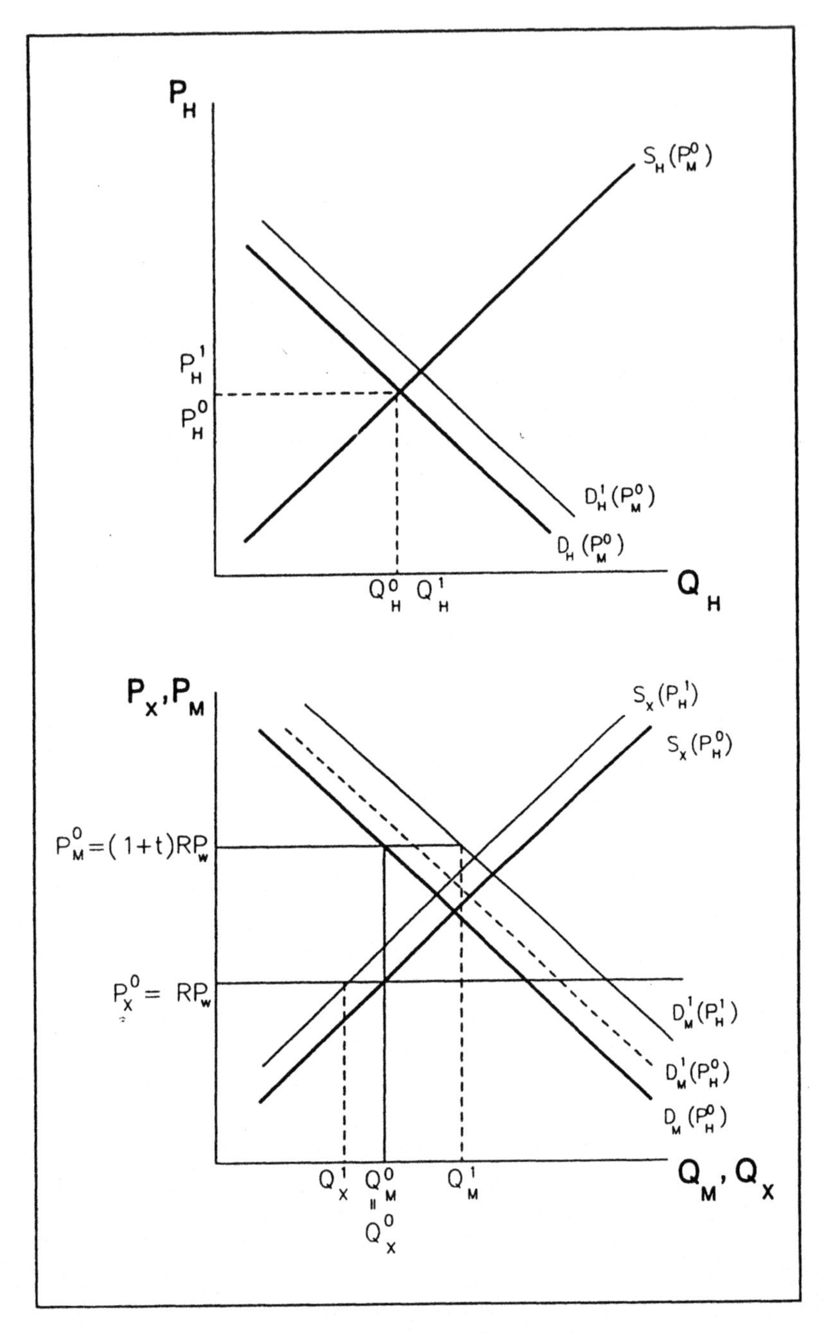

FIGURE 8.2 Partial Equilibrium Effects of a Cut in Defense Spending in an Industry Where Demand Increases

8.2, and surely increasing the price there still further. The additional price increase will also lead to further shifts of supply and demand for trade, and so on. The end result can therefore not be obtained with certainty from the diagram. However, all of these secondary shifts seem unlikely to change in a substantial way the results that are shown in Figure 8.2, which may therefore still be of use in understanding the results of the more complicated interactions captured by the Michigan Model.

Figure 8.3 shows the opposite extreme case, where defense expenditure in an industry is cut substantially and only a small amount of new final demand is created in the same industry, thus reducing total demand. The demand curve in the home sector therefore shifts to the left, to $D^1_H(P^0_M)$, while the demand curve for imports shifts slightly to the right, to $D^1_M(P^0_H)$. The price in the home market therefore falls in this case, to P^1_H, and this shifts both the supply of exports and the demand for imports down. The results, therefore, are a rise in exports and a fall in imports (assuming, as shown, that the initial increase in import demand is small compared to the effect of the drop in the home price).

Here again, there could be further adjustment of prices if there are changes in world prices, the exchange rate, or the tariff equivalent of a nontariff barrier, and in this case the effects would tend to go in the opposite direction from what we discussed in connection with Figure 8.2. However, since over the entire economy the defense cut replaces spending that was only in home sectors with other spending that goes partly to imports, the case of an exchange rate depreciation that was considered there seems the much more likely one.

To sum up, our theoretical analysis suggests that home-sector prices will rise in some sectors and fall in others due to a shift of expenditure out of defense, with corresponding changes in home-sector outputs. As a first approximation, imports rise and exports fall in sectors where demand expands, while the opposite is likely where demand contracts. However, because of the overall shift toward imports with the cut in defense, the currency is likely to depreciate, and this tends to raise prices across the board.

Computational Results

The Michigan CGE model produces results for a wide range of endogenous variables that emerge from the calculations as percentage changes for each of the 29 sectors. Base year data, 1980 in this study, are then used to compute absolute changes for selected variables, e.g., exports, imports, and employment. In what follows we discuss all four

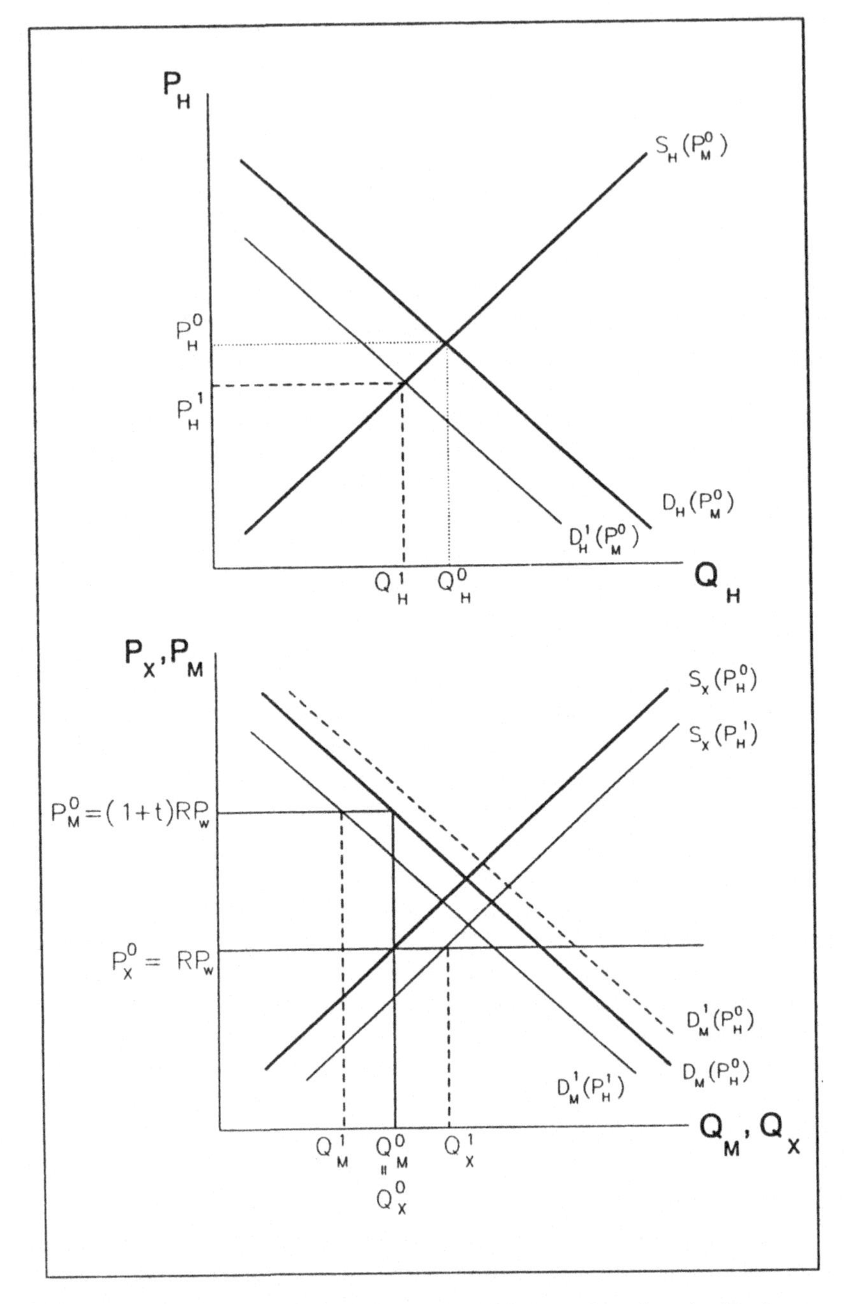

FIGURE 8.3 Partial Equilibrium Effects of a Cut in Defense Spending in an Industry Where Demand Decreases

scenarios, but emphasize the results of the first experiment, that of a shift from defense to all other sources of final demand. The other three scenarios will be discussed subsequently.

Scenario 1: Redistributing Spending Across Total Final Demand. The aggregate results for the United States for each of the four scenarios are presented in Table 8.4. Column 1 refers to the results of redistributing spending across Total Civilian Demand, i.e., consumption, investment and nonmilitary government spending combined. It appears that a 25% reduction in defense spending is fairly painless in the aggregate. That is, there is a marginal reduction in both exports and imports,[11] and only 0.6% of the US labor force would experience some dislocation.

The reduction in U.S. exports is not surprising. Column 1 of Table 8.2 shows domestic demand increasing in a majority of the tradable sectors. This increase in demand will cause an increase in the home price for that industry, leading to a substitution from production for export to production for home use, thus reducing total exports.The change in aggregate imports is somewhat less intuitive. Recall that defense expenditure is assumed to be spent entirely in home sectors and that the shift of expenditure therefore involves an exogenous increase in imports. Given this assumption, it is somewhat surprising that imports decline in the aggregate. One possible explanation is that the fall in the home price for a sector experiencing a reduction in demand is large enough to cause sufficient substitution away from imports in that sector so as to overwhelm the exogenously imposed increase. We will demonstrate in what follows that this is indeed what is happening.

The results discussed thus far are aggregates of the changes that take place in the underlying sectors of the U.S. economy. It is also of interest to analyze the sectoral breakdown of exports, imports, and employment. Tables 8.5 and 8.6 contain the sectoral results for the four experiments. Again, looking at the first scenario, it does not appear that any one industry will be seriously impacted.

Basic metal industries (371 and 372), durable goods sectors (381, 382, 383, 384, and 38A) and community, social and personal services (ISIC 9, which includes government employment) are the only sectors in which employment decreases significantly in percentage terms, as can be seen in partition 1 of Table 8.5. Only three sectors experience a significant decline in absolute employment. Employment in ISIC 9 falls by 329 thousand person-years, which is 1.0% of that sector's 1980 employment. Electric machinery (ISIC 383) and transport equipment (ISIC 384) each fall by roughly 2.8%, or 63 and 64 thousand person-years, respectively.

TABLE 8.4
Summary of Effect on the United States Due to Shifts of 25% in Defense Spending

	Total Civilian Demand	Nondefense Government	Consumption	Investment	Multilateral Demilitarization
Change in Exports					
Value ($ Mill.)	-380.4	-1197.9	-887.8	2303.1	-1531.0
Percent	-0.2	-0.6	-0.4	1.1	-0.7
Change in Imports					
Value ($ Mill.)	-169.3	-912.0	-663.5	2398.9	427.2
Percent	-0.1	-0.5	-0.4	1.3	0.2
Labor Dislocations*					
'000 Person-Years	575.6	456.7	734.5	808.2	596.2
Percent	0.6	0.5	0.7	0.8	0.6
Percent Change in:					
Terms of Trade	0.05	0.07	0.05	0.02	0.12
Effective Exchange Rate#	0.10	0.10	0.10	-0.20	0.20
Prices+	0.10	0.10	0.10	-0.10	0.20

*Refers to the sum of positive changes in home and export sectors within all industries.
#Positive = Appreciation.
+Index of import and home prices.

Source: Authors' calculations.

The aggregate figures for the change in imports, it turns out, tell a very misleading story, as can be seen in partition 1 of Table 8.6. While imports fall in the aggregate, at the sectoral level imports actually rise, as expected, in all but a handful of sectors. It can be seen by comparing column 1 of Table 8.2 with partition 1 of Table 8.6 that all sectors in which imports decline had a decrease in domestic demand. For two sectors in which demand falls, miscellaneous manufacturing (38A) and nonelectric machinery (382), the exogenous increases in imports are enough to outweigh the substitution effect resulting from the reduced home price. As a result, they each experience an increase in imports. This is the case for 16 of the 22 sectors modeled. Of the six remaining sectors experiencing a reduction in demand, five show a negligible decline in imports. The sixth, transport equipment (384), shows a decline of 4.4 percent or $1.4 billion. The decline in this sector alone is enough to offset the combined increase in the other sectors.

The sectoral changes in exports are much less surprising. As can be seen from partition 1 of Table 8.5, 19 of the tradable sectors experience a small decline in exports, with leather products (323) experiencing the largest decline in percentage terms, 1.6%, while the value of exports in food, beverage, and tobacco (310) declines the most, $190 million. The response of these sectors is consistent with the intuition described above. The remaining three sectors, agriculture (1), footwear (324), and electrical machinery (383), each produce more for export once expenditures are redistributed. Intuition would suggest that exports should increase in sectors experiencing a decrease in domestic demand. As noted above, this increase is a result of the fall in the home price. However, this only happens in one of the seven traded sectors in which domestic demand falls. In six of these sectors, the appreciation of the currency (a fall in R in the diagrams) combined with a fall in the world price is sufficient to offset the effects of the fall in the home price.

Scenario 2: Redistributing Spending Across Nondefense Government Spending. The second scenario again reduces military expenditures by 25%, but includes a compensating policy of increasing only nondefense related government spending. In the aggregate, the employment effects of this alternative redistribution are not qualitatively different. This more directed distribution does, however, impact the traded sectors to a much larger extent than does the previous scenario. Exports fall by $1,197.9 million, three times the fall in scenario 1, and imports fall by $912.0 million, more than five times the reduction in scenario 1.

At the sectoral level, from partition 2 of Table 8.5, we can make several general comments regarding the employment changes. First,

TABLE 8.5
Net Changes in Employment in the U.S. Due to Each of Four Scenarios Reducing Military Spending

		Shift 25% of Defense to:							
		Total Civilian Demand		Nondefense Government		Consumption		Investment	
Industry	(ISIC)	%	'000 Person Years	%	'000 Person Years	%	'000 Person Years	%	'000 Person Years
Traded Goods									
Agr.,For., & Fishing	(1)	1.16	40.70	0.70	24.73	1.43	50.20	0.48	16.86
Food, Bev., & Tobacco	(310)	1.53	27.75	-0.22	- 4.06	2.26	40.80	0.19	3.38
Textiles	(321)	0.33	3.68	-0.76	- 8.59	0.30	3.42	1.35	15.10
Wearing Apparel	(322)	1.00	13.06	-0.61	- 8.08	1.62	21.12	-0.06	-0.73
Leather Products	(323)	0.40	0.37	-1.26	- 1.16	0.56	0.51	1.19	1.09
Footwear	(324)	1.51	2.49	-0.35	- 0.58	2.22	3.64	0.34	0.57
Wood Products	(331)	0.33	1.93	0.55	3.23	-0.84	-4.96	4.89	27.91
Furniture & Fixtures	(332)	1.40	6.91	0.25	1.22	0.99	4.91	4.01	19.55
Paper & Paper Products	(341)	0.31	2.32	-0.07	-0.50	0.36	2.68	0.45	3.31
Printing & Publishing	(342)	0.57	8.25	0.80	11.53	0.70	10.11	-0.13	-1.82
Chemicals	(35A)	-0.31	-3.29	-0.46	-5.00	-0.38	-4.11	0.13	1.37

Petrol & Rel. Prod.	(35B)	0.05	0.09	-0.37	-0.63	0.30	0.50	-0.56	-0.94
Rubber Products	(355)	-0.74	-1.97	-1.25	-3.35	-0.82	-2.20	0.03	0.09
Nonmetallic Min. Prod.	(36A)	0.25	1.28	0.61	3.09	-0.96	-4.90	4.86	24.03
Glass & Glass Products	(362)	-0.52	-1.00	-1.32	-2.59	-0.62	-1.20	0.57	1.10
Iron & Steel	(371)	-1.63	-14.02	-2.31	-20.01	-2.13	-18.39	0.97	8.23
Nonferrous Metals	(372)	-2.26	-7.67	-3.58	-12.27	-2.81	-9.56	1.10	3.67
Metal Products	(381)	-1.68	-29.18	-1.91	-33.16	-2.30	-40.10	0.99	17.04
Nonelectric Machinery	(382)	-0.65	-18.79	-1.46	-42.16	-1.56	-45.09	3.69	104.23
Electric Machinery	(383)	-2.75	-63.26	-3.35	-77.21	-3.24	-74.69	-0.29	-6.60
Transportation Equip.	(384)	-2.89	-64.11	-3.44	-76.38	-3.04	-67.47	-1.84	-40.53
Miscellaneous Manufac.	(38A)	-2.04	-35.27	-2.48	-42.86	-2.46	-42.61	0.00	-0.03
Total Traded		-0.50	-129.74	-1.14	-294.80	-0.68	-177.39	0.79	196.87

TABLE 8.5 (contd.)
Net Changes in Employment in the U.S. Due to Each of Four Scenarios Reducing Military Spending

		Shift 25% of Defense to:							
		Total Civilian Demand		Nondefense Government		Consumption		Investment	
Industry	(ISIC)	%	'000 Person Years	%	'000 Person Years	%	'000 Person Years	%	'000 Person Years
Nontraded Goods									
Mining & Quarrying	(2)	0.10	0.93	-0.07	-0.73	0.08	0.80	0.29	2.83
Electric, Gas & Water	(4)	1.23	17.24	0.59	8.33	1.80	25.13	-0.44	-6.17
Construction	(5)	0.70	43.30	1.31	80.99	-0.67	-42.00	5.73	346.42
Wholesale & Ret. Trade	(6)	1.30	260.72	-0.47	-95.28	1.79	357.71	0.90	180.59
Transp., Stor., & Com.	(7)	0.15	7.53	-0.39	-20.21	0.33	16.89	-0.11	-5.83
Fin., Ins. & Real Est.	(8)	1.56	129.11	0.03	2.28	2.26	186.25	0.14	11.85
Comm., Soc. & Pers. Serv.	(9)	-1.04	-329.09	1.02	319.41	-1.16	-367.40	-2.28	-726.56
Total Nontraded		0.18	129.74	0.40	294.80	0.25	177.39	-0.24	-196.87
Total All Industries		0.01	0.00	0.01	0.00	0.01	0.00	0.02	0.00

Source: Authors' calculations.

TABLE 8.6
Net Percentage Changes in Trade in the U.S. Due to Each of Four Scenarios Reducing Military Spending

		Shift 25% of Defense to:							
		Total Civilian Demand		Nondefense Government		Consumption		Investment	
Industry	(ISIC)	Exports	Imports	Exports	Imports	Exports	Imports	Exports	Imports
Traded Goods									
Agr., For., Fishing	(1)	0.02	2.96	0.11	4.86	-0.01	3.27	0.08	0.21
Food, Bev., & Tobacco	(310)	-1.35	2.13	-1.39	0.46	-1.84	3.05	0.67	-0.05
Textiles	(321)	-1.28	1.35	-2.09	0.23	-2.02	1.55	2.37	1.50
Wearing Apparel	(322)	-1.08	2.98	-4.35	0.49	-1.71	4.53	4.33	-0.85
Leather Products	(323)	-1.61	2.95	-3.80	0.10	-2.61	4.38	4.41	-0.12
Footwear	(324)	0.18	2.52	-3.12	0.22	-0.17	3.76	4.48	-0.33
Wood Products	(331)	-0.53	0.98	-0.83	1.16	-0.55	0.71	-0.19	1.91
Furniture & Fixtures	(332)	-0.16	3.39	-1.57	1.65	-0.49	2.67	2.37	7.81
Paper & Paper Products	(341)	0.06	2.05	-0.82	2.59	-0.13	2.46	1.57	-0.02
Printing & Publishing	(342)	-0.13	2.30	-0.73	4.05	-0.42	2.74	1.55	-0.87
Chemicals	(35A)	-0.05	1.42	-0.36	1.52	-0.20	1.89	0.78	-0.49
Petrol & Rel. Prod.	(35B)	-0.15	1.11	-0.48	0.98	-0.27	1.55	0.62	-0.46

TABLE 8.6 (contd.)
Net Percentage Changes in Trade in the U.S. Due to Each of Four Scenarios Reducing Military Spending

		Shift 25% of Defense to:							
		Total Civilian Demand		Nondefense Government		Consumption		Investment	
Industry	(ISIC)	Exports	Imports	Exports	Imports	Exports	Imports	Exports	Imports
Rubber Products	(355)	-0.27	1.15	-0.97	0.97	-0.52	1.90	1.33	-1.58
Nonmetallic Min.	(35A)	-0.26	2.09	-0.96	2.44	-0.51	1.58	1.34	3.83
Glass & Glass Prod.	(362)	-0.23	1.50	-0.73	4.00	-0.51	1.44	1.28	-0.30
Iron & Steel	(371)	-0.51	-0.68	-1.37	1.61	-1.18	-1.59	2.93	0.98
Nonferrous Metals	(372)	-0.34	-0.56	-0.25	2.79	-1.30	-1.74	3.46	1.33
Metal Products	(381)	-0.02	-0.51	-0.71	-0.70	-0.30	-1.46	1.68	3.45
Nonelectric Mach.	(382)	0.21	0.88	-0.35	-0.82	-0.08	-1.39	1.81	11.87
Electric Mach.	(383)	-0.21	-1.73	-0.94	-2.96	-0.57	-2.72	1.85	3.36
Transportation Eq.	(384)	-0.16	-4.35	-0.54	-5.74	-0.25	-4.79	0.55	-1.42
Miscellaneous Manufac.	(38A)	-0.04	0.09	-0.38	-0.27	-0.19	-0.46	0.84	2.61
Total Traded		-0.19	-0.07	-0.58	-0.47	-0.43	-0.33	1.14	1.41

Source: Authors' calculations.

the burden of such a reduction appears to fall disproportionately on the traded sectors. There is a net transfer of 294.8 thousand person-years from traded industries to nontraded industries. ISIC 9 appears to be driving this shift. These results reflect the larger fraction of nondefense government purchases that come from nontraded industries.[12] Second, it should be noted that the burden borne by the traded industries is heavier and more evenly distributed across industries than in scenario 1.

The sectoral impact on exports is more evenly distributed than previously and of a larger magnitude in each industry. The aggregate reduction in imports remains concentrated in the durable goods industries and is, again, largely due to the disproportionately large reduction in demand for goods produced by the transportation equipment industry (384).

Scenario 3: Redistributing Spending Across Consumption. The results of the third scenario reflect a shift in spending from defense to consumption. This shift is intended to represent a reduction in taxes as a response to reduced military expenditures.

The aggregate results in Table 8.4 are once again larger than those reported for scenario 1. The effect on employment is a dislocation of 734.5 thousand workers. The impact on imports and exports is less severe than scenario 2, but still larger than for the shift in scenario 1. Imports and exports each fall by 0.4%, or $663.5 million and $887.8 million, respectively.

This restructuring of final demand shows a slightly weaker impact on traded goods than did the previous scenario. As reported in Table 8.5, there is a shift of 177.4 thousand person-years from traded to nontraded industries. This is, again, a reflection of the higher propensity of consumers to purchase nontraded goods relative to that of the DOD. Private consumers place a much greater emphasis on purchases from wholesale and retail trade (6), and finance, insurance, and real estate (8) than does the DOD. Partition 3 of Table 8.6 shows that employment in wholesale and retail trade (6), and finance, insurance, and real estate (8) increases significantly, while workers in the durable goods industries (381, 382, 383, 384, and 38A) and sector 9 bear the brunt of the dislocations.

The sectoral impact on exports is uniformly negative, reflecting the currency appreciation and increased demand in most sectors. The impact on imports conforms to a priori expectations. In sectors where demand increases, imports increase and, conversely, imports fall in sectors with decreasing demand.

Scenario 4: Redistributing Spending Across Private Fixed Investment. The final unilateral scenario is a shift in spending to private fixed investment. This scenario is intended to mimic a reduction in the budget deficit accompanying a reduction in military expenditures. The reduced budget deficit presumably causes interest rates to fall and consequently encourages private fixed investment. The results for this scenario are strikingly different from the preceding ones. The increase in investment demand leads to an increase in both exports and imports. The number of worker dislocations is also largest for this type of a shift. It is interesting to note, from partition 4 of Table 8.2, that demand increases significantly in only four sectors: furniture and fixtures (332), nonelectric machinery (382), construction (5), and wholesale and retail trade (6). This is due to the high level of concentration of investment expenditures. The expenditure in these four sectors is significantly greater than that of the remaining sectors.

The sectoral results present a very interesting picture. Partition 4 of Table 8.5 indicates that employment increases in 17 of the 22 traded sectors. This happens despite a decline in demand for 20 of the traded sectors. There is also a net transfer of 196.9 thousand person-years from the nontraded sectors to the traded sectors.

The phenomenon of increasing employment accompanying decreasing domestic demand can be explained by the resulting change in exports, noted in partition 4 of Table 8.6. The declining domestic demand, resulting in a lower home price for the good, combined with a depreciation of the dollar leads to an increase in exports in all sectors, with the exception of wood products (331). This increase in exports is in most cases sufficient to offset the employment effects of the reduced domestic demand.

The sectoral effects on imports are driven, to a large extent, by the exogenous increase caused by the shift away from defense purchases. Sectors not receiving an exogenous increase in imports generally experience a decline and, conversely, those with an exogenous increase generally experience increased imports.[13]

Summary

The results of the first three scenarios are qualitatively similar while the fourth is significantly different from the others. The first three scenarios suggest that the burden of shifting expenditures is disproportionately borne by the traded goods industries, while the fourth shifts the burden to nontraded industries. The linear nature of the model is reflected in the first scenario, which is a weighted average of the other three.

It should be noted in all the scenarios that military personnel are included in sector 9, which means that we assume the military employs workers in the same proportion as all other components of sector 9. The results presented above will thus under- or overstate the results according to the difference in labor as a fraction of spending in each component of sector 9. Nonetheless, correction for these inaccuracies would not change the qualitative nature of the results.

Multilateral Reductions in Military Expenditure

In this section, we summarize the results of an experiment similar to scenario 1 above. This experiment involves a *pro rata* shift of 25% of 1985 military expenditures across all categories of final demand for 33 of the 34 countries included in the model.[14] The assumption that military expenditures in most countries are biased towards home produced goods is less applicable in many countries than it is for the United States. Countries such as Australia simply do not possess the necessary industry to satisfy the demands of its government's military. The "buy domestic" assumption is, therefore, assumed to hold only for the United States.

In order to calculate the demand shift parameters for each of the 29 industries in each country, it was necessary to distribute the aggregate military expenditure and GNP data obtained across the industries modelled.[15] The distribution of GNP was accomplished through the use of the input-output tables already employed in the model. The aggregate obtained was distributed to replicate the share in final demand for each of the 29 sectors.

Leontief and Duchin (1983) provide estimates of the proportion of the ACDA data on aggregate military expenditures that correspond to 12 categories. We in turn concorded these categories to our industrial classification. They also provide estimates of the decomposition of the ACDA data by sector for 15 regions of the world. We used these regional breakdowns for each of the 33 countries to correspond to their location within the individual regions.[16]

For comparison with the other experiments, the aggregate results of the multilateral reductions for the United States are listed in column 5 of Table 8.4. Comparing columns 1 and 5, it appears that, in the aggregate, a multilateral reduction in military spending has a somewhat larger impact on the U.S. economy than does a unilateral reduction. The sectoral results, which are available from the authors on request, indicate that, while some industries may experience a larger impact from the multilateral reductions, the differences appear to be fairly small.

Conclusions and Implications

In the long run, a reduction in defense spending is generally regarded to have a positive impact on an economy. In the short run, however, a reduction in defense outlays could result in unemployment and adjustment pressures in at least some sectors of the economy. In order to facilitate a smooth transition, government assistance, if deemed necessary, should be pointed in the right direction. The CGE results that we have reported based on the Michigan Model are useful in assessing the sectoral impact of a reduction in military expenditures.

It is important to note that there is some latitude in choosing whether nondefense government, consumption, or investment spending are to expand in response to reductions in military spending. The decision of which policy to follow will depend on the weights that policy makers assign to the different objectives of government. That is, whether reduced military spending is used to meet other federal spending needs, to reduce taxes allowing for higher consumption or personal savings, or to cut the federal deficit resulting in higher domestic investment, must be decided on the basis of many considerations that lie outside the scope of our study.

In any event, our results suggest that, while the impacts of a 25% unilateral or multilateral reduction in military expenditures do not appear to be large in the aggregate, the sectoral impacts differ significantly depending on the accompanying macroeconomic policy. It also appears that certain specific sectors may bear the brunt of the adjustment costs and therefore would be in need of assistance in the event that reduced military spending may in fact be carried out.

Notes

1. As will become clear from the discussion that follows, we can use our modeling framework to analyze increases as well as reductions in military spending.

2. There may of course be other effects at both the micro and aggregate levels that our modeling approach cannot capture. These effects include the dynamics of adjustment in goods and factor markets and possible impacts working through financial markets and changes in aggregate savings and investment behavior. This suggests the need for a broader and more integrated modeling effort, which is unfortunately something beyond our capability at present.

3. The industries are listed in Table 8.2 and the countries in Deardoff and Stern (1986, pp. 37-38; 1990, pp. 38-39).

4. As will be discussed below, our sector aggregates may obscure technological differences in the production of military and nonmilitary goods in certain sectors.

5. Use of these elasticities is subject to the limitation that they are valid, at most, only for the range of prices for which they were estimated. This should not be a problem for the results reported here, however, for which individual prices changed in most cases on average by only a few percent.

6. Human resources include spending on health and Medicare, income maintenance, Social Security, and education programs.

7. The use of a 1985 sectoral breakdown in military expenditures reflects the availability of the most recent input-output table for the United States. In performing the experiments we use the more disaggregated 1977 input-output table to represent technology. It is assumed that the technology represented there still holds for 1985.

8. Investment is taken to be only gross private fixed investment. Changes in business inventories are considered to be of a more transitional nature and less sensitive to interest rate fluctuations, and hence not affected by a reduction in the budget deficit.

9. For example, in scenario 3, suppose sector 310 is 10% of total civilian demand. Then spending in sector 310 is assumed to increase by $6.48 billion. Similarly in scenario 3, if sector 310 is 10% of consumption, spending in sector 310 increases by $6.48 billion.

10. Of course inputs from other sectors are typically more important than inputs from the same industry represented here. Other than this input-price effect, the Michigan Model does not include any direct effect of the home price on export supply, or vice versa, since capital is assumed specific to each subsector and labor can be hired independently in each.

11. Other experiments in which no "buy American" policy for defense is assumed yield similar but slightly stronger impacts on imports and exports.

12. Recall that the assumption regarding defense purchases was that, within industries, defense purchases were disproportionately from home suppliers. That a greater proportion of defense spending is from traded sectors is consistent with this assumption.

13. Recall that industries with positive investment purchases will receive an exogenous increase in imports, while those with no investment demand do not.

14. Data for Hong Kong are not available, so there is assumed to be no shift in demand within Hong Kong.

15. Data on aggregate military expenditures and gross national product for each country for 1985 were obtained from the U.S. Arms Control and Disarmament Agency (ACDA) publication, *World Military Expenditures and Arms Transfers*, 1987 edition. In some cases, the most recent available data were for 1984.

16. See Grobar and Stern (1989) and Grobar, Stern, and Deardorff (1990) for further details and estimates and analysis of the economic effects of international trade in armaments for 1980.

References

Deardorff, Alan V. and Robert M. Stern (1986), *The Michigan Model of World Production and Trade: Theory and Applications*, Cambridge, MA: MIT Press.

__________ (1990), *Computational Analysis of Global Trading Arrangements*, Ann Arbor, MI: University of Michigan Press.

Dunne, J. Paul and Ron P. Smith. (1984), "The Economic Consequences of Reduced UK Military Expenditure," *Cambridge Journal of Economics*, Vol. 8, pp. 297-310.

Grobar, Lisa M. and Robert M. Stern (1989), "A Data Set on International Trade in Armaments for the Western Industrialized and Developing Countries for 1980: Sources and Methodological Issues," *Weltwirtschaftliches Archiv*, Vol. 125, pp. 748-762.

Grobar, Lisa M., Robert M. Stern, and Alan V. Deardorff (1990), "The Economic Effects of International Trade in Armaments in the Major Western Industrialized and Developing Countries," *Defence Economics*, Vol. 1, pp. 97-120.

Liew, L.H. (1985), "The Impact of Defence Spending on the Australian Economy," *Australian Economic Papers*, Vol. 24, pp. 326-336.

Leontief, Wassily W., and Marvin Hoffenberg (1961), "The Economic Effects of Disarmament," *Scientific American*, Vol. 204, pp. 47-55.

Leontief, Wassily W., Alison Morgan, Karen Polenske, David Simpson, and Edward Tower (1965), "The Economic Impact -- Industrial and Regional -- of an Arms Cut," *Review of Economics and Statistics*, Vol. 47, pp. 217-241.

Stern, Robert M., Jonathan Francis, and Bruce F. Schumacher (1976), *Price Elasticities in International Trade*, London: Macmillan Press.

Steuerle, Eugene C. and Susan Wiener (1990) "Spending the Peace Dividend: Lessons From History," *Urban Institute Policy Paper*.

United Nations, *Yearbook of International Trade Statistics*, Various issues.

United States Arms Control and Disarmament Agency (1988), *World Military Expenditures and Arms Transfers 1987*, U.S. Government Printing Office.

United States Congressional Budget Office (1990), *Summary of the Economic Effects of Reduced Defense Spending*. CBO Staff Memorandum.

Zarembka, Paul and Helen Chernicoff (1973), "Further Results on the Empirical Relevance of the CES Production Function," *Review of Economics and Statistics*, Vol. 53, pp. 106-110.

9

The Collapse of Communism in the USSR: Cold War Victory or Cold War Illusions?

Peter J. Boettke

It has become commonplace among neo-conservative commentators in the West, and even some Russian intellectuals, to argue that the break up of the Soviet empire in the late 1980s was due to Ronald Reagan's military build-up in the early 1980s.[1] By raising the stakes in the international military game, Reagan put the final strain on the Soviet system. The collapse of communism signalled the glorious victory for the West in the Cold War. However accurate this perspective is concerning the weight of the military burden on the former Soviet economy, it does not address the systemic issues and problems surrounding the former Soviet economy. The real question that must be raised is whether the Soviet system could have continued even if no military pressure was exerted by the West.

The neo-conservative perspective on the Soviet problem is untenable because it underestimates the extent to which military power is derived from a prosperous economic base and it overestimated Soviet economic strength.[2] Questioning the neo-conservative hypothesis, however, should not be construed as support for the alternative suggestion that Mikhail Gorbachev was responsible for the break-up.[3] Gorbachev did not become General Secretary to reign over the demise of the Soviet empire. Any view that draws our attention away from the *structural problems* the Soviet system faced throughout its history will fail to grasp the meaning of the Soviet experience with socialism.

The conventional wisdom is guilty of *post hoc ergo propter hoc* reasoning. Just because the collapse of communism occurred after the Reagan build-up, it does not necessarily follow that the build-up caused the collapse. Even if the US and the West had reduced the military stakes in the 1980s, the Soviet economy was doomed to fail. The Soviet system was structurally weak since its founding and doomed to collapse.

The illusion of Soviet economic growth and progress were due to the failings of aggregate economics, in general, and an odd combination of ideas and interests in academic discussions which did not allow dissenting voices to be heard, in particular. In fact, the whole peculiar art of Soviet economic management amounted to the production, and distribution of this illusion.

To illustrate the conflict between western perceptions of socialist industrial achievement and the realities of the former socialist economies, one need only consider the fact that prior to German unification, East Germany was considered the flagship of the socialist industrialized world. Now it is evident to all that the East German economy was a basket case -- incapable of producing anything close to world standards for an industrialized nation.[4]

It is not at all an exaggeration to say that in economic terms the socialist economies of Europe were Third World economies.[5] As George Orwell (1946) pointed out in *Animal Farm*, to the outside world the farm may have appeared as if it was productive and prosperous after the revolution, but inside the farm the animals worked harder and ate less than they ever did before. Unfortunately, the cold warrior mentality in combination with intellectual prejudices blinded scholars, intellectuals and political actors in the West from the real conditions on the farm.

The Ill-Preparation for the Understanding

Our ability to understand the Soviet experience has been distorted greatly by the intellectual trends of the 20th century. The dominant theories in both politics and economics conspired to warp historical interpretations of capitalistic processes and socialist practice. In addition, as the century progressed interest groups developed which served as the guardian of these misunderstandings. Ideas came both to create, and then to serve, the purposes of vested interests which would not allow dissenting opinion to challenge the establishment.

This is not meant to imply that no debate was allowed. Certainly there was debate, but the parameters of the debate were firmly established and unquestioned. For much of the 20th century the basic consensus on either side of the dispute concerning the grand questions of social organization was that capitalism had failed in providing equity and humane social conditions which progressive legislation must correct.[6] Moreover, the Great Depression of the 1930s supposedly demonstrated that capitalism was not only unjust, but also unstable as an economic system. Capitalism, if it was to survive at all, must be subject to democratic forces of control to tame its operations and protect the populace from unscrupulous business and irresponsible speculation. Socialism, in fact, was viewed as a great threat to those who favored capitalism precisely because it was perceived as offering a viable alternative.

This general intellectual climate was reinforced by the theoretical developments in economics. As academic economic theory became more technically sophisticated and rarified in its presentation of its basic theorems, an appreciative or intuitive understanding of the nature of market institutions and their operation became scientifically suspect. The flip-side of the development of the idea of perfect competition, and the strict conditions established for its attainment, was the development of the theory of market failure. Market failures were said to exist whenever capitalist reality did not meet the conditions of the frictionless textbook model of perfect competition.[7] The concepts of externalities, public goods, monopoly and imperfect competition, and macroeconomic instability were developed and used by professional economists to explain why markets may fail to allocate resources in a socially desirable manner. Real existing competitive capitalism generated negative externalities in the form of pollution and other undesirable third party effects, possessed an inherent tendency toward monopolization and waste, could not provide many basic services such as roads and education, and suffered from recurring business cycles. That was the theoretical picture of competitive capitalism that dominated the intellectual landscape for most of the 20th century.

The Great Depression shook an entire generation's faith in the efficacy of capitalist markets. Theory and history both seemed to fundamentally question laissez-faire. Rational planning of the economy came to be viewed not only as the most viable alternative, but the only alternative. The parameters of the debate had shifted drastically by the 1930s. *Laissez-faire* was no longer considered as any kind of option in the economic policy debate. Classical liberal economic policy simply reflected the beliefs of the naive and simple minded. The modern world had become too complex for an 18th century idea to offer anything of value.

John Maynard Keynes (1926, 1933) went so far as to argue that the great social experiments of the time in Germany (fascism) and Russia (communism) would point the way to the future of economic policy. Country after country had abandoned the old presuppositions of classical political economy. Russia, Italy and Germany moved towards establishing a new political economy and their experience must be watched closely. No one could tell which of the new systems would prove itself best, but they nevertheless successfully persuaded thinking men and women in Great Britain and the United States to strive after a new economic plan of their own. Some may still cling to the old ideas of *laissez faire* capitalism, "but in no country of the world today can they be reckoned as a serious force."

Keynes considered himself, and was viewed by others, as a realist in the classical liberal tradition. The Keynesian idea was for government officials to rationally intervene in order to improve the workings and outcomes of the market economy. Keynes's proposal was to combine the socialization of the capital market with the 19th century political traditions of Great Britain. While he saw that the socialization of investment was the only way of securing an approximation of full employment, this change did not require a break with the general traditions of bourgeois society. Moreover, Keynes merely conceived of his theory as an extension of classical political economy and classical liberalism, not a rejection of those systems of thought. Keynes's (1936) advocacy of a greater role of government in planning the economy was, in his mind, a practical attempt to save individualism and avoid the destruction of the existing economic system. Keynes's attitude toward laissez-faire reflected the general consensus of the times among intellectuals, scholars and politicians.

Franklin D. Roosevelt even chose to attack classical economists in his third fireside chat on July 24, 1933. "I have no sympathy," he stated, "for the professional economists who insist that things must run their course and that human agencies can have no influence on economic ills." On December 19, 1936, Roosevelt expressed his complete agnosticism with regard to the truth of any tenet of political economy in a letter to Joseph Schumpeter. He had studied economics for 36 years, Schumpeter was informed, but Roosevelt was "compelled to admit -- or boast -- whichever way you care to put, that I know nothing of economics and that nobody else does either!"[8]

The intellectual *gestalt* of the time could neither appreciate nor tolerate the challenge to economic planning offered by its critics, namely Ludwig von Mises and F. A. Hayek. But without an understanding of even the potential difficulties that economic planning may confront in practice, it would be impossible to make sense out any real world experiment with economic planning. It should not be a surprise that within such a climate of opinion that Soviet practice could not be properly understood. It just could not be that economic planning would not work as envisaged. Economic planning seemed so rational, so scientific, and it had the great potential of providing economic stability and guaranteeing a more equitable distribution of the social pie.

Not only did this intellectual bias fail to appreciate the *economic* problems of planning, it failed miserably to grasp the *political* problems inherent with planning. In the West, this was due to an utterly naive view of the operation of democracy that dominated political science by the early 20th century.[9] The text-book model of democracy portrayed the political system as one in which individual citizens could effectively determine the rules by which they would live. The vote process unambiguously conveyed the necessary information concerning the array of public goods and services demanded and the level of taxes that must be paid. Democracy was an ideal model of self-rule. Faced with market failure, democratic governments could easily set the matter straight. If government action failed, it was not due to any structural weakness in the democratic system -- political actors would just have to gather more information and try harder next time.

Such a view of democratic processes, however, was woefully deficient. And, it possessed a deleterious effect on interpretations of the institutions of socialist policy. The political problems of Stalinism, which were recognized by many early on, were not attributed to the nature of planning per se, but rather to the lack of a democratic tradition in Russian history. Planning, as such, was not seen to possess any threat to political freedom whatsoever. Economic planning, under democracy, would not face any of the problems associated with Stalinism.

Keynes (1944), for example, in reacting to Hayek's (1944) *The Road to Serfdom*, wrote that "I should say that what we want is not no planning, or even less planning, indeed I should say that we almost certainly want more. But planning should take place in a community in which as many people as possible, both leaders and followers, wholly share your own moral position. Moderate planning will be safe if those carrying it out are rightly oriented in their own minds and hearts to the moral issues." So long as "good" people were in charge, nothing was objectionable with economic planning. In fact, economic planning was desirable.

Herman Finer was not as kind to Hayek as Keynes. Finer (1945) accused Hayek's *The Road to Serfdom* of being "the most sinister offensive against democracy to emerge from a democratic country for many decades." The true alternative to dictatorship, Finer assured his audience, was not economic individualism and competition, but a democratic government fully responsible to the people. Economic planning was simply democracy in action.

The level of Finer's misunderstanding of Hayek's basic argument was astonishing viewed from our vantage point today, but at the time it was not. The Mises-Hayek analytical criticism of socialist planning was hardly understood by any professional economist and in many respects has not been fully appreciated even to this day. Moreover, the naive view of democracy that Finer defended in his book only came to be seriously challenged as the theory of public choice developed in the post-World War II era. The mainstream of thought simply did not appreciate, let alone incorporate, the important insights concerning information and incentives in economic and political processes that only became evident with the further development of modern political economy.

Why should it be surprising, therefore, that Sovietology was ill-prepared to understand its subject matter. It possessed neither a sound economic or political theory from which to interpret the unique Soviet facts. The intellectual spirit of the age applauded what the Soviet Union was attempting even if there existed normative disagreements about how they were going about it. Economic failures of the Soviet system were attributed to its backwardness, just as the political problems of the system were attributed to the lack of democratic traditions. What was essentially missing from Sovietology was a thorough examination of the *structural* weakness of socialist institutions.

The Malpractice of Economic Measurement

The degree of ill-preparation was not just limited to a failure to recognize that the problems that plagued the Soviet system were not *in* the system, but rather were *the* system. Several other developments also conspired that prevented many from even recognizing that there were problems at all. The emerging hegemony of macroeconomics in the economic profession and in the public mind was perhaps the most fateful turn of intellectual events in blinding observers of the Soviet economy to the reality of the systemic failure of socialism.

The development of techniques in aggregate economics in the wake of the Keynesian victory in economic thought drew economists attention away from the structural make-up of a system and instead focused their attention on aggregate figures such as gross national product (GNP). Beside the conceptual problem of how one aggregates the data in a world where prices are meaningless, as was the case in the command economies, the approach was a fundamentally flawed one for understanding the industrial structure of any society. Aggregate concepts, such as price level, national product, savings rate and levels of public investment, do not allow the economist to examine how complex production plans in an industrial economy are continually adjusted to match with consumer demands through time. But the mutual adjustment of intertemporal decisions by economic actors to coordinate the plans of producers with consumption preferences of buyers makes up the unique capital structure of any industrial economy. It is the mutual accommodation of suppliers and demanders through a process of competitive bids and offers that economics must explain, and the techniques of aggregate economics simply drew economists attention away from this task. As aggregate economics came to dominate the profession in the 1940s, 1950s and 1960s, the problem became even more acute. Not only did economists not pay much professional attention to the dynamics of capitalist processes of production, they ignored them completely.

An example may illustrate the fundamental problem of aggregate economics in assessing economic systems. Consider the case of a fat man and a muscular man. They may both weigh 225 lbs, but the composition of their bodies is radically different in each individual. One is flabby, the other is fit. To understand the health of either individual it does not much matter what the aggregate weight is, the important point is to examine the *structural composition*.

The Soviet economy was similar to the fat man in my story above. Aggregate growth statistics concealed the flabby and faulty capital structure that was born in Stalin's industrialization. But economists preoccupied with such figures did not appreciate the distinction between sustainable development and non-sustainable development of an economy. Western sovietologists knew of the dangers associated with working with the falsified official statistics on the Soviet economy. But the techniques the CIA developed still focused on gaining some aggregate or macroeconomic measure of performance, rather than encouraging detailed microeconomic analysis of the industrial structure of the Soviet Union.

Not only did the CIA develop techniques which were misleading even in the abstract, but even on their own terms they tended to systematically overstate the capability of the Soviet economy. A comparison of alternative measures of Soviet economic growth is found in Table 9.1, and shows that in the late 1970s and 1980s the CIA

TABLE 9.1
Alternative Measure of Soviet Economic Growth (Average Annual Growth in Percent)

Year	Official Soviet Statistics	Khanin-Selyunin Estimates	CIA Estimates
1951-60	10.3	7.2	5.1
1961-65	6.5	4.4	4.8
1966-70	7.8	4.1	5.0
1971-75	5.7	3.2	3.1
1976-80	4.3	1.0	2.2
1981-85	3.6	0.6	1.8

Source: Revisiting Soviet Economic Performance under Glasnost: Implications for CIA Estimates (Washington, D.C.: SOV 88-10068, 1988), p. 11.

overstated the growth of the Soviet economy as compared to the estimates of Soviet economists Khanin and Selyunin (1987).

But the CIA's performance was actually much worse than these figures would suggest. Whereas the official Soviet figure for the average annual rate of growth of national income in the Soviet economy from 1928 to 1985 was 8.8 percent, the CIA's estimate was 4.3 percent, and Khanin and Selyunin's estimate was 3.33 percent. But this conceals the Soviet decline of the 1970s and beyond. In the 1970s, Khanin and Selyunin estimate that Soviet GNP grew at about 2 percent annual rate of growth, whereas the CIA estimate was 3.7 percent. For the eleventh five-year plan (1981-1985), Khanin and Selyunin estimate a growth rate of .59 percent, whereas the CIA estimates 2 percent average annual growth of Soviet GNP.[10]

Moreover, Khanin and Selyunin date the negative decline of the Soviet economy not to the mid-1970s, but rather 15 years earlier to the beginning of the 1960s. Even if alternative calculations of the Soviet economy may show significant growth, they do not examine the meaning of that growth in terms of the industrial structure created and the employment of scarce resources. As Khanin and Selyunin (1987) pointed out, Soviet growth was achieved through "inordinate resource expenditures. In almost all periods of our history, the use of material resources and fixed assets grew more rapidly than did national income. From 1928 through 1985, material-intensiveness increased by 60% and return on assets fell 30%." Labor productivity grew only modestly throughout this period. The Soviet method of economic management, they argued, was made possible only because of the abundance of resources at the regimes disposal. "But the price was high: living standards fell for decades ..."

This point, however, does not square well with CIA estimates that Soviet per capita GNP converted at US purchasing power equivalents amounted to $8,370 in 1986 or about 49 percent of the US.[11] More recent alternative estimates of Soviet per capita GNP challenge the CIA figures significantly by placing the Soviet economy at somewhere around 25 percent of the US.[12] If the CIA figures were accurate the Soviet economy would have been a maturing industrialized economy, but the reality was that the former Soviet economy provided a standard of living equivalent to a well-developed Third World economy at best. Moreover, if the CIA statistics were correct, then there would not have been any need for a radical economic reform and Gorbachev's rhetoric would have been incomprehensible and unfounded.

Even with revised data international comparisons of per capita GNP systematically overstate the well-being of Soviet citizens. One reason for this bias was that the low quality of Soviet products was not considered. Another reason was that the persistent shortages of goods and the corresponding queuing for even those goods that were available was not reflected in the statistics. And, finally, the per capita GNP statistics do not reveal the low percentage of GNP that went to household consumption in the former Soviet Union. Only about 50 percent of GNP in the former Soviet Union went to household production.[13] Soviet consumers were far worse off than revised statistical estimates indicated.

One significant consequence of these mismeasurement problems was that the military capabilities of the Soviet Union were grossly distorted. If the national income of the former Soviet Union was actually less than a third of the US, the military burden of the empire was much greater than ever estimated by western Sovietologists. Correcting for these alternative calculations of Soviet GNP, and incorporating information from the glasnost era, it is estimated that the military burden represented about 25 percent of GNP in the former Soviet Union.[14] As a result, most western estimates of Soviet military strength were seriously mistaken because the military burden (in terms of the explicit and implicit tax on the population) was understated at the same time that the long-term viability of the Soviet economy was overstated. Correcting the figures challenges previous perceptions concerning the capability of the former Soviet system to engage in a sustained military conflict with the West.[15]

These distortions, though, were not simply the product of poor information and inadequate measurement techniques. The distortions served a very important ideological and interest group function. On the one hand, conservative anti-communists supported the bias toward overestimating Soviet economic and military strength because it reinforced their fears of the impending encroachment of communism throughout the world. The statistics justified large military expenditures to fight the advent of global communism. If the Soviet economy was structurally weak, then the threat of communism would have been rather shallow and would not have justified the military strategy of the Cold War. Only a developing industrial power could supply the economic base and technological innovations that would pose a sustainable threat to western powers. On the other hand, radical intellectuals, even if they despised the Soviet regime, believed in the basic ability of the system of centralized economic planning to promote development. If Soviet economic planning was a failure, then socialism may have been a questionable policy goal to advocate even in more democratic situations. Scholars, intellectuals and politicians of both "left" and "right" persuasion, therefore, possessed an ideological stake in the ability of the Soviet economy to develop and prosper.

These ideas about the efficacy of Soviet economic planning also created an extremely powerful interest group, namely the military-industrial establishment in the West. The military-industrial establishment benefitted directly from the overestimation of Soviet capabilities.[16] Right-wing and left-wing beliefs about the developing Soviet economy provided the needed justification for large appropriations toward armament productions and military research and development. Thus, an iron-triangle was forged of ideas and interests that simply could not, and would not, allow analysis that seriously challenged the Soviet myth of economic success. But, as we have seen, the Soviet system was far from an economic success. More to the point, the Soviet economy may well be the ultimate political economy tragedy of this century.

Concluding Remarks

United States Cold War policy did not contribute to the collapse of communism in the USSR. In fact, Cold War policies may have actually prolonged the Soviet system by affording Soviet leaders the ability to treat economic problems as technological ones for a longer period than otherwise would have been possible by giving Soviet leaders the external enemy they needed to justify the inordinate sacrifices their people had to make to maintain the military burden. At the same time, Cold War policies have distorted the United States economy and strained the public purse.

In the wake of World War II, the United States pursued the twin policies of containment and collective security. George Kennan (1947) argued, in his famous "X" article, that the peculiar mix of Leninist ideology and Russian history posed a serious threat to the West. The Soviet Union's sole intent and purpose was global expansionism. The West, Kennan concluded, must be equally determined and institute a vigilant policy of containment designed to meet head on the Soviet threat to a peaceful and stable world.

In addition, World War II had dealt a serious blow to the American tradition of non-interventionism. Inaccurately referred to as "isolationism," the American tradition of non-intervention was rejected in favor of a policy of collective security to maintain peace. After the alliances of World War II broke down, an anti-Soviet collective security alliance was formed. First, the Truman Doctrine of 1947 pledged United States assistance to friendly nations faced with external aggression, and then in 1949 the North Atlantic Treaty Organization (NATO) was created. NATO was followed by the creation of the Southeast Asia Treaty Organization (SEATO) and the Australia-New Zealand-United States (ANZUS) alliance. In addition, the US made several other bilateral commitments to South Korea, Nationalist China, and Pakistan during the 1950s (See Carpenter, ed., 1989).

The fear of the Soviet threat in combination with the firm belief that the United States was the only country in the immediate aftermath of World War II capable of leading the free world coalition against Soviet aggression, produced an expanding array of global commitments for the United States, and with that the corresponding pressures on the federal budget to meet perceived defense requirements. As I have tried to suggest above, however, a major part of the logic behind the original post-World War II defense strategy was fundamentally flawed in that it was blinded to the structural weaknesses in the Soviet political economy and as a result systematically overstated Soviet capabilities. This was not a benign mistake.

The United States economy has been drastically affected by pursuing these defense policies. A great challenge now faces the US, as Paul Kennedy (1987) states, as to "Whether, in the military/strategical realm, it can preserve a reasonable balance between the nation's perceived defense requirements and the means it possesses to maintain those commitments; and whether as an intimately related point, it can preserve the technological and economic bases of its power from relative erosion in the face of ever-shifting patterns of global production." Kennedy concludes that the United States runs the risk of "imperial overstretch" and decision makers must, therefore, "face the awkward and enduring fact that the sum total of the United States' global interests and obligations is nowadays far larger than the country's power to defend them all simultaneously."

Even now, after so much has changed on the global scene which explodes our past perceptions, it is difficult to find where the so-called "peace dividend" is to be found. Not only did the Cold War strategy threaten the long-term viability of the US economy with "imperial overstretch," but it created the powerful defense industry interest group which has proven almost impossible to break. Large corporations have major defense contracts and employ thousands of individuals, congressional districts have military bases that form the heart of local economies, and millions of individuals work within the military bureaucracy. No politician wants to be responsible for losing the military base or the large government contract in their district or state. The coalition of politicians, beneficiaries and the bureaucracy assures the tyranny of the status quo. Redirecting production from military to civilian demand is a rather daunting task not only for the technological reasons of how one transforms a missile factory into a beer plant, but perhaps even more so for political reasons.

Arguments that the peace dividend will best serve the nation if a new state policy was introduced which deemphasizes defense and instead directs technological development toward solving problems of the environment, public health and community stability, simply by-pass the difficult economic and political problems with government industrial and social policy -- both in terms of the government's ability to achieve its stated aims, and of reversing the policy if it proves faulty once particular interests become entrenched (See, e.g., Markusen and Yudken, 1992). On the other hand, statements by economists who understand the difficulties of government pursuing an effective activist policy, such as Murray Weidenbaum (1991), that the real peace dividend will come from redirecting defense savings in the post-Cold War era away from government-supported consumption and toward the private sector, however correct they are in the abstract, do not adequately address the problem at hand.

Maybe this general failure to adequately address the political and economic problems of the peace dividend on both sides of the political spectrum is because no one (scholar, intellectual or politician) has been able to devise an answer to the difficult problem that entrenched interests present to any existing political economy. Enlightened leaders, a well informed public, or constitutional change do not so much answer the problem as assume it away. The main conclusion to be drawn from the failure of the Thatcher, Reagan and even the Gorbachev periods of proposed change is that political economy reforms within any existing political system that demand a reduced scope for government discretion inevitably stall when the logic of reform confronts the logic of politics. Unfortunately, past choices made under Cold War illusions have structurally distorted the United States economy and weakened its long term viability. If the collapse of communism in the Soviet Union tells us something about the structural failings of the political economy of socialism, then the collapse of state capitalism in the United States should tell us something about the structural shortcomings of the political economy of leviathan and "imperial overstretch."

Notes

This paper draws freely from arguments developed in Boettke, *Why Perestroika Failed: The Politics and Economics of Socialist Transformation* (London: Routledge, 1993).

1. Boris Pinsker, a leading pro-market Soviet intellectual holds the opinion that Reagan's military build-up was the major contributory factor responsible for the break-down of the Soviet empire. This observation is based on a personal conversation with Pinsker on his visit to New York in 1991.

2. Neither does it adequately address the question of the cost to the West of the Cold War. For an examination of this issue see Melvyn Krauss, *How NATO Weakens the West?* (New York: Simon and Schuster, 1986).

3. The idea of Gorbachev as a benevolent liberal reformer became the dominant western perspective after the events of 1989. See, for example, the discussion of Gorbachev in Joshua Muravchik, "Gorbachev's Intellectual Odyssey," *New Republic* (March 5, 1990), pp. 20-25.

4. See the discussion of the economics of German unification in Leslie Lipschitz and Donogh McDonald, eds., *German Unification: Economic Issues* (Washington, DC: International Monetary Fund, 1990).

5. Aggregate measurements of well-being, such as per capita GNP, place the former Soviet Union at about 25% of the corresponding figure in the US economy. See *PlanEcon Report*, 6, No. 52 (December 28, 1990). However, since many goods were not available in the state stores at the official price, such calculations overstate the purchasing power of citizens in a shortage economy.

6. See Mary O. Furner, "Knowing Capitalism: Public Investigation and the Labor Question in the Long Progressive Era," in *The State and Economic Knowledge*, Mary O. Furner and Barry Supple, eds. (New York: Cambridge University Press, 1990), pp. 241-286.

7. For a criticism of the perfect competition model and its impact on economic theorizing, see Israel Kirzner, *Competition and Entrepreneurship* (Chicago: University of Chicago Press, 1973), *Perception, Opportunity and Profit* (Chicago: University of Chicago Press, 1979), and *Discovery and the Capitalist Process* (Chicago: University of Chicago Press, 1985).

8. See William J. Barber, "Government as a Laboratory for Economic Learning in the Years of the Democrat Roosevelt," in *The State and Economic Knowledge*, Mary O. Furner and Barry Supple, eds., pp. 103-137.

9. The founding fathers, however, did not possess such a naive view of democracy. Much of the analysis of modern public choice economics derives inspiration from the work of the founders on constitutional design. See, in particular, James Buchanan and Gordon Tullock, *The Calculus of Consent* (Ann Arbor: University of Michigan Press, 1962).

10. See Richard Ericson, "The Soviet Statistical Debate," Henry Rowen and Charles Wolf, eds., *The Impoverished Superpower* (San Francisco: ICS Press, 1990).

11. *CIA: Handbook of Economic Statistics*, 1987 (Washington, DC: GPO, 1987), pp. 24-25.

12. Soviet per capita GNP in 1990 was estimated to be $5,060 as compared to $21,000 for the US. See *PlanEcon Report*, 6, No. 52 (December 28, 1990), p. 17. Even this figure overstates Soviet GNP because of the unavailability of many goods at official prices. Also see Andres Aslund, "How Small is Soviet National Income?" in *The Impoverished Superpower*, (San Francisco: ICS Press, 1990), pp. 13-61.

13. See Merton Peck and Thomas Richardson, eds., *What Is To Be Done?* (New Haven: Yale University Press, 1991), p.4.

14. See Rowen and Wolf, "Introduction," *The Impoverished Superpower*, (San Francisco: ICS Press, 1990), p. 7.

15. This is not meant to suggest that the former Soviet Union posed no threat to world peace. Clearly, the stock pile of nuclear weapons amassed by the Soviet government could destroy the world several times over, as could those collected in the West. But, two questions immediately emerge concerning Soviet military power when confronted with the revised data. How could the Soviet Union have accomplished its military build-up with such a backward economy, and could these military developments be sustained over time? Without sustainable economic development military power erodes.

16. On the development of the military-industrial establishment in the US, see Seymour Melman, *The Permanent War Economy* (New York: Simon and Schuster, 1974) and *Profits without Production* (New York: Alfred Knopf, 1983) for a critical discussion of the military economy.

References

Carpenter, T., ed. (1989), *Collective Defense or Strategic Independence?*, Lexington, MA: DC Heath and Co.

Finer, Herman (1945), *Road to Reaction*, Chicago: Quadrangle Books.

Hayek, F.A. (1944), *The Road to Serfdom*, Chicago: University of Chicago Press.

Kennan, G. (1947) "The Sources of Soviet Conduct," *Foreign Affairs*, July, pp. 566-582.

Kennedy, Paul (1987), *The Rise and Fall of the Great Powers*, New York: Vintage, pp. 514-515,.

Keynes, John M.(1933), "National Self-Sufficiency," *The Yale Review*, pp. 761-762.

____ (1926), *Laissez-Faire and Communism*, New York: New Republic, Inc., pp. 129-130.

____ (1936 [1964]), *The General Theory of Employment, Interest and Money*, New York: Harcourt Brace Jovanovich, pp. 378-381.

____ (1944), "Letter to Hayek, June 28, 1944," in J.M. Keynes, *Collected Works*, Vol. 27, New York: Cambridge University Press, 1980.

____ (1980), *Collected Works*, Vol. 27, New York: Cambridge University Press, p. 387.

Khanin, Grigory and Vasily Selyunin (1987), "The Elusive Figure," *Novy Mir*, No. 2, translated in *The Current Digest of the Soviet Press*, Vol. 39, No. 25 (1987), pp. 10-12.

Markusen, A. and Yudken, J. (1992), "Building a New Economic Order," *Technology Review*, April, pp. 23-30.

Orwell, George Orwell (1946), *Animal Farm*, New York: Harcourt Brace Jovanovich.

Weidenbaum, Murray (1991), "Policy Decisions for a Post-Cold War Economy," *Business Economics*, Vol. 26, No. 1, pp. 31-33.

10

Estimating Regional Sensitivities to Defense Purchases

Lori L. Taylor

The interrelationships among industries make all industries sensitive to changes in defense purchases. However, some industries, such as those that manufacture arms and ammunition, are clearly more dependent on defense purchases than others. Therefore, employment is more sensitive to changes in defense spending in some industries than in other industries. Further, given the variation in sensitivity to defense purchases among industries and the variation in industry composition among the states, one would expect to find that the impact of changes in defense purchases on employment varies greatly from state to state.

Differential economic effects from defense purchases can have a profound influence on policy for numerous reasons. First, defense purchases have a public works dimension that makes them tools of redistributive policy as well as defense policy. Therefore, legislators from regions with economies that are highly sensitive to defense purchases would seem less likely to favor cuts in defense purchases, *ceteris paribus*, than would legislators from less-sensitive regions. Given these tendencies, one can easily envision situations in which the redistributive effects of changes in defense policy carry more weight in the decision-making process than do the defense impacts of such changes. Further, information about the distribution of economic consequences may be used to direct retraining assistance or alternative aid. Finally, an awareness of defense impacts reduces the noise embodied in employment changes and facilitates distinguishing between sectoral adjustments and business cycles.

Because the distribution of employment impacts arising from changes in defense spending can have so many policy implications, I use input-output analysis to estimate the degree of defense sensitivity for each major industry and each state. I measure the degree of defense sensitivity for each industry by the effect on employment in each industry of a uniform, 1-percent change in real defense purchasing. I then use the measures of industry sensitivity, together with data on industry composition by state, to estimate the degree of defense sensitivity for each state. I find that the industrial composition of Connecticut makes it the state that is most sensitive to defense spending and, therefore, most vulnerable to defense cuts. Similarly, the industrial composition of Delaware makes it the state that is least sensitive to defense purchases. I also illustrate the intrastate variations in defense sensitivity by using data on the industry composition of metropolitan statistical areas in Texas.

Input-Output Analysis

Input-output analysis is an analytic framework that describes the inter-relationship between industries as a system of simultaneous equations.[1] Each equation represents a single industry. The equation for any given industry describes the total value of that industry's output as the sum of the value of that industry's output that is sold to consumers, the value of that industry's output that is used in the industry's own production process, and the value of that industry's output that is sold as an input to every other industry. For example, the 1987 input-output tables of the United States indicate that 83 percent of the output of the aircraft industry was consumed, 12 percent was used in the production of other aircraft, and 2 percent was used as an input by firms providing transportation services.

Because the inputs of one industry come from the outputs of another, input-output tables enable users to trace the ways in which each industry uses the products of every other industry. For example, the input-output table described above also indicates that to produce $1000 worth of output, the aircraft and parts industry requires $26 worth of electronics, $10 worth of rubber and miscellaneous plastics, and $51 worth of business services.

Solving the system of more than seventy equations simultaneously yields the amount of output from each industry that is needed to satisfy the demands of consumers and industry. By changing consumer demand, solving the system of equations again, and comparing the industry output across the two cases, one finds the change in each industry's output that would be necessary to satisfy the change in demand.

As with any economic model, input-output analysis relies on a number of simplifying assumptions to make the complex national economy tractable. Input-output analysis assumes a fixed relationship between factor inputs and constant returns to scale, so that if manufacturing $1's worth of apparel requires 50 cents' worth of textiles, then manufacturing $2's worth of apparel would require $1's worth of textiles. It also implicitly assumes that labor supply is perfectly elastic, so that all industries can increase output without changing relative prices for goods or factors. These assumptions, although reasonable approximations of how the economy responds to marginal changes in demand, become less reasonable as the size of the demand shock increases. Therefore, while input-output analysis can indicate the relative sensitivity of various industries to small shocks in final demand, the technique would prove an unreliable indicator of the consequences of wholesale reform.

Despite its limitations, the input-output approach yields a more accurate picture of defense sensitivity than would an analysis of defense contracts for several reasons. Contract data are notoriously misleading because they indicate only the firms that won contracts, not the locations of the manufacturing plants. For example, the contract data can indicate that a company in St. Louis, Missouri, has won a contract, even though the actual work affects Fort Worth, Texas. The timing of contracts can also make contract data noisy and misleading. Although many contracts result in more than one year's worth of work, the contract data record contracts when they are awarded, not when the work is actually done. Therefore, a firm could work for ten years on a defense project, but the project would appear in the data only one year. Further, contract data do not provide information on subcontracting or other indirect effects. Indirect effects represent half the employment impact of any change in defense purchases. Finally, if defense contractors lose their military customer, many will try to pick up business in civilian aspects of their industry. For example, if a firm in the electronics industry loses a defense contract, other electronics firms may lose business to the increased competition for civilian customers. Therefore, job losses from cuts in defense purchasing affect all firms in an industry. An increase in defense purchases affects all firms in an industry for similar reasons.

The Pattern of Defense Purchases

The input-output table of the United States indicates the distribution of defense purchases by the federal government. In 1987, the federal government spent almost $184 billion, or 4 percent of gross domestic product (GDP), to purchase a wide variety of commodities for the national defense. Table 10.1 presents the major components of defense purchases (expenditures excluding payroll).

The government was a major presence in some industries. The $41.5 billion spent on aircraft for defense purposes represented 23 percent of total defense purchases and 49 percent of total aircraft production. The government was also a big customer for firms that produced ordnance or communication equipment. Defense purchases consumed more than 77 percent of total ordnance production and almost 32 percent of total communications-equipment production. Other industries in which defense purchases were disproportionately large produced materials-handling machinery, miscellaneous machinery, and ships, boats, and tanks.

In many commodity markets, however, defense purchases made the U.S. government a very small player. Direct defense purchases of primary iron and steel accounted for only 0.2 percent of total production. Purchases of food and tobacco represented less than 0.05 percent. Defense purchases from some industries, such as radio and television broadcasting, were insignificant.

However, given the complex interrelationships among industries, the distribution of direct defense expenditures reveals little about industry sensitivity to changes in defense purchases. Some industries that sell little directly to the defense department are exposed to defense cuts indirectly through their customers and suppliers.

Measures of Industry Sensitivity

I measure industry sensitivity to defense purchases as the absolute value of the percentage change in industry output and employment that the input-output table indicates would result from a uniform 1-percent cut in defense purchases.[2] Of course, no one believes that uniform changes in defense purchasing are realistic, but this approach does provide a benchmark estimate of general defense sensitivity.

Not surprisingly, the industries that are most sensitive to defense purchasing sell the lion's share of their output to the defense department. The ordnance industry would lose just over 0.8 percent of its employment if defense purchases were cut by a uniform 1

TABLE 10.1
The Major Components of Defense Purchases in 1987

Industry	Purchases (in millions)	% of Total Production
Construction	10,371.0	1.74
Ordnance	21,702.0	77.04
Food and Tobacco	171.0	0.05
Apparel	463.0	0.73
Miscellaneous Fabricated Textile Products	129.0	0.74
Paper and Allied Products, excluding Containers	107.0	0.13
Printing and Publishing	728.0	0.87
Drugs, Cleaning and Toilet Paper Items	525.0	0.76
Petroleum Refining	1,136.0	0.81
Rubber and Miscellaneous Plastics	337.0	0.40
Primary Iron and Steel	117.0	0.17
Heating and Plumbing Products	544.0	1.24
Screw Machine Products	259.0	0.82
Other Fabricated Metals	436.0	0.93
Engines and Turbines	748.0	5.13
Materials Handling Machinery	1,091.0	13.41
Metal-Working Machinery	250.0	1.22
Special Industrial Machinery	114.0	0.68
General Industrial Machinery	423.0	1.73
Miscellaneous Non-electrical Machinery	2,696.0	14.75
Office Computing and Accounting Machines	3,644.0	6.02
Electric Industrial Equipment	705.0	2.18
Radio, TV and Communications Equipment	25,594.0	31.88
Electronic Components and Accessories	3,330.0	6.79
Miscellaneous Electrical Machinery	461.0	2.25
Motor Vehicles and Equipment	2,670.0	1.31
Aircraft and Parts	41,549.0	48.86
Other Transportation Equipment	7,323.0	24.86
Scientific, Ophthalmic & Photographic Instruments	2,221.0	3.92
Miscellaneous Manufacturing	140.0	0.42
Transportation and Warehousing	9,102.0	3.58
Communications, excluding Radio and TV	2,057.0	1.55
Private Utilities	2,358.0	0.91
Wholesale and Retail Trade	4,404.0	0.52
Real Estate and Rental	363.0	0.05
Hotels, Personal and Repair Services	962.0	0.85
Business Services	22,287.0	3.93

(Continues)

TABLE 10.1 (Contd.)
The Major Components of Defense Purchases in 1987

Industry	Purchases (in millions)	% of Total Production
Eating and Drinking Places	263.0	0.12
Auto Repair and Services	3,863.0	3.72
Amusements	358.0	0.49
Health, Education, and Social Services	720.0	0.15

Source: Survey of Current Business, April 1992, pp. 64-71

percent. The aircraft manufacturing industry would lose almost 0.6 percent of its employment. Other highly sensitive industries manufacture communication equipment, electronic components, ships, and tanks. These industries are more than seven times as sensitive to defense purchases as the national average. Figure 10.1 illustrates the defense-purchasing sensitivity for selected industries. Appendix 1 provides a complete listing of the industry effects.

Industries that supply the most-sensitive industries are moderately sensitive to defense purchases. Manufacturing of engines and turbines -- suppliers to the aircraft and ship, boat and tank industries -- are more than three times as sensitive as the national average. Manufacturers of nonferrous metals -- such as aluminum -- are almost four times as sensitive as the national average. However, manufacturers of electrical and wiring equipment are only slightly more sensitive to defense purchases than the national average.

Steel and iron manufacturing is a striking example of an industry that produces little for the defense department directly but is moderately sensitive to defense purchases because it supplies the defense contractors. The government buys only 0.2 percent of total iron and steel production to use for defense purposes. A 1-percent cut in those purchases would have a negligible effect on the industry. However, purchases by the five most-sensitive industries (ordnance, aircraft, communications equipment, electronics, and ships and tanks) represent 6 percent of total iron and steel production. A 1-percent cut in purchases by just those five industries would have thirty times the effect of a cut in direct defense purchases alone. When all the interrelationships among industries are considered, steel and iron

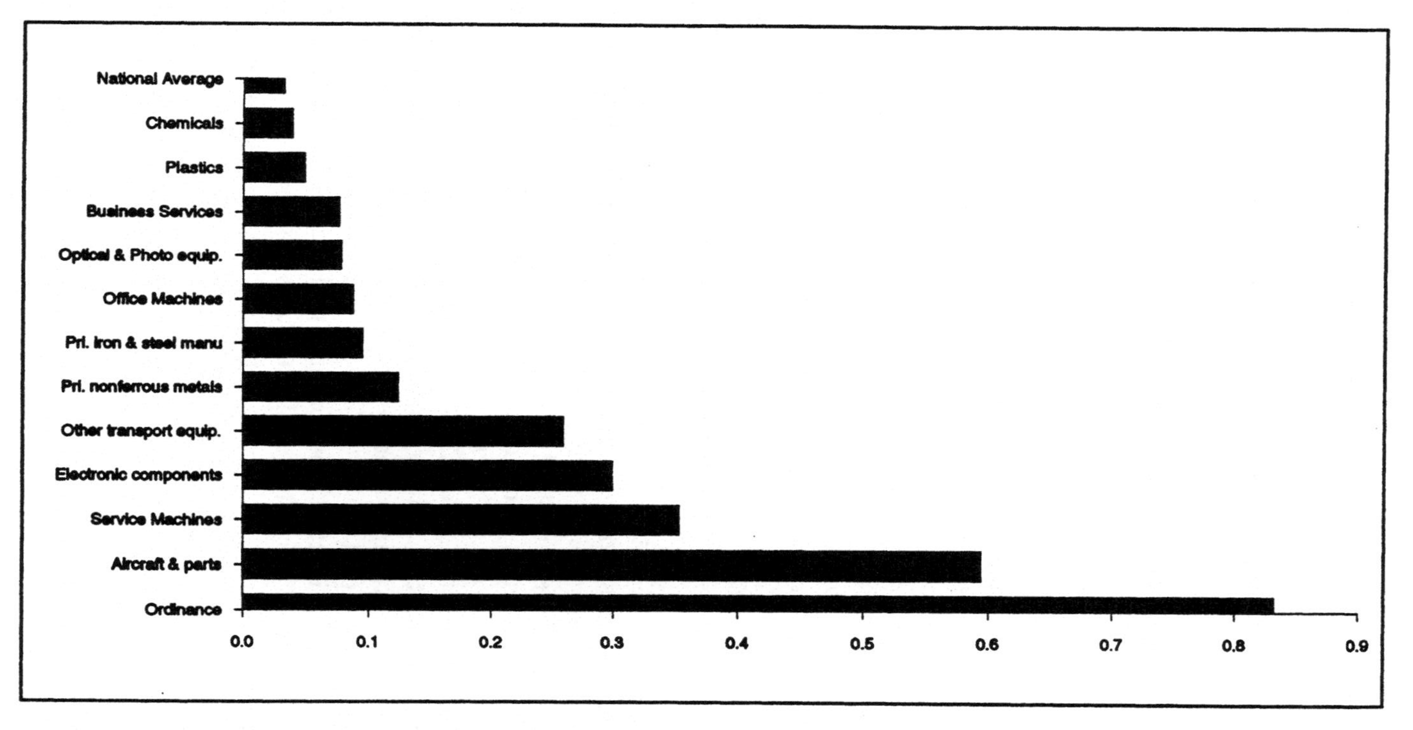

FIGURE 10.1 Defense Sensitivity For Selected Industries

manufacturers are almost three times as sensitive to defense purchases as the national average.

Even industries that sell little to the U.S. Department of Defense or its suppliers are sensitive to defense purchases through multiplier effects. If defense purchasing fell, demand for consumer goods and services would fall slightly while the former employees of defense-related industries looked for new work. For example, retail and wholesale trade stands to lose 0.02 percent of its employment if real defense purchases decrease by 1 percent, making that industry roughly two-thirds as sensitive to defense purchasing as the national average.

Across industries, the U.S. economy is relatively insensitive to defense purchasing. Using the benchmark estimates, the U.S. would lose slightly more than 0.03 percent of its employment if all defense purchases declined by 1 percent. The low level of defense sensitivity nationwide is completely consistent with the small role that defense purchases play in the national economy. Recall that in 1987 near the peak of President Reagan's defense build-up, defense purchases accounted for only 4 percent of gross domestic product.

State Sensitivity

Although the nation as a whole is relatively insensitive to defense purchasing, sensitivity among industries varies substantially. Because industrial composition varies from state to state, sensitivity among states also varies substantially. States with high concentrations of ordnance or aircraft manufacturing are much more sensitive to defense purchases than are states without such concentrations.

State estimates of sensitivity to defense purchases can be derived by combining the industry measures of defense sensitivity with information on the industrial composition of employment in each state if one assumes that all states use the same production technologies.[3] For example, if the input-output table indicates that national employment in aircraft manufacturing would decline 0.6 percent if defense purchases declined 1 percent, then by assumption, Texas employment in aircraft manufacturing would also decline 0.6 percent. The best estimate of total employment losses for each state would be the sum of the expected losses in each industry within that state, and each state's sensitivity to defense purchases would be the total employment losses through defense cuts divided by the state's total

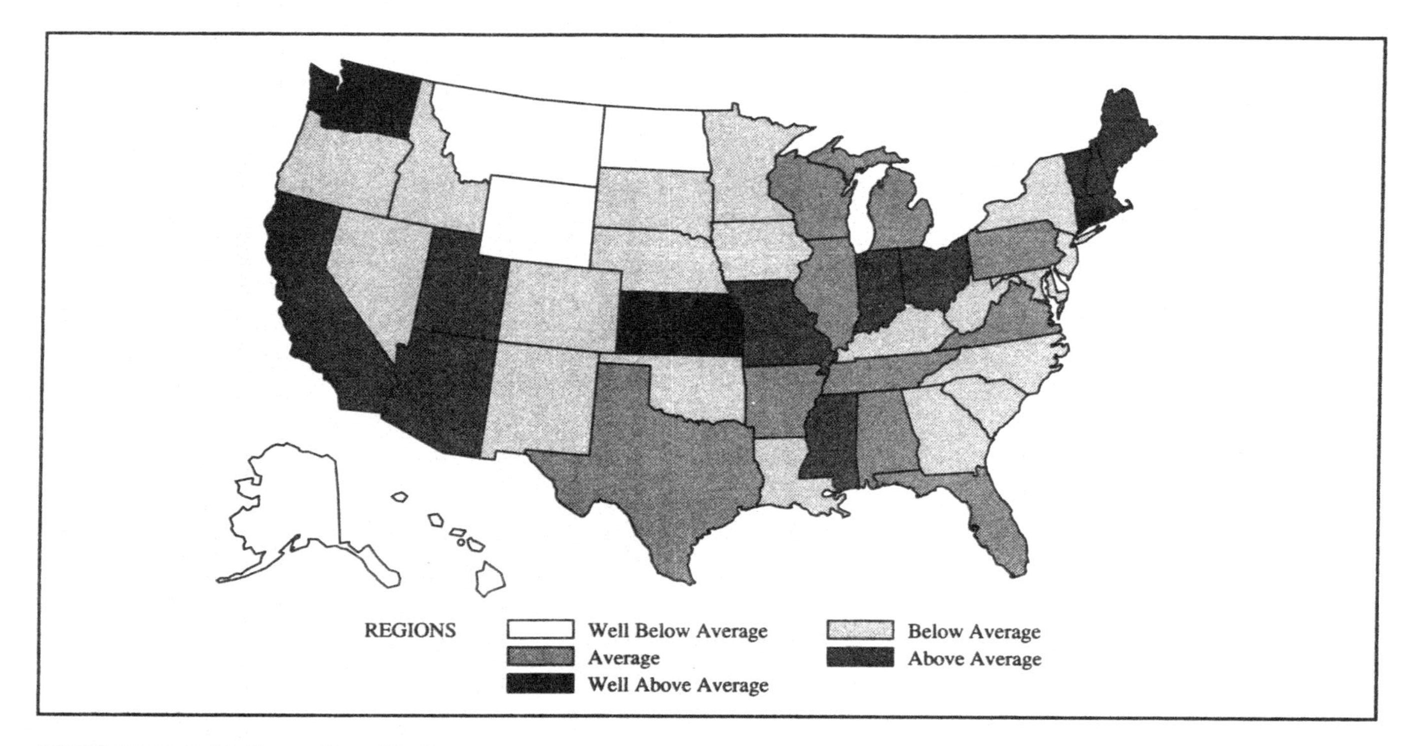

FIGURE 10.2 Defense Sensitivity

nonfarm employment. Figure 10.2 illustrates the defense sensitivity of the states. The supporting data are in Appendix 2.

The relatively high concentrations of transportation equipment manufacturing in Connecticut, Washington, and Kansas make these three states the most sensitive to defense purchases. Connecticut, which is the most defense-sensitive state in the union, is 60 percent more sensitive than the national average. Washington and Kansas are more than 25 percent more sensitive than the national average.

At the other end of the spectrum are Alaska, Delaware, and Wyoming. These states are one-third less sensitive than the national average because their economies have only a small proportion of industries that are highly sensitive to defense purchases. For example, the aircraft and parts industry represents less than 0.01 percent of nonfarm employment in Delaware. Montana, North Dakota, and Hawaii also have state economies that are well below average in defense sensitivity.

Between the two extremes are states with economies that are more similar to the national economy. The states that are above average have somewhat elevated concentrations of employment in highly sensitive industries or in those industries' major suppliers. States that are below average have relatively low concentrations of employment in these industries. For example, the employment share of electronics manufacturers is at least twice the national average in Arizona, California, Indiana, Massachusetts, New Hampshire, and Vermont. Manufacturers of aircraft and ships, boats, and tanks are disproportionately represented in the economies of all the above-average states except Massachusetts, New Hampshire, Ohio, and Vermont. Indiana, Ohio, and Rhode Island have relatively large concentrations of employment in industries that supply the defense contractors, such as primary and fabricated metals. In contrast, the states that are below average in defense sensitivity generally have relatively high concentrations of employment in industries that are only weakly sensitive to defense purchases, such as food or textiles manufacturing.

Digressing slightly, Figure 10.2 also illustrates an interesting geographical pattern to the distribution of defense sensitivities. As a general rule, states in the Upper Midwest are less sensitive than states in the South and Mid-Atlantic regions, which in turn are less sensitive than states in New England.

Intrastate Sensitivities

Although defense sensitivity is negligible in many states, specific communities within those states might still experience significant job losses through defense purchasing cuts. Analysis at the state level blurs significant employment changes at the local level. Some communities would experience job losses significantly greater than their state's average. Other communities may lose no jobs at all. The state employment effects are better estimates of local employment effects when all parts of the state are integrated into a single economy. In states with many regional economies, such as California or Texas, local economic effects may differ dramatically from the state average.

To illustrate the potential for considerable differences in defense sensitivity within states, consider the three largest metropolitan statistical areas (MSAs) in Texas -- Houston, Dallas, and Fort Worth. The economies of the three MSAs are very different. Stereotypically, Houston has an energy and petrochemicals economy, Dallas has an electronics and banking economy, and Fort Worth has an industrial manufacturing economy.

Applying the estimates of industry sensitivity to the industrial composition of the three MSAs reveals that they also have very different sensitivities to defense purchases (Table 10.2). Fort Worth is more than twice as sensitive to defense purchases as Houston and nearly twice as sensitive as Dallas. In turn, Dallas is at least 30 percent more sensitive than Houston. Based on its industrial composition, Fort Worth is more than twice as sensitive to defense

TABLE 10.2
Defense Sensitivities for Metropolitan Areas in Texas

City	Employment	Sensitivity
Houston	1386.9	0.028
Dallas	1309.8	0.037
Fort Worth	533.1	0.071

Source: Bureau of Labor Statistics and author's calculations.

spending as Texas as a whole and at least 30 percent more sensitive to defense spending than Connecticut.

An examination of the cities' economies quickly reveals the reasons for this striking disparity. Of the three MSAs, Houston has the smallest concentration of employment in the most defense-sensitive industries. Only 2 percent of Houston's labor force produces transportation equipment, electronics, instruments, or fabricated metals.[4] In contrast, almost 9 percent of Dallas' and 11 percent of Fort Worth's employment is in these durable goods industries. Fort Worth is more sensitive than Dallas because most of its manufacturing is in aircraft and parts, while most of Dallas' manufacturing is in electronics. As indicated in Figure 10.1, the aircraft and parts industry is almost twice as sensitive to defense purchases as the electronic components industry.

Conclusions

Because it represents only 4 percent of GNP, even substantial changes in defense purchases could have negligible effects on the national economy. Input-output analysis indicates that a uniform 1-percent cut in defense purchasing would reduce employment nationally by less than 0.03 percent. Therefore, the nation's sensitivity to defense purchases is relatively low. However, despite the nation's relative insensitivity to defense purchases, there are industries, states, and communities that are sensitive.

Some sensitive industries seem obvious. The ordnance industry, which manufactures arms and ammunition and sells 77 percent of its output to the defense department, is more than 20 times more sensitive to changes in defense purchases than the national average. However, other industries that sell little to the defense department become sensitive to defense purchases through multiplier effects. In fact, those interrelationships between industries make all industries at least a little sensitive to defense purchases.

Because of their diversification, states and cities are not nearly as sensitive to defense purchases as are many industries. However, differences in industrial composition make some states and communities more sensitive to defense purchases than others. At the two extremes, Delaware is only one-third as sensitive to defense purchases as Connecticut. Based on industrial composition, Fort

Worth is more than twice as sensitive to defense purchases as Texas and more than two and one-half times as sensitive to defense purchases as Houston.

Notes

The views expressed in this article are those of the author and should not be attributed to the Federal Reserve Bank of Dallas or the Federal Reserve System. The author thanks Kelly A. Whealan for research assistance.

1. For a more detailed discussion of input-output analysis, see Miller and Blair (1985).

2. The relative magnitude of the sensitivity measure is unaffected by the sign of the demand change.

3. For tractability, I combine some industry categories to create a set of twenty-nine industries that are common to most states. For example, the defense sensitivity of the furniture and fixtures industry equals the sensitivity of the household furnishings industry plus the sensitivity of the other furniture and fixtures industry, weighted by the national employment in the two industries. All combinations are consistent with standard industry classifications.

4. Ordnance is not an industry category that is reported at the metropolitan level. Some ordnance employment is classified in transportation equipment.

Appendix 1

Estimates of Defense Sensitivity by Commodity/Industry

Industry	Employment	Change in Employment	% Change in Employment
Forestry and Fisheries	4.0	0.001	0.028
Agricultural, Forestry & Fisheries	80.0	0.009	0.011
Metal Ores Mining	20.0	0.023	0.111
Coal Mining	161.8	0.080	0.049
Oil and Gas Extraction	261.3	0.129	0.049
Stone and Clay Mining	77.6	0.027	0.034
Chemical and Fertilizer Mining	16.7	0.008	0.046
Construction	4922.1	1.323	0.027
Ordnance	76.5	0.637	0.832
Food and Tobacco	1620.4	0.050	0.003
Fabrics, Yarn, and Thread	729.7	0.190	0.026
Misc. Textiles & Floor Coverings	50.9	0.011	0.022
Apparel	906.5	0.095	0.010
Misc. Fabricated Textile Products	192.3	0.058	0.030
Lumber and Wood Products, excluding Containers	712.8	0.262	0.037
Wood Containers	41.9	0.011	0.025
Household Furniture	305.4	0.038	0.012
Other Furniture and Fixtures	210.4	0.049	0.023
Paper and Allied Products, excluding Containers	474.4	0.152	0.032
Paperboard Containers & Boxes	201.8	0.066	0.033
Printing and Publishing	1506.2	0.429	0.028
Chemicals	278.9	0.111	0.040
Plastics and Synthetic Materials	168.2	0.083	0.049
Drugs, Cleaning and Toilet Paper Items	372.9	0.044	0.118
Paint and Allied Products	210.7	0.088	0.042
Petroleum Refining	163.9	0.056	0.034

Appendix 1 (Contd.)

Estimates of Defense Sensitivity by Commodity/Industry

Industry	Employ-ment	Change in Em-ployment	% Change in Employ-ment
Rubber and Misc. Plastics	843.3	0.564	0.067
Leather Tanning and Finishing	14.1	0.002	0.015
Footwear and Other Leather	111.5	0.010	0.009
Glass and Glass Products	153.6	0.062	0.040
Stone and Clay Products	656.3	0.275	0.042
Primary Iron and Steel	438.4	0.418	0.095
Primary Non-ferrous Metals	341.0	0.426	0.125
Metal Containers	55.4	0.010	0.018
Heating and Plumbing Products	615.5	0.302	0.049
Screw Machine Products	435.1	0.350	0.080
Other Fabricated Metals	219.4	0.180	0.082
Engines and Turbines	90.5	0.094	0.104
Farm and Garden Machinery	93.6	0.011	0.011
Construction & Mining Machinery	133.7	0.024	0.018
Materials Handling Machinery	57.7	0.088	0.153
Metal-Working Machinery	311.4	0.222	0.071
Special Industrial Machinery	151.5	0.022	0.015
General Industrial Machinery	227.1	0.165	0.073
Misc. Non-electrical Machinery	305.6	0.703	0.230
Office Computing and Accounting Machines	462.0	0.405	0.088
Service Industry Machines	177.2	0.040	0.022
Electric Industrial Equipment	279.6	0.193	0.069
Household Appliances	135.9	0.018	0.013
Electric Wiring/Lighting Equipment	195.1	0.075	0.038
Radio, TV and Communications Equipment	82.9	0.293	0.353
Electronic Components and Accessories	602.7	1.809	0.300

Appendix 1 (Contd.)

Estimates of Defense Sensitivity by Commodity/Industry

Industry	Employ-ment	Change in Em-ployment	% Change in Employ-ment
Misc. Electrical Machinery	93.7	0.049	0.052
Motor Vehicles and Equipment	866.6	0.224	0.026
Aircraft and Parts	678.2	4.033	0.595
Other Transportation Equipment	472.3	1.225	0.259
Scientific, Ophthalmic, and Photographic Instruments	511.1	0.401	0.078
Miscellaneous Manufacturing	370.5	0.056	0.015
Transportation and Warehousing	3163.0	2.079	0.066
Communications excluding, Radio and TV	902.3	0.322	0.036
Radio and TV Broadcasting	225.4	0.052	0.023
Private Utilities	925.6	0.368	0.040
Wholesale and Retail Trade	20637.6	4.590	0.022
Finance and Insurance	3271.0	0.456	0.014
Real Estate and Rental	1247.0	0.115	0.009
Hotels, Personal and Repair Services	2164.1	0.579	0.027
Business Services	6399.7	4.917	0.077
Eating and Drinking Places	6105.8	0.744	0.012
Auto Repair and Services	795.4	0.389	0.049
Amusements	221.4	0.046	0.021
Health, Education, and Social Services	11375.8	0.311	0.003
Government Enterprises	3138.0	0.943	0.006

Appendix 2

Estimates of Defense Sensitivity by State

Alabama	0.0316	Montana	0.0214
Alaska	0.0196	Nebraska	0.0250
Arizona	0.0369	Nevada	0.0245
Arkansas	0.0307	New Hampshire	0.0357
California	0.0388	New Jersey	0.0294
Colorado	0.0303	New Mexico	0.0245
Connecticut	0.0538	New York	0.0278
Delaware	0.0172	North Carolina	0.0277
Florida	0.0310	North Dakota	0.0218
Georgia	0.0301	Ohio	0.0370
Hawaii	0.0222	Oklahoma	0.0278
Idaho	0.0239	Oregon	0.0281
Illinois	0.0317	Pennsylvania	0.0327
Indiana	0.0400	Rhode Island	0.0363
Iowa	0.0285	South Carolina	0.0281
Kansas	0.0422	South Dakota	0.0238
Kentucky	0.0291	Tennessee	0.0311
Louisiana	0.0277	Texas	0.0311
Maine	0.0346	Utah	0.0353
Maryland	0.0275	Vermont	0.0366
Massachusetts	0.0356	Virginia	0.0306
Michigan	0.0316	Washington	0.0495
Minnesota	0.0293	West Virginia	0.0242
Mississippi	0.0352	Wisconsin	0.0328
Missouri	0.0357	Wyoming	0.0189

References

Interindustry Economics Division (1992), "Annual Input-Output Accounts of the U.S. Economy, 1987," *Survey of Current Business*, Vol. 72 (April), pp. 55-71.

Miller, Ronald E., and Peter D. Blair (1985), *Input-Output Analysis: Foundations and Extensions*, Englewood Cliffs, NJ: Prentice-Hall.

U.S. Department of Commerce, Bureau of Economic Analysis (1987), *Annual Employment Averages by S.I.C.*.

U.S. Department of Labor, Bureau of Labor Statistics (1987), *Employment and Wages: Annual Averages 1987*, Bulletin 2370 Washington, D.C.: Government Printing Office, March.

PART FOUR

Effects on Less Developed Countries

11

Defense Spending and Economic Growth in Developing Countries

Basudeb Biswas

Economic implications of defense spending can be studied from different perspectives. One basic concept of economics is that given our technical knowledge and endowment of resources, more production of one commodity results in less production of some other commodity. More real spending in the military sphere leads to a reduction of funds for production of civilian goods. This basic fact is reflected in high hopes of receiving a "peace dividend" from less spending on defense following the end of the Cold War. According to the *Human Development Report* (United Nations Development Programme, 1992), worldwide military spending has been falling in the late 1980s as shown in Table 11.1.

Industrial countries decreased their total military spending from about $838 billion in 1987 to $762 billion in 1990 in constant 1988 U.S. dollars. The corresponding figures for the developing countries are $132 billion in 1987 and $123 billion in 1990.

The same analysis that applies to the choice between military goods and civilian goods can also be applied to the choice between production for current consumption and production for future consumption. Defense spending cannot contribute to a nation's ability to produce more economic goods and services in the future. More public expenditure in the military sector leads to crowding out of private investment and less investment on public goods like health, education, and scientific research. Thus, from both the short-run and the long-

TABLE 11.1
Trends in Global Military Spending

	Developing Countries	Industrial Countries	World	Developing Countries as % of World
Military Expenditures (US$ Billions)				
1960	35	385	420	8.3
1980	137	618	755	18.1
1984	155	750	905	17.1
1987	132	838	970	13.6
1990	123	762	885	13.9
Annual Growth Rates (%)				
1960-70	7.9	3.5	4.0	
1980-90	-1.1	2.1	1.6	
1980-84	3.1	5.0	4.6	
1984-87	-5.2	3.8	2.3	
1987-90	-2.3	-3.1	-3.0	

Source: United Nations Development Programme, *Human Development Report*, (New York: Oxford University Press, 1992).

run points of view a decline in military spending will attain the primary objective of development, that is, to benefit people.

A possible beneficial effect of defense expenditure lies in its role in creating effective demand when there is slack in the economy. Within the Keynesian framework of macroeconomic analysis, government expenditure on goods and services including defense is an important force in the determination of output and employment. From this perspective, military spending or any other form of government spending has the potential of achieving full employment output.

The approach of this study about the impact of military expenditures on economic growth is somewhat different from those mentioned above. Treating defense expenditures as autonomous, mainly determined by strategic consideration and threat and security, one can argue that defense expenditures may have developmental side effects. The argument runs in the following manner. The military is an organized sector and helps building of the infrastructures and contributes to technological progress. The military sector helps in the process of modernization through establishment of allocative efficiency improving institution. The civilian sector gets the benefits of the economic "spin-off" from the military sector. It is also hypothesized that factor productivities may be greater in the military sector than in the civilian sector. In an earlier work, Biswas and Ram (1986) focused on this dimension of the relation between military expenditure and economic growth and estimated parameters within a production function framework. Results obtained in that analysis were compared with those of Rothschild (1977), Benoit (1978), Frederiksen and Looney (1982), Lim (1983), and Deger and Sen (1983), and Leontief and Duchin (1983). The Biswas and Ram study was based on data for the periods 1960-70 and 1970-77, and a sample of 58 less-developed countries was taken. The main objective of this study is replication of the empirical part of the earlier study. The present study is based on a sample of 74 LDCs and covers the period from 1981 to 1989 during the first part of which there was an increase in military spending and a decrease in the second half (Table 11.1).

The main point emerging from this work is that, in contrast with the results reported in Biswas and Ram (1986), the defense outlays seem to have a positive effect on economic growth for 1981-89.

Evidence in the Conventional Framework

We start with a simple neoclassical production function in which labor (L), capital (K), and military spending (M) enter as "inputs" into a single aggregated output (Y). By taking total derivatives and manipulating the expression, one can derive the following growth equation:

$$\dot{Y} = \beta_0 + \beta_1\left(\frac{I}{Y}\right) + \beta_2\dot{L} + \beta_3\dot{M} + U \ , \tag{1}$$

where $\dot{Y}$ is the annual rate of growth of total output (GDP), I/Y is the investment-output ratio, $\dot{L}$ *and* $\dot{M}$ are, respectively, the annual rates of growth of the labor force and the military expenditure variables, and U is the classical stochastic disturbance term. β_1 reflects the marginal product of capital, and β_2 and β_3 are the elasticities of output with respect to labor and military expenditures. Equation (1) is used as the basic empirical equation in this section.

The sample covers 74 countries, and the period extends from 1981 through 1989.[1] Following the World Bank's classification, low-income and middle-income LDCs are treated separately, and pooled sample estimates are also reported.[2]

TABLE 11.2
Results on the Relation Between Military Expenditures and Economic Growth in LDCs, 1981-89: Conventional Models[a]

	$\frac{I}{Y}$	$\dot{L}$	$\dot{M}$	R^2
1981-89				
Full sample	0.121**	0.568*	0.081	0.20
(N = 74)	(2.977)	(1.743)	(3.036)	
Low-income LDCs	0.146**	-0.472	0.052	0.26
(N = 30)	(2.090)	(-0.697)	(2.237)	
Middle-income LDCs	0.117*	0.526	0.229**	0.30
(N = 44)	(1.940)	(1.337)	(3.074)	

[a]Dependent variable is the average annual rate of growth of GDP over the period. A constant term is included in all regressions, but its estimates are not reported. Numbers in parentheses are t-statistics.

*Significant at the 10% level.

**Significant at least at the 5% level.

Source: Author's calculations

The estimates in Table 11.2 indicate that defense expenditure has a significantly positive effect on economic growth. This is in contrast with the result of the earlier study by Biswas and Ram (1986). However, when one looks at the estimates for the low-income and the middle-income groups separately, the quantitative effect is much less in the low-income countries.[3]

Military Expenditures and Economic Growth: An Augmented Neoclassical Model

We briefly mentioned some hypotheses about the manner in which increased defense spending may affect growth favorably or unfavorably. Most researchers probably recognize two important mechanisms through which military expenditures may affect economic growth: (a) the military sector may, for a variety of reasons, generate positive or negative externalities for the rest of the economy, and (b) there may be important factor productivity differences. The conventional framework represented in equation (1) can be rationalized in terms of an "external effect," but it cannot throw light on a possible productivity differential. The model described below was specified by Feder in the context of a study of the role of exports in growth.[4] The Feder model has been adapted as a two-sector framework to assess the externality effect of military expenditures and the factor productivity variation between the military and the civilian sectors. The model is built on the neoclassical production-function framework and leads to a linear regression equation similar to the conventional specifications. The basic features of the model have been explained in Biswas and Ram (1986) and are briefly mentioned here.

In contrast with a one-sector framework of the conventional model, the economy is now divided into two sectors. The military sector output is designated as M and the civilian sector output is designated as C. Assume that labor (L) and capital (K) are the only inputs in each sector. The relative marginal products of labor and capital may differ across the two sectors and the size of the military sector output may act as an "externality" factor for the civilian sector. The basic equations can be written as follows:

$$Y = C + M \tag{2a}$$

$$C = C\,(L_c\,, K_c\,, M) \tag{2b}$$

$$M = M(L_m\,, K_m) \tag{2c}$$

where the lowercase subscripts c and m denote sectoral inputs. Postulating that the total input usage is given,

$$L_c + L_m = L \quad \text{and} \tag{3c}$$

$$K_c + K_m = K \tag{3d}$$

Using input subscripts to denote partial derivatives of the production functions with respect to the inputs, let

$$\frac{M_L}{C_L} = \frac{M_k}{C_K} = (1 + \delta) \tag{4}$$

Equation (4) indicates that the ratio of respective marginal factor productivities in the two sectors deviates from unity by a factor δ. $C_m\ (=\frac{\partial c}{\partial m})$ would represent the marginal externality effect of military output on the civilian sector. If $C_m > 0$ and/or $\delta > 0$, increased military output will imply a higher rate of growth of total output Y, which is the sum of M and C for a given usage of L and K. Taking the total differentials of equations (2a), (2b), (2c), (3c), and (3d) one can write the following:

$$dY = dC + dM \tag{5a}$$

$$dC = C_L dL_c + C_k dK_c + C_m dM \tag{5b}$$

$$dM = M_L dL_m + M_k dK_m \tag{5c}$$

$$dL_c + dL_m = dL \tag{6a}$$

$$dK_c + dK_m = dK \tag{6b}$$

As explained by Biswas and Ram (1986), the model yields the following econometric specifications:

$$\frac{dY}{Y} = C_k \frac{I}{Y} + C_L \frac{dL}{Y} + (\frac{\delta}{1+\delta} + C_m) \frac{dM}{Y} \tag{7}$$

$$\dot{Y} = \alpha(\frac{I}{Y}) + \beta\ (\dot{L}) + [\frac{\delta}{1+\delta} + C_m][\dot{M}\ \frac{M}{Y}] \tag{8}$$

In equation (8), as in equation(1), a dot over a variable denotes its rate of growth, and $\frac{I}{Y}$ *and* $\frac{M}{Y}$ are the conventional notations for the ratios of investment and military spending to the total output.[5] Equation (8) enables a test of hypothesis that both C_m and δ are zero. In that case, the coefficient of $\dot{M}\ (\frac{M}{Y})$ is zero and the expression reduces to the standard growth equation. To estimate separately the externality effect C_m and the relative factor productivity differential δ, further manipulation is needed. Making one simplifying assumption that the elasticity of civilian output with respect to military output is constant, one gets the following form

$$\dot{Y} = \alpha\ (\frac{I}{Y}) + \beta(\dot{L}) + (\frac{\delta}{1+\delta})[\dot{M}(\frac{M}{Y})] + \theta\dot{M} \tag{9}$$

where θ is the elasticity of civilian output with respect to military output, that is, $\theta = C_M\ (\frac{M}{C})$. Equation (9) allows the externality effect C_m and the relative factor productivity differential δ to be separately identified.

Average variable values for the period 1981-89 are used. Average growth of real military expenditures is derived by fitting an exponential trend function to the constant dollar expenditures given in SIPRI year books. Equations (8) and (9) are estimated to provide information regarding the impact of military expenditures on overall economic growth through the externality effect and/or due to the sectoral factor productivity differential.

Empirical Tests for the Augmented Model

Table 11.3 presents estimates of equations (8) and (9) for the full sample and also for the subsamples for 1981-89. Estimated coefficients of $\dot{M}\,(\frac{M}{Y})$ for equation (8) for the full sample and for the subsamples are statistically significant. For equation (9), none of the estimated coefficients of $\dot{M}$ or $\dot{M}(\frac{M}{Y})$ for the full sample or for the subsamples are significant. That is consistent with the estimates in Table 11.2

TABLE 11.3
Results on the Relation Between Military Expenditure and Economic Growth in LDCs, 1981-89: Augmented Growth Model

	$\frac{I}{Y}$	$\dot{L}$	$\dot{M}(\frac{M}{Y})$	$\dot{M}$	R^2
Full sample	0.137**	0.573*	0.018**		0.22
(N = 74)	(3.351)	(1.786)	(3.413)		
	0.136**	0.573*	0.016	0.008	0.22
	(3.264)	(1.773)	(1.463)	(0.156)	
Low income LDCs	0.184**	-0.387	0.013**		0.30
(N = 30)	(2.537)	(-0.585)	(2.617)		
	0.189**	-0.384	0.015	-0.010	0.30
	(2.442)	(-0.570)	(1.235)	(-0.193)	
Middle income LDCs	0.129**	0.558	0.040**		0.30
(N = 44)	(2.155)	(1.426)	(3.091)		
	0.122**	0.515	0.023	0.131	0.32
	(2.031)	(1.317)	(1.242)	(1.27)	

Source: Author's calculations

that indicate a positive overall effect of military expenditures on growth. However, for the extended equation (9), neither the coefficient of $\dot{M}$ nor that of $\dot{M}(\frac{M}{Y})$ is significant at any reasonable level in any of the samples. Perhaps collinearity between these two variables lowers the precision of the estimates. Therefore, while one may say that the overall effect of military outlays on LDC growth is positive, it is difficult to ascertain whether it is the externality effect or the factor-productivity differential that is more important.

Concluding Remarks

This work was motivated by the consideration of replicating an earlier study by Biswas and Ram (1986) about the impact of military expenditures on economic growth. Econometric results are often fragile. In Leamer's (1983, p. 43) terms, "if we are to make effective use of our scarce data resource, it is therefore important that we study fragility in a much more systematic way." With a view to improving the quality of prior research, this work uses the same model but a more recent data set.

Conventional estimates reported in Table 11.2 indicate a positive effect of military expenditures on economic growth for the full sample and for both subsamples. The augmented model supports that proposition represented in equation (8). However, the extended model of equation (9) indicates no significant externality effect or factor-productivity differential. It is possible that high correlation between $\dot{M}$ and $\dot{M}(\frac{M}{Y})$ lowers the precision of the estimates, and it is difficult to judge whether it is the externality effect or the factor-productivity differential that is more important. On the whole, one may say that, in contrast with the results obtained by Biswas and Ram (1986), the more recent data indicate the positive effect of military outlays on LDC growth. However, caution is obviously needed in drawing strong inferences from such results.

Notes

I would like to thank Rati Ram for specific comments which I have incorporated in the present version. Of course, the author alone is responsible for any remaining errors or shortcomings. The financial support of the economics department of Utah State University is gratefully acknowledged. Competent research assistance was rendered by Sarita Mohapatra and Joon-Ho Lee.

1. Data on military expenditures are taken from Stockholm International Peace Research Institute (SIPRI), *World Armaments and Disarmament, SIPRI Yearbook* (Oxford University Press, New York, 1987, 1991). Data on labor force growth and growth of GDP are from World Bank, World Development Report 1991, and all other variables are from World Bank, World Tables, 2nd ed. (Baltimore: John Hopkins University Press, 1991).

2. Following the terminology in World Bank, *World Development Report* 1989, a low income developing country is defined as one with a per capita GNP of US $580 or less in 1989 (on the basis of conventional exchange rates); middle-income LDCs are those having per capita GNP of more than $580 but less than $6000 in 1989.

3. The coefficient of I/Y is positive and statistically significant. However, its magnitude appears small. Also, as may be expected, the labor coefficient is not significant for low-income LDCs.

4. Feder's methodology is detailed in Gershon Feder, "On Exports and Economic Growth," *Journal of Development Economics*, Vol. 12 (February-April 1983), pp. 59-73. See also Feder (1983), pp. 61-68.

5. For example, $\dot{Y}$ stands for ΔY/Y, and similar remarks apply to L and M. Feder's notation in this respect, as in some others, is different. He uses a dot over the variable to denote its absolute increase, not its rate of growth.

Appendix A

Sample Countries:

Argentina, Bangladesh*, Benin*, Bolivia, Botswana, Brazil, Burkina Faso, Burundi, Cameroon, Central Africa, Chad, Chile, Columbia, Congo, Costa Rica, Cote D'Ivore, Dominican Republic, Ecuador, Egypt, El Salvador, Ethiopia, Gabon, Ghana, Greece, Guatemala, Haiti, Honduras, Hungary, India, Indonesia, Iran, Jamaica, Kenya, Madagascar*, Malawi, Malaysia, Mali*, Mauritania*, Mauritius, Mexico, Morocco, Mozambique*, Nepal*, Nicaragua, Niger*, Nigeria*, Oman, Pakistan*, Panama, Paraguay, Peru, Philippines, Poland, Portugal, Rwanda, Senegal, Sierra Leone*, Somalia*, South Korea, Sri Lanka*, Syria, Tanzania*, Thailand, Togo*, Trinidad and Tobago, Tunisia, Turkey, Uganda*, Uruguay, Venezuela, Yugoslavia, Zaire*, Zambia*, Zimbabwe.

*Low-income LDCs.

Appendix B

Country	$\dot{M}$	$\frac{M}{Y}$	$\frac{I}{Y}$	$\dot{L}$	$\dot{Y}$
Argentina	-7.429	4.688888	18.37777	1.4	-0.3
Bangladesh*	5.464	1.466666	14.98888	2.6	3.5
Benin*	-0.283	1.957142	17.73333	3.2	1.8
Bolivia	-4.405	3.7	15.37777	2.7	-0.9
Botswana	11.688	2.955555	29.12222	3.4	11.3
Brazil	1.13	1.23333	24.47777	2.2	3
Burkina Faso*	4.357	2.911111	23.65555	2.6	5
Burundi*	-2.372	3	17.29999	2.9	4.3
Cameron	2.558	1.8666666	27.75555	3.2	3.2
Central Africa*	-1.398	2	13.8	2.7	1.4
Chad*	58.932	6.06	8.128568	2.4	6.5
Chile	0.5454	7.933333	20.44444	1.7	2.7
Colombia	9.283	2.055555	24.81111	2	3.5
Congo	1.495	2.7	36.93333	3.4	3.9
Costa Rica	-0.302	0.577777	30.41111	2.4	2.8
Cote D'Ivore	0.44	1.111111	11.42333	4.1	1.2
Dom. Republic	-5.976	1.444444	27.51111	2.3	2.4
Equador	3.694	1.744444	26.4	2.7	1.9
Egypt	-4.422	6.255555	36.2555	2.5	5.4
E. Salvador	-5.36	4.077777	31.3333	1.4	0.6
Ethiopia*	5.8503	9.188888	13.17777	3	1.9
Gabon	2.056	3.022222	38.37777	3.7	1.2
Ghana*	7.0474	0.688888	18.67777	3.4	2.8
Greece	-0.907	6.533333	24.65555	0.4	1.6
Guatemala	3.052	2.577777	14.64999	2.9	0.4
Haiti*	1.1143	1.285714	14.72222	1.9	-0.5
Honduras	13.255	4.588888	18.85555	3.5	2.3
Hungary	5.33	2.9	30.76666	-0.2	1.6
India*	7.3082	3.311111	24.38888	2.1	5.3
Indonesia*	-44.124	3.3	30.21111	2.1	5.3
Iran	-6.613	3.457142	21.66666	3.5	3.4
Jamaica	-8.537	1.2375	26.34999	1.3	1.2
Kenya*	-0.835	3.177777	24.5	3.9	4.1
Madagascar*	-7.003	2.311111	12.5	2.9	0.8
Malawi*	-4.853	2.244444	18.33333	3.4	2.7
Malaysia	-2.299	6.522222	21.66666	2.6	4.9
Mali*	6.052	2.528571	22.74444	2.5	3.8

Appendix B (contd.)

Country	$\dot{M}$	$\frac{M}{Y}$	$\frac{I}{Y}$	$\dot{L}$	$\dot{Y}$
Mauritania*	-16.082	7.475	29.01111	2.4	1. 4
Mauritius	2.587	2.77777	27.4	1	5.9
Mexico	-7.578	0.575	27.7	2.1	0.7
Morocco	0.053	5.411111	31.28888	2.6	4.1
Mozambique*	7.153	9.983333	20.61111	2.7	-1.4
Nepal*	13.924	1.366666	21.83333	2.6	4.6
Nicaragua	1.121	15.94444	29.41427	3.4	-1.6
Niger*	3.7436	0.722222	14.66666	3.4	-1.6
Nigeria*	-14.794	1.533333	16.25555	3.4	-0.4
Oman	4.384	21.34444	29.925	4.7	12.8
Pakistan*	7.986	6.622222	19.55555	3.2	6.4
Panama	9.743	1.711111	24.44444	2.2	0.5
Paraguay	0.135	1.266666	31.13333	3.2	2.2
Peru	-0.064	6	31.97777	2.3	0.4
Philipines	-5.5	1.744444	27.65555	2.5	0.7
Poland	3.0848	3.111111	31.52222	0.7	2.5
Portugal	2.846	3.3	36.36666	0.6	2.5
Rwanda*	-1.237	1.825	16.66666	3.2	1.5
Senegal	9.296	2.6	23.06666	3	3.1
Sierra Leone*	-19.834	0.8	13.88888	2.4	0.6
Somalia*	-12.827	3.055555	27.4	3	3
South Korea	6.3171	5.177777	22.05555	1.2	9.7
Sri Lanka*	23.302	2.5	26.36666	1.5	4
Syria	-10.646	14.16666	31.06249	3.6	1.6
Tanzania*	3.981	4.288888	21.21249	3.1	2.6
Thailand	2.064	4.755555	33.87777	1.9	7
Togo*	10.657	2.477777	25.28888	3.5	1.4
Trinidad & Tobago	-9.05	2.571428	12.60555	1.7	-5.5
Tunisia	5.517	4.88888	34.76666	2.5	3.4
Turkey	2.107	4.544444	30.53333	2.4	5.1
Uganda*	-5.448	3.511111	12.04444	3.2	2.5
Uruguay	-6.647	2.833333	19.08888	0.6	0.1
Venezuela	-3.952	2.511111	29.4	2.8	1
Yugoslavia	-1.284	3.944444	45.57777	0.7	1.3
Zaire*	-1.687	1.666666	11.67777	3.1	1.9
Zambia*	-7.254	3.488888	17.95555	3.7	0.8
Zimbabwe	5.244	6.311111	23.24444	3.5	2.7

$\dot{M}$ = Annual rate of growth of military expenditure.

$\dot{L}$ = Annual rate of growth of labor force.

$\dot{Y}$ = Annual rate of growth of gross domestic product.

$\frac{I}{Y}$ = Investment output ratio.

$\frac{M}{Y}$ = Military expenditure output ratio.

References

Benoit, Emile. (1978), " Growth and Defense in Developing Countries," *Economic Development and Cultural Change,* Vol. 26 pp. 271-80.

Biswas, Basudeb and Rati Ram (1986), "Military Expenditures and Economic Growth in Less Developed Countries: An Augmented Model and Further Evidence," *Economic Development and Cultural Change*, Vol. 34, 361-372.

Deger, Saadat and Somnath Sen. (1983), "Military Expenditure, Spin-Off and Economic Development," *Journal of Development Economics*, Vol. 13, 67-83, esp. 67.

Feder, Gershon. (1983), "On Exports and Economic Growth." *Journal of Development Economics*, Vol. 12, pp. 59-73.

Frederickson, Peter C. and Looney, Robert E. (1982), "Defense Expenditures and Economic Growth in Developing Countries: Some Further Empirical Evidence," *Journal of Economic Development*, Vol. 7, pp. 113-26.

Leamer, Edward E. (1983), "Let's Take the Con Out of Econometrics," *American Economic Review*, Vol. 23, pp. 31-43.

Leontief, Wassily and Faye Duchin. (1983), *Military Spending: Facts and Figures, Worldwide Implications and Future Outlook*, Oxford University Press, p. 66.

Lim, David. (1983), "Another Look at Growth and Defense in Less-Developed Countries," *Ecònomic Development and Cultural Change*, Vol. 31 pp. 377-84.

Rothschild, Kurt W. (1977), "Military Expenditure, Exports and Growth," *Kyklos*, Vol. 26, pp. 804-13.

Stockholm International Peace Research Institute (SIPRI). *World Armaments and Disarmament, SIPRI Yearbook, 1987 & 1991*. New York: Oxford University Press.

United Nations Development Programme. (1992), *Human Development Report*. New York: Oxford University Press.

World Bank. (1989), *World Development Report*. New York: Oxford University Press.

World Bank. (1991), *World Development Report*. New York: Oxford University Press.

World Bank. (1991), World Tables (2nd ed) Baltimore: John Hopkins University Press.

12

Arms Imports and Third World Growth in the 1980s

Robert E. Looney and Peter C. Frederiksen

During the 1980s both defense spending and arms imports declined in many developing countries (DCs), especially in the Middle East and to a lesser degree in South Asia and Northern Africa[1]. In large part, the reductions in defense allocations resulted from growing fiscal problems which forced governments to reorder their spending priorities. It is apparent for the developing world as a whole that countries are indeed examining the potential benefits of reduced defense allocations. Depending on the relative impact of defense spending, the concomitant resource reallocation may significantly affect the economic performance of these countries. This paper examines whether future "peace dividends" are likely to stimulate or to retard third world economic growth. To do this, we examine whether (a) military spending and arms imports helped or hindered growth in the 1980s, (b) military spending/arms imports were associated with changes in external debt, and (c) military expenditures impacted uniformly between groups of countries. We hypothesize that DCs will exhibit large variations in how defense spending has impacted economic performance. In turn these variations, it is believed, reflect the underlying health of the individual country, i.e., its ability to absorb the potential adverse effects associated with changes in defense spending patterns.

Literature Survey

Much has been written recently on the causes and consequences of militarization in the DCs. While much of the early work was anecdotal and biased toward the standard "guns vs. butter" analogies, a rapidly growing literature has attempted to identify the impact of defense spending on various aspects of economic development and growth. Many of the studies assumed that since defense consumes large quantities of technical and managerial manpower, there will be a significant opportunity cost to defense spending. Unfortunately, no consensus on the effect of defense on the economy has yet emerged.[2] Even recent studies have failed to quell the debate. For example, Biswas and Ram (1986) recently concluded that "military expenditures neither help nor hurt economic growth in LDCs to any significant amount."

Another recent interest has focused on causality. While most of the early studies assumed causation from defense to growth, Joerding (1986) and LaCivita and Frederiksen (1991) have shown that, as expected, causality and the lag length (from the independent to the dependent variables) differ among countries.

The economic effect of planned cuts in defense has not been limited to DCs. In a 1992 article, Roth (1992) examined how the planned cuts in United States' defense spending and the growing budget deficits will affect employment in the U.S. Among his generalizations, Roth felt that (a) the US economy could easily absorb the displaced workers (active-duty, DoD civilians, and defense industry workers), (b) outlays will not fall as fast as authorizations and will thus act as a modified stabilizer, and (c) the state of the U.S. economy will have a significant impact on the severity of worker dislocation.

Another avenue of research has been to use sub-groups of DCs and examine the impact of defense spending within each group. This type of research argues that by creating a stable economic environment, added defense expenditures may actually stimulate higher rates of investment, technological process, technology transfer and hence overall growth. Frederiksen and Looney's (1983) study based on Benoit's (1978) work grouped countries based on a broad range of economic variables to reflect resource availability. Later studies, which enlarged the sample, used later data, or grouped countries using other criteria (such as savings and investment or foreign exchange availability, import elasticity, and investment productivity) found that for the relatively richer group there was a positive effect from defense on growth but in the constrained group there were statistically insignificant results between defense and growth.[3]

Dividing DCs according to producers and non-producers of at least one major weapon system indicated that producers experienced positive economic impacts from military expenditures while non-producers experienced declines in growth and investment.[4] Broadly similar results were obtained by grouping according to regime type[5] or the legitimacy of government.[6]

Recently, analysis has branched into more complex issues and studies have used both time series and simultaneous models estimated by two and three stage least squares regression techniques. These studies have attempted to incorporate the demand for military expenditures as well as their impacts to determine feedbacks from one to the other. The results[7] tend to confirm the results which were obtained by the more naive models discussed above.

In short, the research so far demonstrates a somewhat consistent pattern whereby certain groups of DCs -- usually the more successful, the more stable, or who are producing arms -- seem to derive some positive impacts from military spending. For the other group, on the other hand, it seems that defense spending has little impact on the economy.

A major limitation to the studies cited above is that they are very aggregative and any generalizations to a specific country is hazardous at best. One exception is Lebovic and Ishaq's (1987) study of defense spending in the Middle East. Using a pooled time-series, cross-sectional analysis on various groupings of Middle Eastern states, they found that higher military spending tended to suppress economic growth in the non-oil states during the 1973-1984 period.

Babin (1989) incorporated the time variable since some relationships which might exist over the long-run disappear in the short-run or vice versa. As Babin concludes, one cannot assume that defense spending will have an immediate, or even short-term, effect on national economic performance. Along these lines, Kick and Sharda's (1986) analysis indicated that an increase in the military manpower ratio has a positive effect on infrastructure and social welfare but that the impact occurs with a long (12 year) lag. Militarization, whether measured in expenditures or size of the military, contributes to economic development.

In summary, although there is no broad consensus as to impact (positive, negative, or none) or causality (defense to growth, growth to defense, or feedback), there is some agreement as to the channels in which defense expenditures transmit impacts to the general economy.[8] These include:

Resource Allocation Effects. Increases in military expenditures divert or re-allocate resources away from domestic civilian investment, public expenditures on government capital investment and current account expenditures on non-military inputs.

Resource Mobilization Effects. Increases in military

expenditures can influence domestic savings through the following linkages: reduced social services, additional taxes, an increase in the social discount rate, and inflation.

Spin-off Effects. Military expenditure may impact economic growth through spin-off effects on human capital (from military training, education and modernization) and on investment productivity through technology transfers).

Aggregate Demand Effects. If underutilized productive capacity exists, an increase in aggregate demand from military expenditures can result in increased output and a rise in capacity utilization and profit rates, in turn inducing an increase in investment rates.

Debt Accumulation Effect. This effect is the impact on current performance of debt accumulation from past imports of military goods and services.

Methodology and Results

Given the conflicting nature of the impacts of these factors, we do still not know whether, a priori, military expenditures promote or hinder economic growth. The net outcome is likely to differ across countries and through time. This paper examines the relationship between defense (and particularly arms imports) and growth during the 1980s.

Factor Analysis

As a first step, we factor analyzed[9] a set of twenty-five economic variables[10] to get a broad overview of the relationship between defense expenditures, arms imports, debt, and economic performance for the 1980s. The results, which appear as Table 12.1, indicate five main trends/factors[11] in the data:

> ***Factor 1: Debt/Arms Imports.*** The main trend in the data was represented by the high correlation between the arms imports share of total imports and the ratio of total external debt to exports. Several structural variables, the resource balance and the share of savings in GDP (1989) were also included in this factor. The resource balance roughly corresponds to the current account in the balance of payments.
>
> ***Factor 2: Growth.*** Many of the overall measures of macroeconomic growth in the 1980s were highly correlated. High growth was also strongly correlated with the share of national resources devoted to investment.

TABLE 12.1
Military Expenditure, Growth, External Debt Variables and Factor Loadings with Eigen Values > 2

VARIABLE		FACTOR				
		Debt Arms Imports	Growth	Public Spending Debt	Military Spending	Debt Service
Debt/Exports	89	0.888*	-0.190	0.011	0.063	0.167
Res Bal/GDP	89	-0.803*	-0.266	0.052	0.034	0.173
Savings/GDP	89	-0.798*	0.193	-0.013	0.277	0.064
Arms Imp	80-79	0.775*	0.008	0.056	0.395	0.063
Arms Imp	72-89	0.771*	0.032	0.138	0.412	0.038
GDP Growth	80-89	0.038	0.899*	-0.026	0.246	-0.063
Imp Growth	80-89	-0.078	0.862*	0.080	0.059	-0.065
Priv Cons	80-89	0.041	0.790*	0.162	0.049	0.157
Invest Growth	80-89	0.052	0.757*	-0.336	0.040	-0.231
Invest/GDP	89	-0.287	0.547*	-0.078	0.363	-0.106
Govt Cons	80-89	0.186	0.540*	-0.227	0.110	-0.219
Govt Exp/GNP	80-89	-0.158	0.060	0.847*	0.004	-0.063
Govt Exp/GDP	72-79	-0.010	-0.001	0.831*	0.251	-0.079
Debt/GDP	80	0.383	-0.069	0.687*	0.128	0.267
Debt/GDP	89	0.489	-0.316	0.629*	0.065	0.210
Exports/GDP	89	-0.469	0.050	0.620*	-0.128	-0.232
Govt Cons/GDP	89	0.134	-0.029	0.556*	-0.261	-0.221
Av Milex/GE	72-79	0.082	0.299	-0.087	0.865*	-0.049
Av Milex/GE	80-89	0.075	0.057	-0.287	0.818*	-0.073
Milex/GNP	80-89	0.077	0.162	0.379	0.802*	-0.046
Milex/GNP	72-79	0.121	0.219	0.336	0.787*	-0.036
Interest/Exp	80	-0.212	-0.012	-0.025	-0.021	0.900*
Debt Serv/Exp	80	-0.199	-0.044	0.006	0.060	0.877*
Debt Serv/Exp	89	0.436	0.085	0.084	0.108	0.737*
Interest/Exp	89	0.076	-0.155	-0.089	-0.097	0.710*
Eigen Values		**5.470**	**5.140**	**3.464**	**3.299**	**2.138**

*denotes factor loadings over 0.50.

Source: Authors' calculations based on oblique factor rotation.

Factor 3: Public Spending/Debt. This factor depicts the close relationship between government expenditures and the overall external debt burden. Included in this factor is the share of exports in GDP, which may indicate that countries with a high share of resources allocated to exports are relatively credit worthy.

Factor 4: Military Expenditures. This factor primarily depicts the % of the central government budget allocated to military spending and the "military burden", (the % of GDP allocated to the military). Interestingly, arms imports as a share of total imports is only weakly correlated with these variables.

Factor 5: Debt Service. This factor is comprised of four measures of debt servicing -- interest payments and total debt service as a share of exports in 1980 and 1989.

The factor scores for the 62 countries in the sample appear as Table 12.2. Since the individual country scores have a mean of zero, they provide an index of the relative country ranking. As anticipated, the Middle East countries have by far the highest defense burdens, while many of the Latin American countries score relatively highly in terms of their debt service burden. The economic successes of the East Asian countries is apparent by the Factor 2 scores.

The next step was to determine the relationship between growth and defense for the sample set in the 1980s. Specifically did the net impact of military expenditures (a) produce a positive or neutral effect in countries facing few relative resource constraints and (b) produce a negative impact on growth in those countries which were relatively resource constrained.

To group the countries, we used the Factor 2 score: countries with a factor score less than zero were classified as low growth (and presumably resource constrained) and countries with factor scores greater than zero were considered high growth (and presumably relatively resource unconstrained).

The mean values of the 25 economic and defense expenditure variables (used in the factor analysis) appear as Table 12.3. Both groups had relatively similar defense burdens, although the share of the central budget allocated to defense was considerably lower in the high growth group during the 1980s (11.4% versus 15.6%). In contrast, the high growth group had considerably lower shares of their total imports accounted for by arms imports in both the 1970s and 1980s. As expected, income growth was much greater in the high growth group; perhaps of greater significance was that this group maintained

TABLE 12.2
Factor Loadings for Individual Countries

COUNTRY	FACTOR				
	Debt Arms Imports	Growth	Public Spend-ing Debt	Military Spending	Debt Service
Tanzania	2.10	0.05	0.01	-0.13	0.05
Somalia	5.63	-0.49	0.17	0.88	-0.26
Malawi	0.61	0.28	0.49	-0.85	0.85
Burundi	1.31	0.84	-0.76	-0.42	-0.29
Madagascar	0.93	-0.82	-0.80	-0.24	1.32
Nigeria	-0.70	-2.72	-0.57	0.59	-0.84
Zaire	0.12	-0.10	-0.20	-0.09	0.00
Mali	1.02	0.98	-0.42	-0.20	-0.69
Niger	0.31	-1.32	-0.65	-0.98	0.21
Upper Volta	0.75	0.60	-1.49	-0.26	-1.38
Rwanda	0.63	0.38	-1.31	-0.64	-1.14
India	0.50	1.06	-1.14	0.40	-0.29
China	-0.91	2.15	-0.78	2.03	-1.32
Haiti	0.13	-1.24	-1.04	-0.48	-1.35
Kenya	0.11	0.61	0.29	-0.53	0.45
Pakistan	0.67	1.21	-0.42	1.13	-0.13
CAR	0.61	-0.23	-0.35	-0.92	-1.32
Ghana	0.33	0.16	-0.86	-1.18	0.07
Togo	0.16	0.21	1.20	-0.74	-0.41
Zambia	0.25	-1.11	1.44	0.87	0.00
Sri Lanka	0.07	0.84	0.27	-0.97	-0.60
Indonesia	-0.69	0.75	-0.63	0.18	0.00
Mauritania	0.44	-0.50	2.35	1.18	0.32
Bolivia	0.26	-1.10	-0.34	0.25	1.60
Egypt	1.13	0.68	2.40	3.68	0.06
Senegal	0.16	0.29	0.15	-0.69	0.45
Zimbabwe	-0.27	-0.39	0.36	0.48	-1.53
Philippines	-0.36	-0.34	-0.63	-0.09	1.12
Ivory Coast	0.00	-0.43	1.35	-1.12	1.18
Dominican Rep	-0.42	0.27	-0.78	-0.46	-0.23
Morocco	0.16	0.60	0.46	0.72	1.10
Papua New Guinea	0.04	0.37	1.03	-1.44	-0.61
Honduras	0.20	-0.03	-0.10	-0.44	-0.17
Guatemala	0.05	-1.59	-1.67	-0.15	-1.17
Congo	0.11	-0.15	2.37	-0.06	-0.06
Cameroon	-0.06	0.07	-0.72	-0.57	-0.44

TABLE 12.2 (Contd.)
Factor Loadings for Individual Countries

	FACTOR				
COUNTRY	Debt Arms Imports	Growth	Public Spend-ing Debt	Military Spending	Debt Service
Peru	-0.22	-1.14	-0.57	1.81	0.80
Ecuador	-0.03	-0.46	-0.52	0.58	1.37
Paraguay	-0.34	0.01	-1.12	-0.07	-0.42
El Salvador	0.32	-0.57	-1.31	0.33	-1.19
Colombia	-0.42	0.31	-1.09	-0.54	0.77
Thailand	-0.73	1.74	-0.51	0.38	-0.28
Jamaica	-0.48	0.10	1.42	-1.11	0.00
Tunisia	-0.40	0.29	1.04	-0.58	-0.59
Turkey	-0.11	1.24	-0.22	0.62	1.33
Panama	-0.22	-1.30	1.81	-0.91	-1.16
Chile	-0.76	-0.18	0.18	0.58	1.30
Costa Rica	-0.18	0.72	0.38	-1.34	0.58
Mauritius	-0.60	2.03	0.59	-1.83	-1.09
Mexico	-0.48	-0.29	-0.61	-1.00	2.54
Argentina	-0.12	-1.41	-0.35	0.64	1.74
Malaysia	-1.39	0.72	1.07	0.24	-1.26
Algeria	-0.18	0.26	0.25	-0.04	1.08
Venezuela	-1.05	-0.50	0.13	-0.30	0.94
Brazil	-0.68	0.65	-0.64	-0.71	2.77
Hungary	-1.06	-0.17	1.25	0.92	-0.11
Uruguay	-0.61	-0.97	-0.30	-0.14	0.10
Yugoslavia	-1.80	-0.98	-1.72	3.03	-0.62
Gabon	-0.97	-0.61	1.48	-0.23	-0.92
Trinidad	-1.17	-2.57	0.51	-0.45	-1.73
Portugal	-0.68	1.06	0.65	0.01	-0.28

Source: Derived from analysis in Table 12.1

relatively high rates of investment growth during both periods while in the low growth group the rate of capital formation fell from 4.5% in the 1970s to -4.4% in the 1980s. These growth patterns were also reflected, albeit to a lesser extent, in exports, government consumption, and private sector consumption.

In terms of the relative size of the public sector, the low growth group had a higher ratio of government expenditures to GNP in the

TABLE 12.3
Mean Values, 25 Economic and Defense Variables, High and Low Growth Country Groups

Variable		Growth Group		
		Low	High	Total
Military Expenditures:		Percent(%)		
% Central Budget	72-79	12.5	12.9	12.7
% Central Budget	80-89	15.6	11.4	13.4
% GNP	72-79	2.9	2.6	2.8
% GNP	80-89	3.0	2.8	2.9
Arms/Total Imports	72-79	4.9	2.5	3.6
Arms/Total Imports	80-89	4.5	3.1	3.8
Growth In:				
GDP	80-89	0.9	3.7	2.4
Investment	80-89	- 4.4	3.0	- 0.5
Govt Consumpt	80-89	0.1	3.8	2.1
Imports	80-89	- 4.0	1.9	- 0.9
Private Consumpt	80-89	1.2	3.4	2.4
Composition of Expenditures:				
Govt Exp/GNP	72-79	23.9	21.8	22.4
Govt Exp/GNP	80-89	21.4	26.6	24.2
Govt Consmt/GDP	89	12.0	12.8	12.5
Investment/GDP	89	15.4	23.4	19.7
Savings/GDP	89	13.3	18.9	16.3
Exports/GDP	89	24.2	26.5	25.4
Resource Bal/GDP	89	- 2.0	- 4.6	- 3.4
External Debt:				
Total Debt/Exp	89	433.8	240.9	331.2
Total Debt/GNP	80	51.2	41.2	45.9
Total Debt/GNP	89	101.4	62.2	80.6
Debt Service/Exp	80	23.0	19.6	21.2
Debt Service/Exp	89	24.7	26.0	25.4
Interest/Exp	80	11.7	10.0	10.8
Interest/Exp	89	11.8	10.8	11.3

Source: Based on Factor 2 Score in Table 12.2. Military variables from United States Arms Control and Disarmament Agency, *World Military Expenditures and Arms Transfers* (Washington, D.C.: US Arms Control and Disarmament Agency, various issues). All other data from World Bank, *World Development Report* (New York: Oxford University Press, various issues).

1970s than the high growth countries (23.9% versus 21.8%) but this fell to 21.4% in the 1980s, while increasing to 26.6% for the high growth group. As might be imagined, the high growth group were able to allocate a relatively large part of their resources to investment, and while they had a higher savings rate the differences were not as great as those associated with investment.

Several diverse patterns characterize the indebtedness of the two groups of countries. The low growth countries have considerably higher debt burdens, both in terms of the total debt/GNP ratio and total external debt to export ratio. In addition, these gaps widened during the 1980s. However, the debt service ratios do not reflect this pattern, with the high growth countries having the highest ratio of debt service to exports in 1989. These patterns suggest that much of the debt in the low growth group is concessional and/or of a longer term nature.

Other than their rate of macro-aggregate growth, the two groups seem to have their greatest differences with respect to their pattern of debt -- especially the ratios of debt to exports and GNP.

Discriminant Analysis

To assess the extent to which the pattern of debt differentiates high from low growth countries, a discriminant analysis[12] was performed using the set of variables used in the factor analysis. Countries were initially classified as 0 or 1 based on their factor 2 score, and the discriminant analysis (using a stepwise selection process) determined the extent to which our set of economic/military variables could correctly classify high and low growth countries.

The results of the analysis[13] indicated that GDP growth in the 1980s was the most significant variable differentiating the two groups. However, the only other statistically significant growth variable was the rate of growth of exports -- the seventh and last variable entered in the stepwise procedure. The next most important variable was the share of defense expenditures in the central government budget, followed by the share of investment in GDP, and the resource balance share of GDP. Arms imports as a % of total imports in 1972-79 was the fifth most important discriminating variable, followed by the two export variables. Interestingly, none of the debt variables were statistically significant in differentiating the high growth from low growth countries.

Our profile of high and low growth countries is therefore largely based on relative resource constraints -- especially differences in the proportion of resources allocated to investment (domestic resource constraint), and the rate of growth in exports (the external resource constraint). In addition the high growth countries devote considerably less of their central government budgets to defense and allocate a much lower share of their imports to armaments. On the basis of the seven significant discriminating variables, every country except Mexico were classified correctly and the probabilities of correct placement into the respective group were usually associated with high levels of confidence. The resulting discriminant scores provide a ranking of countries in terms of relative resource constraints (with countries the least resource constrained having the highest negative discriminant score).

Regression Results

Our next step was to determine the impact of defense expenditures on growth in the two groups of countries (as defined in terms of discriminant scores). To do this, a simple Benoit-type growth model of the form:

Growth = f(Invest., Resource Flow, Military Exp., Arms Imports)

was estimated using linear regression analysis. In this model, growth is seen largely as a function of investment and foreign resource flows. Military expenditures and arms imports are added to the regression equation to assess their impact on overall economic growth. The growth variable (GDPG) is the growth of GDP from 1980-89, and the investment variable (GDIG) is the rate of growth of gross capital formation. The resource flow, military expenditures, and arms imports variables (DEBT, MILEX, and ARMSIMP, respectively) are the factor 3,4 and 1 scores for each country. Operationally, these factor scores provide good proxy measures since little multicollinearity exists between the factors.

The results of the regression analysis appear as Table 12.4. Initially, we estimated the model for the entire sample (Eq. 1). The results suggest that both debt and military expenditures contributed to overall economic expansion. On the other hand, arms imports do not appear to have any impact on growth during the 1980s.

To see if these patterns were similar for the sub-groups of countries, two additional sets of regressions were performed. The first set (Table 12.4, Eqs. 2-8) gradually eliminated the relatively resource constrained/low growth countries from the sample set. The results indicate that, as in the case of the total sample, investment, debt and military expenditures were all statistically significant in contributing

TABLE 12.4
Regression Results

	Independent Variables -- t-statistics						
EQUATION	GDIG	DEBT	MILEX	ARMSIMP	df[a]	$R^{2,b}$	F[c]
1. Full Sample	7.62**	3.16**	2.52*	-0.87	49	.56	17.7
Eliminating Resource Constrained Countries							
Discriminant Score:							
2. < 2.5	5.89**	2.10*	3.72**	-1.51	43	.58	17.2
3. < 1.5	5.01**	1.61	4.36**	-2.20*	37	.63	18.7
4. < 1.0	4.57**	-0.01	5.26**	-2.44*	31	.67	18.8
5. < 0.5	2.83**	-0.74	5.61**	-2.47*	28	.67	17.6
6. < 0.0	3.02**	0.68	5.35**	-2.32*	27	.68	17.4
7. < -0.5	1.80	-1.82	5.33**	-2.51*	20	.72	16.2
8. < -1.0	1.97	-0.68	5.44**	-2.06	13	.72	12.0
Eliminating Resource Unconstrained Countries							
Discriminant Score:							
9. > -2.5	6.21**	3.26**	1.52	0.08	45	.45	10.9
10. > -2.0	5.81**	3.43**	1.80	0.08	41	.45	10.3
11. > -1.5	5.33**	3.18**	1.68	0.18	35	.46	9.2
12. > -1.0	4.74**	3.16**	1.40	0.05	31	.39	6.7

TABLE 12.4 (Contd.)
Regression Results

EQUATION	Independent Variables -- t-statistics						
	GDIG	DEBT	MILEX	ARMSIMP	df[a]	$R^{2,b}$	F[c]
Discriminant Score:							
13. > -0.5	4.06**	3.03**	1.18	0.54	24	.39	5.5
14. > 0.0	2.97**	3.54**	1.14	0.87	17	.42	4.9
15. > 0.5	2.80**	3.50**	0.85	0.83	16	.43	4.7

[a]degrees of freedom
[b]adjusted
[c]F-statistic
**indicates that the coefficient (not reported) was statistically different from zero at the 99% level of confidence
*indicates that the coefficient was statistically different from zero at the 95% level of confidence.

Source: Authors' calculations.

to overall expansion. However, as more and more of the low growth countries were eliminated, the debt variable ceased to have a significant impact on growth. In addition, as the proportion of high growth/resource unconstrained countries increased, the military expenditure term became increasingly important in contributing to economic growth. The arms import variable tended to impact negatively on growth, although the effect was fairly weak and statistically significant for only five of the seven regressions.

The second set of regressions (Eqs. 9-15) sequentially eliminated the high-growth countries and a different pattern emerged. For the resource constrained countries, investment and debt played an important role in economic growth. In contrast to the relatively richer countries, neither defense expenditures or arms imports were statistically significant in explaining the overall rate of economic growth in the 1980s.

The relationship of arms imports to overall growth is an interesting one. The results found here are somewhat counter-intuitive. On the one hand, our results indicate that arms imports retard growth in the relatively richer countries (who allocate a much lower proportion of total imports to armaments). On the other hand, arms imports appear to have a neutral effect for the resource constrained countries. While somewhat beyond the scope of this paper, part of the explanation may be attributed to the original factor analysis where arms imports were highly correlated with the share of the debt burden (debt to total exports ratio). This pattern suggests that the resource constrained countries finance much of their arms imports through increases in external debt. As such, these funds may simply augment or add to foreign exchange holdings -- foreign exchange otherwise unavailable and consequently of low opportunity cost.

Conclusions

Conventional wisdom suggests that large outlays on defense divert scarce resources away from directly productive investment ("guns versus butter") and human capital formation (education and health). While this view might make intuitive sense, it does not necessarily follow that increased military expenditures will actually reduce overall economic growth in developing countries as a whole. The counter-argument for DCs suggests that defense expenditures may in fact be an economic stimulus. Military expenditures finance heavy industry (armaments), the acquisition of advanced technologies, provide employment, and the like. Defense expenditures or a large military establishment may also attract investment and thus enhance the country's foreign exchange position. The results which we have obtained in this paper are consistent with this dual view of defense expenditures. The findings are also consistent with earlier studies for the periods prior to 1980. Roughly the same picture has carried over into the 1980s: the more abundantly resource endowed countries appear to have derived positive net benefits to growth from increased defense expenditures. For the relatively poorer group of nations, military spending has no significant impact -- either positive or negative.

For those who advocate cutting defense spending to increase economic growth, such a policy might not always be successful. As Richards and Waterbury (1990) note:

"We may estimate, counterfactually, the returns on alternative uses of the monies devoted to defense, but practically nowhere in the world is there any assurance that reduced defense budgets would result in increased outlay on say, social welfare or infrastructure. Defense outlays are laden with the symbols and sentiments of national pride and survival. People seem prepared to accept disproportionate public investment in defense. They and their leaders find less justification in using equivalent resources to reduce adult illiteracy or line irrigation ditches."

Notes

1. United States Arms Control and Disarmament Agency, *World Military Expenditures and Arms Transfers 1990* (Washington, D.C., U.S. Arms Control and Disarmament Agency, 1991), Figures 2 and 6.

2. For an excellent review, see Steve Chan, "The Impact of Defense Spending on Economic Performance: A Survey of Evidence and Problems," *Orbis*, Vol. 29, No.3, Summer 1985, pp. 403-34; see also Saadat Deger and Robert West, "Introduction: Defense Expenditure, National Security and Economic Development in the Third World," in Saadat Deger and Robert West, eds., *Defense, Security and Development* (London: Francis Pinter, 1987), pp. 1-16.

3. See Frederiksen and Looney (1982, 1985), and Looney and Frederiksen (1986).

4. Following the classification of Neuman (1984), and Looney and Frederiksen (1987).

5. See, for example, Looney (1988).

6. See Looney (1990).

7. See, for example, Looney (1989).

8. The following draws on West (1991).

9. For a general overview of this technique and interpretation of results, see Rummel (1970).

10. Economic variables are from the World Bank, *World Development Report, 1991* (New York: Oxford University Press, 1991). Defense Expenditures were derived from: United States Arms Control and Disarmament Agency, *World Military Expenditures and Arms Transfers, 1990* (Washington: U. S. Arms Control and Disarmament Agency, 1991) and *World Military Expenditures and Arms Transfers 1972-1982* (Washington: U. S. Arms Control and Disarmament Agency, 1984). The variables (%) include (in order of listing in Table 12.1): (1) total external debt/exports, 1989; (2) resource balance/GDP, 1989; (3) savings/GDP, 1989; average arms imports/total imports, (4) for 1980-1989 and (5) 1972-1979; (6) average annual rate of GDP growth, 1980-1989; (7) the average annual rate of growth of imports, 1980-1989; (8) the average annual rate of growth in private consumption, 1980-1989; (9) the average annual rate of growth in gross capital formation, 1980-1989; (10) investment/GDP, 1989; (11) the average annual rate of growth in government consumption, 1980-1989; average government expenditures/GNP, (12) for 1980-1989 and (13) 1972-1979; total external debt/GDP, (14) for 1980 and (15) for 1989; (16) exports/GDP, 1989; (17) government consumption/GDP, 1989; military spending/ central government budget, (18) for 1972-1979 and (19) for 1980-1989; average military expenditure/ GNP (20) for 1980-89 and (21) for 1972-1979; (22) interest payments on the external debt/exports, 1980; debt service payments/exports (23) for 1980 and (24) for 1989; (25) interest payments/exports, 1989.

11. Selected on the basis on having Eigen values greater than 2.0. See Rummel (1970).

12. Based on variables used in factor analysis. See *SPSS, SPSS/PC + Advanced Statistics 4.0* (Chicago: SPSS Inc., 1990) for a description of the discriminant program and its interpretation.

13. The statistically significant variables (Wilks' Lambda in parentheses) which formed the discriminant function (in order of importance) were: [1] GDP growth 1980-89 (0.569); [2] military expenditures as % of central government budget 1980-89 (0.467); [3] investment/GDP, 1989 (0.400); [4] resource balance/GDP, 1989 (0.340); [5] arms imports/total imports, 1972-1979 (0.297); [6] exports/GDP, 1989 (0.285); [7] export growth 1980-89 (0.271).

References

Babin, Nehma (1989), "Military Spending, Economic Growth and The Time Factor," *Armed Forces and Society*. Vol. 15, pp. 249-62.

Benoit, Emile (1978), "Growth and Defense in Developing Countries," *Economic Development and Cultural Change*, Vol. 26, No. 2, pp. 271-80.

Biswas, B., and Ram, R. (1986), "Military Expenditures and Economic Growth in Less Developed Countries: An Augmented Model and Further Evidence," *Economic Development and Cultural Change*, Vol. 34, pp. 361-42.

Chan, Steve (1985), "The Impact of Defense Spending on Economic Performance: A Survey of Evidence and Problems," *Orbis*, Vol. 29, pp. 403-34.

Deger, Saadat, and Robert West (1987), "Introduction: Defense Expenditure, National Security and Economic Development in the Third World," in Saadat Deger and Robert West, eds., *Defense, Security, and Development*, pp. 1-16, London: Francis Pinter.

Frederiksen, Peter C., and Robert E. Looney (1985), "Another Look at the Defense Spending and Development Hypothesis," *Defense Analysis*, Vol. 1, pp. 205-10.

_____ (1983), "Defense Expenditures and Economic Growth in Developing Countries," *Armed Forces and Society*, Vol. 9, pp. 633-46.

_____ (1982), "Defense Spending and Economic Growth in Developing Countries: Some Further Empirical Evidence," *Journal of Economic Development*, Vol. 2, pp. 113-125.

Grobar, Lisa M., and Richard C. Porter (1989), "Benoit Revisited: Defense Spending and Economic Growth in LDCs," *Journal of Conflict Resolution*, Vol. 33, pp. 318-45.

Joerding, Wayne (1986), "Economic Growth and Defense Spending: Granger Causality," *Journal of Development Economics*, Vol. 21, pp. 35-40.

Kick, Edward and Ban Sharda (1986), "Third World Militarization and Development," *Journal of Developing Societies*, Vol. 2, pp. 49-67.

LaCivita, Charles J., and Peter C. Frederiksen (1991), "Defense Spending and Economic Growth: An Alternative Approach to the Causality Issue," *Journal of Development Economics*, Vol. 35, pp. 117-26.

Lebovic, James, and Ashfaq Ishaq (1987), "Military Burden, Security and Needs, and Economic Growth in the Middle East," *Journal of Conflict Resolution*, Vol. 31, pp. 106-38.

Looney, Robert, E. (1990), "The Role of Military Expenditure in the African Economic Crisis," *Jerusalem Journal of International Relations*, Vol. 12, pp. 76-101.

_____ (1989), "Impact of Arms Production on Third World Distribution and Growth," *Economic Development and Cultural Change*, Vol. 38, pp. 145-53.

_____ (1988), "Political Economy of Third World Military Expenditures: The Impact of Regime Type on the Defense Allocation Process," *Journal of Political and Military Sociology*, Vol. 16, pp. 21-30.

Looney, Robert E. and Peter C. Frederiksen (1987), "Impact of Latin American Arms Production on Economic Performance," *Journal of Economic, Social, and Political Studies*, Vol. 23, pp. 309-20.

_____ (1986), "Defense Expenditures, External Public Debt, and Growth in Developing Countries," *Journal of Peace Research*, Vol. 23, pp. 329-38.

Neuman, Stephanie (1984), "International Stratification and Third World Military Industries," *International Organization*, Vol. 38, pp. 167-97.

Richards, Alan, and John Waterbury (1990), *A Political Economy of the Middle East: State, Class, and Economic Development*, Boulder: Westview Press.

Roth, Theodore R. (1992), "The Impact of Defense Spending on Employment in the United States," *Armed Forces and Society*, Vol. 18, pp. 383-405.

Rummel, R. J. (1970), *Applied Factor Analysis*, Evanston, Ill.: Northwestern University Press.

SPSS Inc. (1990), *SPSS / PC + Advanced Statistics 4.0*, Chicago: SPSS Inc.

United States Arms Control and Disarmament Agency (1991), *World Military Expenditures and Arms Transfers: 1990*, Washington, D.C.: U.S. Arms Control and Disarmament Agency.

_____ (1984), *World Military Expenditures and Arms Transfers: 1972-1982*, Washington. D.C.: U.S. Arms Control and Disarmament Agency.

West, Robert (1991), "The Impacts of Military Expenditure on Economic Growth: Review of Research and Empirical Evidence," Paper presented in January at *U.S. Institute of Peace Conference*, Conflict Resolution in the Post-Cold War Third World.

World Bank (1991), *World Development Report, 1991*, New York: Oxford University Press.

PART FIVE

Related Issues of Importance

13

Deterring Terrorism Through Reputation Building

John L. Scott

The conventional wisdom is that governments should not negotiate with terrorists because to do so encourages future terrorism. Given that an incident has occurred, the gains from negotiation are similar to the usual economic gains from trade. The terrorist has a hostage (for example) that is more valuable to the government which it faces than to the terrorist, hence there are gains from trade. If all this is common knowledge then bargaining theory predicts a settlement with the government paying the terrorist at least the terrorist's value and at most the government's value, the actual payment being indeterminant. Sandler, Tschirhart, and Cauley (1983) draw conclusions regarding the nature of the eventual settlement. Selten (1988) uses game theory to analyze the equilibrium properties of the settlement. Islam and Shahin (1989) use a static model to address the optimal mix of media attention and bargaining for hostages in the optimal settlement. Lapan and Sandler (1988, p.21) look at the bargaining question under perfect information and conclude that "reputational effects are important only under imperfect information." Scott (1991) empirically tests a reputation hypothesis and finds evidence of reputation building.

We demonstrate that governments cannot build reputations in models of complete information but may attempt reputation building with incomplete information. With complete information, the threat not to negotiate with terrorists is a bluff which is always called in the absence of credible pre-commitments.

We first show that reputation building does not occur in models with complete information. We then present a model with incomplete information, derive the appropriate decision rules, then the equilibria. In the following section we discuss the sensitivity of the results to the model's parameters and offer conclusions.

Chain Stores and Terrorists

Suppose that there are N terrorist attacks which might take place. Further suppose that the government who is the target of these attacks would rather negotiate in a single incident than refuse to negotiate. Consistent with the conventional wisdom, we might conjecture that the government should resist the temptation to negotiate in order to build a reputation which might deter future attacks. Suppose that the government establishes a non-binding no-negotiation policy. Consider the Nth period. If a terrorist attack occurs, the government will surely negotiate because a reputation is useless at game's end. The Nth terrorist should realize this and attack. Hence, we have determined the outcome of the final period without reference to the earlier periods. Now consider the next-to-last period. The government realizes that the final period's outcome is independent of period N-1, so there is no incentive to attempt to build a reputation (by refusing to negotiate) in period N-1. Thus, the government should negotiate if attacked in period N-1. The terrorist, realizing this, attacks and is met with negotiation. Therefore, the final two periods are independent of the earlier periods and feature terrorist attacks and government negotiations. Continuing this process of backward induction, we see that all N terrorists attack and the government negotiates with each. Thus, as Lapan and Sandler (1988) state, there is no scope for reputation building in models of complete information.

We will show that reputation building is possible in a model of asymmetric information. Our complete information specification is similar to Selten's (1978) chain store paradox in which a monopolist may fight entry into its market. The paradox is that, though it seems intuitive that reputation building (fighting entry at first to discourage future entry) might be an optimal strategy, the unique subgame perfect equilibrium has the monopolist never fighting entry. However, Kreps and Wilson (1982) show that if the potential entrants entertain doubts as to the motivations of the monopolist, reputation building is possible. With a small probability that the monopolist is not a profit maximizer, or derives satisfaction from fighting entry, a wedge is driven into the complete information model and reputation building is possible.

The Model

The model employed in this study is similar to Kreps and Wilson's (1982). Suppose that there are two types of government, weak and strong. The government's type is unknown to the terrorist. The terrorist views the government type as randomly determined, drawn from a distribution of types which is common knowledge. After the government type is chosen, the terrorist decides whether or not to attack. If the terrorist does not attack, his payoff is 0, and the government's payoff, regardless of type, is 'a' ($a > 1$). If the terrorist attacks, the weak government decides whether or not to negotiate. If the weak government does not negotiate, he instead elects to counterattack in an attempt to regain hostages and bring the terrorist to justice. We assume that negotiations are binding. Given that an attack takes place, if the weak government negotiates, the payoff to the terrorist is b ($0 < b < 1$) and the payoff to the weak government is 0. If the weak government counterattacks, the payoff to the terrorist is $b-1$ and the payoff to the government is -1. The strong government differs from the weak government in that the strong government's only pure strategy contingent on attack is counterattack. Given that an attack takes place, the payoff to the terrorist is $b-1$ and 0 to the strong government.

Our model differs from Kreps and Wilson's in two respects. Our model has two periods rather than Kreps and Wilson's arbitrarily long (finite) game. We impose this restriction because we wish to show why incomplete information is necessary to theoretically justify government reputation building. Justifying the conventional wisdom and explicitly stating the prior assumptions behind it requires only two periods. Secondly, we remove a dominated strategy from one of the government types. This is done to avoid some equilibria that are not intuitively pleasing.

The differences in the payoffs of the two types of governments may be justified in at least two ways. First, differences in risk preference might separate the two types. The payoff to the government from counterattacking is an expected payoff since with counterattack there is a chance of loss of innocent lives. Thus counterattack can be viewed as a risky strategy, while negotiation is, in any single period of the game, less risky. Even when all governments are risk averse, some governments may prefer the expected utility of counterattack in single period games. Other governments might view the losses associated with losing innocent lives as too great to justify using the risky strategy of counterattacking. Terrorist uncertainty about risk preference might, then, be the origin of the incomplete information in the model. Another more obvious difference in the payoffs of the two types is in personal preferences of policy makers. These preferences may or may not be driven by public sentiment.

Payoffs in the game must represent the payoffs to decision makers involved in the war on terrorism for the model to represent real world terrorism. The equilibria we derive are independent of comparisons of magnitudes of payoffs across players. In other words, the equilibria do not depend on whether the government's payoff from some final outcome is greater than the terrorist's payoff. The most important characteristic of the payoffs is the order of the payoffs for a player across the various possible outcomes. The magnitudes of the payoffs are not so important as their order in determining equilibria; therefore, though we make assumptions regarding relative magnitudes, these assumptions contribute mainly to increasing tractability and not to determining the characteristics of the equilibria. We feel that the payoffs reasonably abstract the order and (where possible) comparative magnitudes of the preferences of governments and terrorists engaged in real world conflict. We will explore the sensitivity of the equilibria to changes in magnitudes and orderings of the payoffs after the equilibria have been derived.

Some definitions are in order before formal analysis is attempted.

{T1, T2, W, S} = the set of players. T1 is the terrorist which may potentially attack in period 1. T2 is the terrorist which may potentially attack in period 2. W is the weak type of government. S is the strong type of government.

{W, S} = the set from which the true type of government is drawn. W is the weak type of government. S is the strong type of government.

Ps = the probability that the government's type is S.

{C1, N1, C2 , N2} = the set of pure strategies of W (Counterattack on round 1 if attacked, negotiate on round 1 if attacked, counterattack on round 2 if attacked, negotiate on round 2 if attacked).

{A1, D1} = the set of pure strategies of T1. (Attack on round 1, do not attack on round 1.)

$\{C_{1W}, C_{2W}\}$ = the strategy set of the weak type. (Counterattack on round 1 with probability C_{1W}, counterattack on round 2 with probability C_{2W}).

A_1 = the strategic choice of T1. (Choose A1 with probability A_1.)

{A2C1, A2N1, A2D} = three possible pure strategies for T2. Attack on round 2 given counterattack occurred on round 1, attack on round 2 given that negotiation occurred on round 1, attack on round 2 given that there was no attack on round 1.

$\{A_{2C1}, A_{2N1}, A_{2D}\}$ = the strategy set of T2. (Choose A2C1 with probability A_{2C1}, choose A2N1 with probability A_{2N1}, choose A2D with probability A_{2D})

A notational rule that we follow is that strategic choices are subscripted, pure strategies and other parameters are not. It is straightforward to use only the definitions not involving period 2 if the game has only one period.

Analysis

Decision Rules

One Round Game. If the game were played only once, clearly a weak type should negotiate and a strong type should not negotiate in a subgame perfect Nash equilibrium. Hence, if the terrorist knew the government's type, the terrorist would attack if and only if the government were weak. Thus with only one repetition of the game, the outcome depends on the probability distribution of government types and the payoffs. The terrorist should attack if the expected value of attacking is greater than the expected value of inactivity:

$$\text{Attack if } (b-1)Ps + b(1-Ps) \geq 0. \text{ That is, if } b \geq Ps. \quad (1)$$

Second Round Given No Attack Was Made in First Round. If the terrorist did not attack in round 1, his round 2 decision rule is the same as that of the terrorist in a one period game (see (1)). This is due to the fact that we use subgame perfection in both games and the terrorist has no more information in the second period (if no attack is made in the first) than the terrorist in the one period game.

Second Round Given Negotiation in First Round. If negotiation was met in round 1, clearly the government's type is weak. Hence the terrorist should attack with probability $A_{2N1} = 1$.

Second Round Given Counterattack in First Round. In any subgame perfect equilibrium the weak type must negotiate if attacked in round 2. The strong type will, of course, counterattack in round 2. We now derive the terrorist's decision rule given that he has been counterattacked in round 1. Given that the terrorist has seen counterattack on round 1 he should attack in round 2 if

$$P(S\backslash C1)(b-1) + P(W\backslash C1)b > 0. \quad (2)$$

Rewriting using Bayes' Law, our decision rule becomes

$$A_{2C1} = 1 \text{ if } [P(C1\backslash S)P(S)(b-1) + P(C1\backslash W)P(W)(b)] / [P(C1\backslash S)P(S) + P(C1\backslash W)(1-P(S))] > 0. \quad (3)$$

Since $P(C1\backslash S) = C_{1S}$, $P(C1\backslash W) = C_{1W}$, and $P(S) = Ps$, the above expression may be rewritten in terms of these strategies and the parameter Ps, which are common knowledge:

$$A_{2C1} = 1 \text{ if } [C_{1S}Ps(b-1) + C_{1W}(1-Ps)(b)] / [C_{1S}Ps + C_{1W}(1-Ps)] > 0. \quad (4)$$

The strong type's strategy space contingent on counterattack contains only the pure strategy (counterattack), $C_{1S} = 1$. Thus, we have:

$$A_{2C1} = 1 \text{ if } [Ps(b-1) + C_{1W}(1-Ps)(b)] / [Ps + C_{1W}(1-Ps)] > 0. \quad (5)$$

Since $Ps \geq 0$ and $C_{1W} \geq 0$, we know that the denominator of (5) is non-negative. Note that $Ps + C_{1W}(1\text{-}Ps) = 0$ if and only if $Ps = C_{1W} = 0$. If $Ps = 0$ then the terrorist has no need of deriving a conditional probability for his round 2 decision in the first place, since it is known that the type is weak and this type will not counterattack on round 2. Hence for purposes of deriving the terrorist's round 2 decision rule we may assume without loss of generality that $Ps > 0$. Thus, without loss of generality, $Ps + C_{1W}(1\text{-}Ps) > 0$. So the terrorist's round 2 decision rule becomes

$$A_{2C1} = 1 \text{ if } Ps(b\text{-}1) + C_{1W}(1\text{-}Ps)(b) > 0. \tag{6}$$

That is, i. $A_{2C1} = 1$ if $C_{1W} > Ps(1\text{-}b)/b(1\text{-}Ps)$. (7i)
Similarly, ii. $A_{2C1} = 0$ if $C_{1W} < Ps(1\text{-}b)/b(1\text{-}Ps)$, (7ii)
and iii. $A_{2C1} \in [0, 1]$ if $C_{1W} = Ps(1\text{-}b)/b(1\text{-}Ps)$. (7iii)

First Round. We now derive the terrorist's decision rule for round 1. The terrorist strictly favors attack in round 1 if attack gives a greater expected payoff than inactivity (which has a payoff of 0). That is,

$$A_1 = 1 \text{ if } P(C1)(b\text{-}1) + P(N1)b > 0. \tag{8}$$

The axioms of probability and our definitions give us

$$P(C1) = PsC_{1S} + (1\text{-}Ps)C_{1W} = Ps + (1\text{-}Ps)C_{1W}. \tag{9}$$

Similarly,

$$P(N1) = Ps(1\text{-}C_{1S}) + (1\text{-}Ps)(1\text{-}C_{1W}) = (1\text{-}Ps)(1\text{-}C_{1W}). \tag{10}$$

Hence our decision rule becomes

$$A_1 = 1 \text{ if } [Ps + (1\text{-}Ps)C_{1W}](b\text{-}1) + (1\text{-}Ps)(1\text{-}C_{1W})b > 0. \tag{11}$$

This simplifies to

$$A_1 = 1 \text{ if } b^2 > Ps \tag{12}$$

The terrorist's first round decision rule in its entirety is:

$$A_1 = 1 \text{ if } b^2 > Ps,\ A_1 = 0 \text{ if } b^2 < Ps, \text{ and } A_1 \in [0, 1] \tag{13}$$

if $b^2 = Ps$.

Equilibria

Equilibrium if $b \leq Ps$. If $b \leq Ps$ this game has one stable equilibrium (one connected set, that is). By stable equilibrium we refer to the Cho and Kreps (1987) equilibrium domination criterion. The equilibrium depends on the relative size of b and Ps. If $b \leq Ps$ the following is an equilibrium.

Strong Government:	Counterattack in both periods if attacked. ($C_{1S} = 1$, $C_{2S} = 1$)
Weak Government:	Counterattack in the first period if attacked, negotiate in the second period if attacked. ($C_{1W} = 1$, $C_{2W} = 0$)
Terrorist:	Do not attack in the first period. Attack in the second period if and only if negotiation was encountered in the first period. ($A_1 = 0$, $A_{2C1} = 0$, $A_{2N1} = 1$, $A_{2D} = 0$)

We now demonstrate that this is an equilibrium.

We first demonstrate that the proposed equilibrium is a Nash equilibrium. Suppose that the terrorist will not attack in either period. Then any government strategy is a best reply.

Suppose that both governments will counterattack the terrorist in the first period. Then the terrorist should not attack in the first period. Should the terrorist attack in the second period? Since the terrorist has learned nothing because he did not attack in the first period, he makes his decision based only on the relative magnitudes of Ps and b. His decision rule will be the same as the decision rule for the one period game (see (1)). We have assumed that $b \leq Ps$. Thus, following the one period decision rule we find that a terrorist's best reply to the strategy of the government $A_2 = 0$, enforcing the proposed equilibrium. Thus the proposed strategies are a Nash equilibrium.

The aforementioned equilibrium is also subgame perfect. For a demonstration of subgame perfection, we need only look to the final round, since the only proper subgames involve each government's second round decision of whether to counterattack or to negotiate. Clearly the proposed strategies are Nash equilibria for these subgames. Hence the previous equilibrium is also subgame perfect.

We now demonstrate that this proposal is sequential. Suppose that in the first period the terrorist deviates from his proposed strategy. Is it rational for the weak type to deviate from his proposal? If W deviates, then the terrorist's strategy prescribes another attack on round 2 (since the terrorist knows that only W can play N1, the beliefs that the terrorist must entertain to enforce attack are trivial). And here perfection prescribes that W negotiate on round 2. Hence if attack is met with negotiation by W, his total payoff is 0 (for 2 successive rounds of negotiation). Suppose that W holds to the proposed strategy. Then he will receive -1 for the first round and the rational terrorist will reply with no attack on round 2, giving type W a payoff of 'a'. Hence the total payoff of holding to the proposed equilibrium is a-1 for W. This is greater than the payoff of 0 for deviating from the proposed strategy (because $a > 1$). Thus the proposed strategy is a sequential equilibrium.

Since it is only possible for the weak type to deviate from the proposal, given a terrorist deviation, the equilibrium domination criterion is vacuous, hence the proposal is trivially stable in the sense of Cho and Kreps (1987).

Equilibrium if b > Ps. If $b > Ps$, the following is an equilibrium.

Strong Government: Counterattack in both periods if attacked ($C_{1S} = C_{2S} = 1$).

Weak Government: Counterattack in the first period with probability $Ps(1- b)/b(1-Ps)$.
Negotiate in the second period if attacked.
($C_{1W} = Ps(1-b)/b(1-Ps)$, $C_{2W} = 0$)

Terrorist: Do not attack in the first period if $b^2 < Ps$, attack in the first period if $b^2 > Ps$, randomize arbitrarily if $b^2 = Ps$. Attack in the second period if negotiation was encountered in the first period. If counterattacked in the first period, attack in the second with probability (a-1) / a. Attack in period 2 if no attack was made in period 1. ($A_{2N1} = 1$, $A_{2C1} = (a-1)/a$, $A_{2D} = 1$)

We now demonstrate that this is a subgame perfect Nash equilibrium. First of all, perfection will insure that the weak government will negotiate if attacked on round 2. Now suppose that there is no attack on round 1. $b > Ps$ insures that the expected payoff to the round 2 terrorist, $(b-1)Ps + b(1-Ps)$, is positive. Hence round 2's terrorist should attack if there was no attack on round 1. Given the weak government's proposed first period strategy, (7iii) applies; hence, any terrorist round 2 strategy is a best reply. That is, $A_{2C1} = (a-1)/a$ is a best reply.

Suppose that the terrorist chooses the strategy $A_{2C1} = (a-1)/a$. What is the government's round 1 best reply to attack in this case? The government's best reply to the terrorist's round 1 strategy is based on (1) the immediate round 1 payoff and (2) the expected payoff which this strategy will yield in round 2. This payoff is

$$-1 + [0(A_2) + a(1-A_2)] = -1 + a - aA_2. \tag{14}$$

A government strategy of $A_2 = (a-1)/a$ yields makes this expected payoff to counterattack on round 1 equal to zero. Hence $C_{1W} \in [0, 1]$ is a best reply. Is $C_{1W} = Ps(1- b)/b(1-Ps)$ contained in [0, 1]? Clearly, $b > Ps > 0$ implies $Ps(1- b)/b(1-Ps) \in [0, 1]$, hence $C_{1W} = Ps(1- b)/b(1-Ps)$ is a best reply to $A_2 = (a-1)/a$. Round 1's terrorist decision rule has been derived earlier (see (13)). Thus it is demonstrated that the proposal is a subgame perfect Nash equilibrium.

This equilibrium is trivially sequential and stable, since under this equilibrium there are no out of equilibrium moves for the government or the terrorists -- all actions are possible under the equilibrium strategies.

The stable equilibrium for the two period game will be one of these two, depending on the relative size of b and P . Since we list all possible orderings of the b and Ps and derive unique best replies for each player under each ordering, we have exhaustively listed the set of equilibria. In each equilibrium the weak government counterattacks with some positive probability in the first round -- in other words, some reputation building is present. In the first equilibrium, the weak government never negotiates in period 1. This requires that the probability that the government type is strong is sufficiently high. A weaker assumption -- that the terrorist is almost (but not completely) certain that the government's type is W -- does not yield this hard line policy by the government. However, in equilibrium the weak government will always refuse to negotiate with some positive probability. The smaller the doubt that the government is strong (the larger Ps) the smaller the probability of counterattack in equilibrium (the smaller C_{1W} in equilibrium). This result is important for two reasons. First of all, with full information, the weak government always negotiates in equilibrium. But a small amount of doubt about the government's type makes refusing to negotiate some of the time a government best reply. Thus, the conventional wisdom that refusal to negotiate with terrorists (with some positive probability) will avert future terrorism only requires that the terrorist have a small amount of incomplete information. Secondly, the more certain the terrorist feels that the government glories in counterattack (i.e. the greater Ps), the less likely the government will need to counterattack. As Schelling (1956: p. 282) states,

> The sophisticated negotiator may find it difficult to seem as obstinate as a truly obstinate man. If a man knocks at a door and says that he will stab himself on the porch unless given $10, he is more likely to get the $10 if his eyes are bloodshot.

Sensitivity to Parameter Changes. Exploration of the sensitivity of these results to parameter changes serves to illustrate the importance of the assumptions about the order and magnitudes of the payoffs. Some might argue that the payoff to the terrorist for an unsuccessful attack is greater than the payoff from not attacking, basing this on the assertion that terrorists prefer media exposure to losses of manpower and equipment if each may be had with certainty. The results of this change are immediate. Attack becomes a dominant strategy so that reputation building by the government is not possible -- counterattack is pointless. Rational terrorists would certainly encourage this opinion (Schelling's "bloodshot eyes"). It might also be the case that $a < 1$. What guidance does our intuition give us concerning the magnitude of a, the payoff to the government if no attack occurs? Clearly 'a' should be greater than the payoff to negotiation. In addition, one might argue that in more risk averse countries, 'a' is greater than the payoff of counterattacking due to the great uncertainty associated with counterattacking. If 'a' is less than the payoff of counterattack, then reputation building is a vacuous concept *because counterattack is preferred at all stages of the game over not being attacked.* A more heroic assumption of this model is that $a > 1$ (i. e. the payoff from not being attacked is greater than the negative of the payoff associated with launching a counterattack). If this is not the case, reputation building in the two period game is in trouble since one period's losses due to counterattack will never be made up. In the two period game, negotiation becomes the dominant sequential equilibrium strategy. $a<1$ implies, however, that the satisfaction that the government derives from not being attacked is less than the regret that the government feels from counterattacking and possibly losing innocent lives.

Conclusions

The conventional wisdom that governments should build reputations as not bargaining with terrorists holds in models of incomplete information. In our model, both of the two equilibria have early government counterattacks discouraging later terrorist attacks. This does not hold with complete information. Our model's origins are found in Selten's (1978) chain store model and Kreps and Wilson's (1982) incomplete information adaptation of the chain store model. The conventional wisdom is caught in the chain store paradox.

Beyond the reputation building results, we have demonstrated that models of terrorism may be built from existing economic models, simplifying the task of deriving optimal policies for dealing with terrorism.

References

Cho, In Koo and David Kreps (1987), "Signaling Games and Stable Equilibria," *Quarterly Journal of Economics*, Vol. 102, pp. 179-221.

Islam, Mohammed, and Q. Shahin (1989), "Economic Methodology Applied to Political Hostage-taking in Light of the Iran-Contra Affair," *Southern Economic Journal*, Vol. 55, pp. 1019-1024.

Kreps, David and Robert Wilson (1982), "Reputation and Imperfect Information," *Journal of Economic Theory*, Vol. 27, pp. 253-279.

Lapan , H.E. and Todd Sandler (1988), "To Bargain or Not To Bargain: That Is The Question," *American Economic Review*, Vol. 78, pp. 16-21.

Nelson, P. S. and John L. Scott (1992), "Terrorism and the Media: An Empirical Analysis," *Defence Economics*, Vol. 3, pp. 329-339.

Sandler T., John Tschirhart, and Jon Cauley (1983), "A Theoretical Analysis of Transnational Terrorism," *The American Political Science Review*, Vol. 77, pp. 36-54.

Scott, J. L. (1991), "Reputation Building in Hostage Taking Incidents," *Defence Economics*, Vol. 2, pp. 209-218.

Schelling, T. C. (1956), "An Essay on Bargaining," *American Economic Review*, Vol. 46, pp. 281-306.

Selten, R. (1978), "The Chain Store Paradox," *Theory and Decision*, Vol. 9, pp. 127-159.

______ (1988), "A Simple Game Model of Kidnapping," in R. Selten, *Models of Strategic Rationality*, Dordrecht; Boston: Kluwer Academic Publishers, pp. 77-93.

14

The Prospect of Stable World Peace and Its Global Economic Consequences

Anandi P. Sahu and Robert T. Kleiman

The demise of Cold War and the collapse of the Soviet Union have raised new hopes for a stable world peace. Suddenly, the world no longer appears to be divided into two armed camps, occasionally teetering at the brink of nuclear annihilation. There is a widespread belief that the new military and geopolitical realities provide an unprecedented opportunities for the West to reap the "peace dividends." As a result, academic scholars, journalists and policymakers[1] are trying to find answers to two very pertinent questions: how large is the peace dividend? and how best can it be harvested?

Economic Consequences of Stable Peace in the U.S.

From the point of view of economic prosperity, the new found world peace, even if it turns out to be stable, is not an unmixed blessing. In view of the decreased threat from the former Soviet Union to the Western nations, there is a strong desire in the U.S. to decrease defense spending. This desire has been growing stronger in face of the unprecedented budget deficit and the need to spend on infrastructure and other neglected domestic programs in the U.S. As the possibility for a significant increase in government revenues through taxes appears rather remote, defense cuts appear to be an obvious option.

McKinsey & Co. has estimated that Department of Defense (DOD) procurement and research and development expenditures, in real dollars, will decline from $117 billion in 1990 to $68 billion in 1995. Reductions in defense spending in the U.S. can have some serious implications. First, if the decrease in defense expenditures is not matched by increased private sector or government spending, there would be a decline on output and employment, due to a decline in aggregate demand. This adverse outcome, however, is not inevitable if the level of demand is maintained. Meyer and Raines[2] in fact show that if the level of aggregate demand is maintained, GDP actually increases due in large part to increases in investment and private capital. However, while the overall economy may not be adversely affected if the level of aggregate demand is maintained, this is not true for certain regions of the economy that are heavily dependent on the defense industry. The logic also applies to the industries and firms that are dependent on the defense sector as a major source of demand for their products and services. California is already said to be reeling from the lay-offs in defense related industries, and California is by no means unique. As Taylor's study[3] suggests several states are highly sensitive to defense cuts. Thus, the federal government should tread with care -- keeping government spending constant is not sufficient to avert regional hardships.

Anticipated Changes in Government Spending Patterns

The reduction in defense spending is very likely to be accompanied by changes in the pattern of both the total federal spending as well as expenditures on defense. It is only natural that reduced budget will force the federal government to reprioritize the spending of federal dollars.

Changing Mix of Defense Purchases. The defense department and the Congress would need to establish a new set of priorities where to spend the reduced dollars. In setting these new priorities, they will have to take into account the new world order. The most likely outcome is less expenditures on development of star wars technology and inter-continental ballistic missiles, and more on readiness of the U.S. troops for rapid deployment -- say, to handle regional conflicts -- and modernization of often used weapons than to manufacture costly military hardware which are mere white elephants.

Making the Transition Smooth. The federal government is bound to play a key role in making the transition to reduced level of defense expenditures as smooth as possible. It seems likely that reduction in defense spending will be accompanied by increases in domestic spending on items such as rebuilding of the nation's transportation infrastructure and expenditures on retaining workers and education. A House Armed Services Committee panel has recommended a plan aimed at better integration of the defense industry with the nation's commercial industrial base. Under this plan, 25% of savings in the defense budget would be earmarked for maintaining defense facilities and skills by shifting their focus to civilian uses. However, losers in the defense cut scenario will not necessarily recoup their losses under the new pattern of government expenditures -- a weapons engineer may not be eligible for hiring by a construction firm engaged in rebuilding infrastructure. The Office of Technology Assessment expects 530,000 to 920,000 private-sector defense jobs to be eliminated by 1995. The help from increased government expenditures on worker retraining may not be sufficient to compensate many workers now lucratively employed in defense related industries. Nevertheless, shifting employees from defense related industries to civilian positions provides at least a partial answer. Under the very best of circumstances, some pain appears unavoidable.

Can the U.S. Businesses Adjust?

Government spending on defense has been providing a powerful source of demand for some segments of the defense industry. The ordnance industry in particular will be very adversely affected -- 77% of its products were bought by the defense department in 1987.[4] Furthermore, some firms in the aerospace industry, such as McDonnell Douglas or Lockheed, have generated more than half of their revenues from defense contracts as opposed to passenger aircraft. Certainly, firms that are heavily dependent on the defense sector would face a revenue loss in the near term. These companies face a difficult strategic dilemma: diversify aggressively into nondefense (i.e, civilian) businesses or tough out the contraction with the hope that cutbacks will not affect them as severely as their competitors.

Conversion to Civilian Uses. Can firms in the defense industry channel their productive capacity to design and manufacture civilian goods? The answer to this question depends on the innovativeness of the firms as well as technical constraints under which they may be operating. The track record of defense contractors in commercial business ventures is not good. The capabilities required to succeed in civilian business are fundamentally different from those needed to design and produce weapon systems. Firms involved in the defense industry often lack adequate knowledge of commercial products, production methods, advertising and distribution, and customer demand. In addition, the cushion offered to aerospace firms by the commercial airline market is diminishing. The aggregate backlog of the largest commercial manufacturers continues to decline. As a result of their own financial problems, some airlines are postponing deliveries, and a few (for example, Northwest) are canceling some orders.

On the other hand, firms with superior research and development capabilities as well as those with operating flexibility may, in fact, not suffer at all. For example, a firm that used to design interactive video systems (Flight Safety International) to train pilots of war planes is now reconfiguring the system to provide the thrill of three dimensional interactive video journey through outer space for visitors of Disneyland for a handsome fee. Such a firm is even likely to expand the global market for its product as the new product may not be considered to have major security implications for the United States -- specially in light of warm political relations among countries.

Consolidation and Downsizing of Firms. Given the reduced defense budget, the competition for defense dollars is going to increase and it may not be as easy in future to sell expensive toilet seats and hammers to the defense department. Weaker firms would find it difficult to compete with stronger, more efficient and innovative firms. As a result, only the strongest companies will survive. Firms in the defense industry have started to get this message loudly and clearly, and some have already merged or have been bought out. For example, in the fourth quarter of 1992, Lockheed purchased General Dynamic's fighter operations, General Electric sold its aerospace operation to Martin Marietta, and FMC took control of Harsco's military vehicles unit. This trend is likely to continue and the Wall Street may continue to force the discipline of the financial markets on weaker defense firms. However, the survivors may do very well.

Defense companies will also attempt to cut their costs by reducing excess capacity. Smaller but more competitive positions can be achieved through consolidation, asset sales, and, if necessary, by closing down unneeded facilities. There will be an increased emphasis placed on improving manufacturing efficiency in order to obtain greater productivity from a smaller workforce. Firms that concentrate on those markets where they have the strongest competitive position stand the best chance of surviving, and even prospering, during a period of reduced military demand.

While it is rather difficult to provide a dollar figure for an optimal federal defense expenditure, it is difficult to visualize a scenario in which defense spending is not an important, if not dominant, component of the federal government expenditures. Thus, even at the reduced level, there would be a significant demand for defense goods and services. However, as the composition of the defense spending is likely to change, distribution of benefits, among different segments of the defense industry, from defense purchases is also likely to be altered.

Composition of GDP and Living Standard

As discussed earlier, most studies suggest the U.S. economy at the national level remains relatively unaffected by changes in defense purchases.[5] Some have even argued that excessive defense spending even leads to an economic decline.[6] At the same time, a cursory look at the U.S. economic history reveals that periods of war often led to economic prosperity in the U.S. -- World War II is said to have even rescued the U.S. from the Great Depression. However, the linkage between defense spending and economic expansion is not equally strong during peace and war periods. The latter link appears considerably weaker as several studies in this volume have suggested. Even so, is an economy based on production of civilian goods not better from the point of view of realizing the highest possible standard of living achievable by the country's citizens?

One may roughly define the standard of living of a country in terms of real per capita consumption. Once we take this into account, it becomes clear how defense spending may allocate greater resources toward production of military hardware and less toward production of consumer goods. While production of a tank generates income for the firm and workers involved in production of the tank, it can not be used for civilian consumption. However, if the tank could be exported it would be beneficial like export of any other product. One may, therefore, argue that domestic consumption of military goods and services reduces the potential for a higher standard of living. Thus, even if a reduction in defense spending does not bring a huge "peace dividend" -- it does not increase the total GDP a lot -- it has the potential for raising the real standard of living for the U.S. and other economies that reduce their defense expenditures, and transfer the released resources to civilian production.

Weidenbaum (1991) argues that real peace dividend will come from a shift from *government supported* consumption toward the *private* sector consumption. Others would argue, as does the Clinton administration, that the government expenditure can serve as a catalyst for the private sector growth if the government consumption is in the form of investment expenditures on items such as infrastructure and education. Meyer and Raines, in fact, find that defense cuts generate economic growth through increases in savings and investment. Whether the private sector should make all the investment decisions or some investment decisions are more efficiently handled by the federal government continues to be debated along ideological lines. We believe that government should play a limited, but necessary role, where social investment is the most efficient way of enabling aggregate capital formation, and thus promoting economic growth at the national level.

Global Peace, Trade and Growth

As pointed out above, an individual economy may benefit economically, even in terms of standard of living, if it produces and exports defense products. However, the importing countries may not. The reduction in global tension has led to warming of relations not only between the two Super Powers, but also among other nations. This change in the world political environment is conducive to greater spread of international trade and economic cooperation, leading to a spread of prosperity globally.

Implications for Developing Countries. The global warming of political relationships will also have favorable economic fallouts for the developing nations. An economically backward country like Vietnam will benefit from the change in the political climate. Economic cooperation between Vietnam and industrialized countries will benefit both. While Taiwan and South Korea serve as examples of economic miracles of the Cold War, China and North Korea may become the new success stories in the world of stable peace. African countries, instead of being pawns in the Super Power war games, may also benefit from the thaw.

Emergence of Economic Rivalries. While peace will alter the general world economic environment, it will have a significant impact on the roles played by major economic players. The military rivalries between the East and the West is likely to be replaced by economic rivalries. Already, Germany and Japan are considered to be major economic rivals to the U.S. The world is becoming divided into giant trading blocks; the proposed North American free trade zone and the European Community are reflections of emerging rivalries. However, from these economic rivalries, a new global economic cooperation may emerge ultimately.

Possible Change in the U.N. Role. As pointed out earlier, the reduced resources would be more directed towards increasing mobility and speed with which the U.S. armed forces can reach areas of armed conflicts globally. The role that the United Nations plays in such conflicts is also likely to be drastically altered eventually, with some possibility of the U.N. having its own armed forces to enforce Security Council resolutions. The Security Council itself may be expanded to include countries such as Japan, Germany, Brazil and India to reflect the new political realities. The U.N. may also play a more active role in solving human sufferings, without regard for *national sovereignty* -- Somalia may merely be a first step. While the United Nations may be able to serve as a super government ultimately, at least in the near term, industrial nations of the world led by the U.S. would continue to *enforce* peace globally, mostly with the consent of the U.N.

Conclusion

While the end of Cold War has not necessarily ushered in an era of eternal global bliss, it may have changed the character of the military conflict -- a change from dealing with the prospect of devastating thermonuclear war to many small conflicts. While peace dividends can translate into domestic prosperity and a higher standard of living, a *complete* transfer of resources from war efforts to peaceful uses may be premature. The U.S. will maintain a fair level of military expenditures and, as a result, the most efficient firms in the defense industry will survive the defense cutbacks.

Notes

1. See, for example, Weidenbaum (1991, 1992), and Reynolds (1992).
2. See Meyer and Raines (Chapter 5).
3. See Taylor (Chapter 10).
4. See Taylor (Chapter 10).
5. See Weidenbaum (1990), and Meyer and Raines (Chapter 5).
6. See Kennedy (1987).

References

Kennedy, Paul (1987), *The Rise and Fall of Great Powers*, New York: Random House.

Reynolds, Alan (1992), "The Sky Is Not Falling," *Forbes*, Vol. 149, March 30, 1992, pp. 152.

Weidenbaum, Murray (1990), "Defense Spending and the U.S.Economy: How Much Change is in the Offing?" *Defence Economics*, Vol. 1, pp. 233-242.

_____ (1991), "Policy Decisions for a Post-Cold War Economy," *Business Economics*, Vol. 26, No. 1, pp. 31-33.

_____ (1992), "Can Defense Contractors Survive the New World Order?" *Business & Society Review*, Summer, pp. 50-55.

About the Contributors

Charles H. Anderton is an associate professor of economics at the College of the Holy Cross in Worcester, Massachusetts. He has written articles about the economic aspects of conflict for various academic journals and books.

H. Sonmez Atesoglu is an associate professor of economics at Clarkson University, Potsdam, New York.

Basudeb Biswas is a professor of economics at Utah State University. He is the author of many articles on international trade and economic development published in refereed journals.

Peter J. Boettke is a National Fellow (1992-93) at the Hoover Institution on War, Revolution and Peace and an assistant professor of economics at New York University. He is the author of *Why Perestroika Failed: The Politics and Economics of Socialist Transformation* and *The Political Economy of Soviet Socialism: The Formative Years, 1918-1928.*

Alan V. Deardorff is a professor of economics and public policy in the Department of Economics and Institute of Public Policy Studies, University of Michigan, Ann Arbor. His published work includes a number of articles and books dealing with the pure theory of international trade and the more applied modelling of international economic policy. He and Professor Stern have collaborated for over two decades in the development and applications of the Michigan general equilibrium computational model of world production and trade.

J. Paul Dunne is a lecturer in economics at the University of Leeds, UK. He has published numerous articles on the economic effects of military spending, the problems and potentials of conversion, and in other areas of applied economics. He has also edited *Quantitative*

Marxism and jointly edited *The British Economy After Oil* and *Structural Change in the UK Economy*.

Peter C. Frederiksen is a professor of economics in the Defense Resources Management Institute, Naval Post-Graduate School, Monterey, California. He has authored numerous articles on defense spending and economic growth and also economic development in general.

Jon D. Haveman is an assistant professor in the Department of Economics, Krannert School, Purdue University, W. Lafayette, IN. His primary research interests are in the analysis of the welfare effects of customs union formation and the effects of changing trade patterns on U.S. labor markets.

Robert T. Kleiman is an associate professor of finance at Oakland University. He is the author of numerous articles on finance in academic and professional journals. He has also been a consultant to several firms and, government and private institutions.

Robert E. Looney is a professor of economics in the Department of National Security Affairs, Naval Post-Graduate School, Monterey, California. He has authored numerous books and articles on various aspects of economic development.

Laurence H. Meyer is a professor of economics at Washington University and a research associate at the University's Center for the Study of American Business. He is also president of Laurence H. Meyer & Associates, an economic consulting firm specializing in macroeconomic forecasting and policy analysis.

Michael J. Mueller is an associate professor of economics at Georgia Southern University and adjunct professor of economics and associate member of the Institute for Research on Environment and Economy at the University of Ottawa, Ottawa, Canada.

Edward A. Olszewski is a professor of physics at the University of North Carolina-Wilmington. He is the author of several articles on economics with an emphasis on quantitative expertise in time series analysis.

James E. Payne is an assistant professor of economics at Eastern Kentucky University, Richmond, Kentucky. He is the author of many articles pertaining to defense economics, macroeconomics, monetary theory and economic development.

Fredric Q. Raines is an associate professor of economics at Washington University. He is a consultant on several projects studying transition problems for specific industries and communities vulnerable to cuts in defense spending. His current research focuses on economic conversion and the role of R&D in economic growth.

Rati Ram is a professor of economics at Illinois State University.

Kevin L. Ross is an assistant professor of economics at the University of North Carolina-Wilmington. He is the author of many articles on international trade, finance and macroeconomics.

Anandi P. Sahu is an associate professor of economics at Oakland University, Rochester, Michigan. He has published many articles on monetary theory and macroeconomic issues. He is also co-editor of *The Economic Legacy of the Reagan Years: Euphoria or Chaos?*

John L. Scott is an assistant professor of economics at Northeast Louisiana University. He is the author of several papers on both theoretical and empirical aspects of terrorism and crime.

Robert M. Stern is a professor of economics and public policy in the Department of Economics and Institute of Policy Studies, University of Michigan, Ann Arbor. He has published numerous articles and books over the past 35 years on a wide variety of topics, including international commodity problems, the determinants of comparative advantage, price behavior in international trade, balance-of-payments policies and the computer modelling of international trade and trade policies.

Lori L. Taylor is a senior economist with the Federal Reserve Bank of Dallas in Dallas, Texas. She is the author of a number of papers on public finance including "Reduced Defense Purchasing: Anticipating the Impact on State and Industry Employment," in the November 1990 issue of the Federal Reserve Bank of Dallas' *Economic Review*.

Subject Index